Uniforms & Traditions of the LUFTWAFFE

Volume 2

by
John R. Angolia
& Adolf Schlicht

1st Edition

Published by R. James Bender Publishing,
P.O. Box 23456, San Jose, California 95153
Phone: (408) 225-5777
Fax: (408) 225-4739

Designed by Roger James Bender
Cover photo by Jack Christiansen, Items
courtesy of Harper Noehren,
Eric Queen and Al Burnes

Printed in the United States of America

ISBN No. 0-912138-71-8

TABLE OF CONTENTS

ACKNOWLEDGEMENTS

The authors and publisher wishes to correct a grave oversight that occurred in Volume I of this work with the omission of a much-needed credit to David Littlejohn. Mr. Littlejohn, noted author and historian, provided valuable input into the first three chapters of Volume I, and further assisted in other areas of the entire work. He should have been acknowledged by Assisted by David Littlejohn in Volume I. It is our sincere wishes that this oversight, albeit one volume late, has been corrected.

Individuals:

Ailsby, Chris
Alexander, Bob
Anconetani, Joe
Anderson, Ed
Anderson, Paul
Augustson, Hilde
Azzi, Gustavo
Barrows, Al
Bart, Terry
Bartlett, Sam
Beardsley, R.
Biasutti, Claudio
Bilheimer, Pete
Bock, Gernot
Bossiere, Bob
Bowerman, Brian
Breuker, Anton
Buhs, Andre
Burnes, Al
Buske, Jack
Callewaert, Ghislain
Carlson, LTC Terry
Catella, Francis
Chaney, Tom

Charita, Josef
Clark, Larry
Clark, Mike
Colarossi, Greg
Conway, John
Cook, David
Cook, Stan
Coulson, Ron
Coy, John
Crother
Cullember, Jerry
Curren, R. LaRue
Davis, LTC Bill
de Diego, Rafael
Dedman, Jim
Delich, Dave
Deuster, Dieter
Dietz, Jeff
Dinsmore, Gayle
Embre, Ray
Farlowe, Chris
Farnes, COL (Ret.) Keith
Fellows, George
Feltrin, Leonard

Fernandez, Gaston
Fisk, MAJ Ken
Floch, Johannes
Frailey, Don
Fuselier, Greg
Geiger, Mike
Gerber, Gary
Gibbons, Mark
Gokoo, Chuck
Goodapple, Terry
Govoni, Riccardo
Gray, John
Griggs, Bill
Grohs, Earl
Grünberg, Arnold
Hackney, Clint
Halcomb-Smith, Jill
Haley, Jim
Heckler, Dan
Heitzer, Thomas
Hodgin, John
Howard, Bill
Huet, Bill
Huet, Tony
Huff, John
Hungen, Heinz v.
Innes, George
Ishihara, Hidetake
Kerby, Steve
Korolevich, Mike
Kousoulas, Capt. (Ret.) Christos
Lafayette, Dick
Lautenschläger, Uwe
Liban, Jim
Lott, Art
Lyons, Bob
Mandley, Gordon
Manion, Ron
Mathias, Dr. Andre

McClintock, George
McGuire, Tom
Meldahl, Andrew
Mesturini, Franco
Meyer, Wolfgang
Miklosko, David
Moran, Mike
Morris, Mike
Morris, William
Mundhenk, Richard
Myers, G.
Neal, A. J.
Noehren, Harper
Petroni, Steve
Plettinck, Pete
Pohl
Queen, Eric
Rodachy
Rode, Karl
Roeckelein, Horst
Rupert, Steve
Selzer, Hermann
Simon, Thierry
Skötte, Anders
Soltys, Trevor
Spronk, Otto
Stadnicki, Ed
Stone, Joe
Swearingen, Ben
Tabbitt, John
Tannahill, Ian
Taugourdeau, Alain
Treend, Bob
Ulric of England
Walker, Gary
Weiblen, Jerry
Winebrenner, Walt
Wood, Gary
Xilas Historical Col.

Institutional:

Bundesarchiv/Miltärarchiv, Freiburg, Germany
Imperial War Museum, London, England
Luftwaffe Museum, Uetersen, Germany
Library of Congress, Washington, D.C.
Military Museum, Brussels, Belgium
National Archives, Washington, D.C.

The first 500 copies of the First Edition are serial numbered. This collector's volume is No. _49_.

CHAPTER • 21
OFFICIALS OF THE LUFTWAFFE

The officials did not possess the status of soldiers, but were nevertheless members of the Armed Forces. The categorization of the officials is very complex with all its subtleties, and difficult to explain and understand.

As with the other two services of the Armed Forces, the Luftwaffe, too, utilized officials to perform administrative duties. Besides administration, many technical services and duties for the direct or indirect support of the troops were performed by officials. They were correctly termed "Armed Forces officials of the Luftwaffe" (Wehrmachtbeamte der Luftwaffe), but commonly addressed simply as "officials" (Beamte).

Those officials of the Air Administration (Luftfahrtverwaltung) of the Reich Air Ministry, which belonged to the new Luftwaffe, were transferred to the Luftwaffe with the collective term "Armed Forces officials of the Luftwaffe" by an order (LV 35, No.37) dated 28 February 1935, to be effective by 1 March 1935.

Officials had the status not of soldiers, but rather as "Members of the Armed Forces" (Wehrmachtangehörige) or "Members of the Luftwaffe" (Angehörige der Luftwaffe). Active officials served in a dual status—subject to military laws and regulations as members of the Luftwaffe, while at the same time to the Reich Civil Service laws according to their status as Reich Civil Service officials (Reichsbeamte). The active officials and the officials of the body of reserves had a rank as determined by comparison to a defined soldier's grade. The exception to the rule were the officials of the Luftwaffe Forestry Service, which possessed the general rank of officers or NCOs.

Unlike their officer counterparts, officials were not regarded as superiors in a military sense, even when certain groups of officials were authorized to give professional directions in the form of orders to soldiers on duty within their immediate field of function. However, since about 1938, the status of military superiors (to include military and in certain defined cases even disciplinary authority) was gradually conferred upon certain groups of officials in special positions of units and headquarters.

8

There were repeated considerations of the High Command to transform the status of officials to a status as soldiers, but without any success due to the opposition of the officials which wanted to retain their special status. Eventually in 1944, judicial officials and some branches of the administrative officials were transferred to an officer status to the newly constituted Special Troop Service, but on a voluntary basis only.

When a soldier was appointed (on a voluntary basis only) as a Luftwaffe official, he was required to resign as an active soldier. However, he could retain his former military rank on a reserve status. As with soldiers, there were active officials and officials of the body of reserves (des Beurlaubtenstandes—d.B.).

Since the end of 1940, the collective group of Supplementary Officials (Ergänzungsbeamte) was constituted and composed of the officials of the body of reserves, the officials at disposal (z.V.) and the Wartime Officials (Beamte auf Kriegsdauer—a.Kr. or a.K.). This group was renamed "Supplementary Armed Forces Officials" (Ergänzungs-Wehrmachtbeamte). The supplementary officials did not have the status of Reich Civil Service officials. As members of the Armed Forces they served in an exclusively military status. As far as their duties in their respective functions were concerned, they were equal to the active officials.

Besides the officials in uniform there were officials which were not granted a uniform, e.g. to a large extent the officials of the lower career.

Careers (Laufbahnen): The term "Laufbahn" (career) was used with two very different meanings:

a. In its strict meaning Laufbahn was used for classification of the four groups of officials. Each of these groups was based on different conditions mainly subject to the educational level needed for appointment in one of the groups as follows:

- High grade career (höherer Dienst): a university degree was required.
- Elevated career (gehobener mittlerer Dienst or gehobener Dienst): an educational level between high school and college, with an additional two to three years of practical training was required.
- Medium career (einfacher mittlerer Dienst or mittlerer Dienst): a high school diploma and an apprenticeship of a trade was required.
- Lower career (unterer Dienst or einfacher Dienst): a grade school education without any further qualification was required.

NOTE: The last name term was introduced by an order (RGBl 1939 Part I, page 371) dated 28 February 1939 to take the place of the first name term.

All officials of the first two careers held officer rank. The possibility to rise from NCO rank to officer rank existed in the medium career. NCOs could be appointed as officials of the medium and elevated careers after 12 years of service as soldiers, and after graduating from two years of additional training at special schools (Fachschule—trade school). They were termed "Versorgungsanwärter" (roughly, aspirants for employment as official).

Each of the four careers was distinguished by a distinctive colored piping or the lack of piping about the collar patches.

    b. Laufbahn was also used to denote the branches (Fachlaufbahn or Fachrichtung as the technical branches were usually termed) comparable to the soldier's branches of arms or services. The officials of one branch did include one, several or all of the four careers. Each of the branches had its own conditions of admission, and regulations for training and examination.

The branches were distinguished by "secondary colors" (Nebenfarben) in addition to the official's dark green basic branch color (Waffenfarbe). The secondary colors were displayed as the inner (upper) base color of the shoulder boards. However, there were several branches grouped with the same branch colors.

NOTE: 1) There were branches with other basic branch colors than dark green and/or without a secondary color—to be discussed in another chapter. 2) In the subsequent chapters the term "career" will be used to denote the service groups as a. above, and "branch" to denote the branches of officials as b. above.

Uniform, Branches and Titles: By order (L.P./L.D. No.30327/34 geh. Kdos. D IV, 2b) dated 6 September 1934 the officials of the Air Administration, the future officials of the Luftwaffe, were grouped with a determined military rank.

By an order about the "Uniform of the Luftwaffe after De-camouflage" (Der Reichsminister der Luftfahrt L.D. No.30573/35 geh.Kdos. D IV, 3 Az.64.e.10.) dated 1 March 1935 the uniform of the officials was determined as follows:

- basic branch color: dark green (except for the officials of the Reich Air Traffic Control Service); secondary color of all branches: bright red
- Officials of Officer Rank:
  - collar patches: as before, but with three-pointed pips in lieu of gulls
  - shoulder boards: as officers of equal rank, but with a double underlay—lower one dark green, upper one bright red (including officials of general officer rank)
- Officials of NCO rank:
  - collar patches: with three-pointed pips; the 5mm wide tress on the bottom and outer side of the patches was retained for the collar patches of greatcoats, but was abolished on those of the tunic and the flyer's blouse.
  - shoulder straps: as for NCOs, and with dark green piping (without any secondary color).
  - Tresse around the collar of tunics and blouses as prescribed for NCOs.

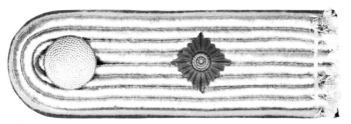

Shoulder board for an official the equivalent of an Oberleutnant. The basic branch color is dark green, and the secondary color is red.

Oberzahlmeister Jawoll tries his hand at cooking.

In the years that followed, the uniform accouterments were considerably altered by introduction of shoulder boards for certain officials of NCO rank, by the differentiation of the careers, and by introduction of secondary colors.

    1. Branches and Secondary Colors: Introduction orders and dates have not been found for most of the branches. The following orders about

the secondary colors are comprehensive lists of branches and colors, which had previously been introduced.

The secondary colors were displayed as the upper (inner) underlay of shoulder boards, and with some branches as the color of the collar patches. The latter will be discussed in the section "Uniforms" and is indicated in the following lists by an asterisk (*). The lower career officials were accorded a secondary color only when the shoulder straps were replaced by shoulder boards (order of 2 November 1940).

Order (LV 35, No.423) dated 26 July 1935: secondary color bright red (hochrot) for all branches.

Order (LV 35, No.786) dated 23 October 1935: Lower career officials without a secondary color. All other officials with secondary colors as follows:

Black: All officials of the RLM, regardless of branches. However, this was changed to the respective branch color shortly after the alteration of the black branch color of soldiers of the RLM to the color of the basic branch as per order (LV 39C, Nr.846) dated 10 September 1939.

Bright Red: Administrative (non-technical) officials

Light Brown: Officials of technical branches

Dark Blue: Construction Service; this was changed to bright red at a later date, and designated Construction Administrative Service.

Golden Yellow: Meteorological officials; later transferred to the Reich Weather Service

Wine Red: Judicial officials

Apple Green: Pharmacists; later designated Pharmaceutical Service

Shoulder boards with other secondary colors as previously introduced were permitted for wear until 31 December 1935.

Order (LV 39B, Nr.29) dated January 1939: Renaming of the Operational Technical Service (betriebstechnischer Dienst [B], constituted in 1938) as Machine and Electric Technical Service (maschinen- und elektrotechnischer Dienst).

Order (LV 40, Nr.569) dated 10 May 1940, changes as follows:

White: Officials of general officer rank; exceptions were Supreme Reich Court Martial (crimson*), and other Judicial officials (wine red*).

Bright Red: General Administrative Service (Allgemeiner Verwaltungsdienst), Construction Administrative Service (Bauverwaltungdienst or bautechnischer Verwaltungsdienst), Agricultural Service (Landwirtschaftsdienst), Surveying Service (Vermessungsdienst)—renamed Surveying-technical Administration Service at a later date, Technical Machine Service (maschinentechnischer Dienst), Technical Electric Service (elektrotechnischer Dienst)

Crimson*:	Supreme Reich Court Martial (Reichskriegsgericht)
Wine Red*:	Judicial Service (Justizdienst)
Pink:	Photo Service (Bilddienst—Bi), Motor Transport Service (Kraftfahrdienst—K), Ordnance Service (Waffendienst—W), Weapons and Ammunition Service (Waffen- und Munitionsdienst—W.u.M.), Technical Aircraft Service (flugzeugtechnischer Dienst—Fl; also termed Flugzeugdienst), Cartographic Service (kartographischer Dienst), Lithographic Service (lithographischer Dienst)
Golden Brown:	Signal Service (Nachrichtendienst—N)
Orange:	Special School Service (Fachschuldienst)—As the titles of the branch were introduced by an order of 2 February 1938 it may be concluded that the branch was constituted shortly before, Librarian Service (Bibliotheksdienst), Medical Service (Medizinaldienst), Veterinary Service (Veterinärdienst), Pharmacists (Apotheker), Chemists (Chemiker), officials of the Luftwaffe War Science Section (kriegswissenschaftlicher Dienst der Luftwaffe), Psychologists (Psychologen)—later renamed Psychological Examination Service (Psychologen)
Blue-grey:	Reich Weather Service (Reichswetterdienst)—Meteorologist's aspirants and soldiers of the branch, which were termed "weather service soldiers" (Wetterdienstsoldaten) remained in status of soldiers and wore a golden yellow branch color.
Dark Brown:	Reich Flight Safety Service (Reichsflugsicherungsdienst)—subdivided into Operational Service (Betriebsdient—Fs/B), and Technical Service (Technischer Dienst—Fs/T)

Changes resulting from order (LV 40, No.895) dated 8 July 1944:

Bright Red:	Craftmen's Service at clothing depots (handwerklicher Dienst bei Bekleidungsämtern)
Pink:	Other craftsmen's service
Black*:	Order (LV 44, No.1189) dated 19 August 1944: Officials of the Construction-technical Administrative Service, which were transferred to the department of the Chief of the Luftwaffe Construction Service (Luftwaffen-Bauwesen) per order (r.d.L. Chef Luftwehr Az.11 b 41 No.5254/44 g. LD Ag II 11) dated 10 June 1944.

Details about the constitution of the following branches have not been found:

Bright Red:	Operational-technical Administrative Service (Betriebstechnischer Verwaltungsdienst)
?	Military Geological Service (wehrgeologischer Dienst)
?	Replacement Service (Wehrersatzwesen)

2. Titles: The titles of the officials were termed "Amtsbezeichnungen" ("position designations"). The titles are a very complex matter as most of the branches had their own distinguishing titles or prefixes to generally used titles. Even as there were tendencies to standardize the titles of some branches, this effort had little success. If officials of the technical and the non-technical branches carried the same name, the titles of the technical officials of the lower, medium and elevated careers were differentiated by the prefix "Technischer" (technical) to the title.

A definite coordination of the titles with branches was possible only for some branches. The titles of the officials of the lower and medium careers in relation to ranks were altered several times, e.g., by an order (LV 39A, No.263) dated 4 September 1939.

Officials of the medium and elevated careers which were on temporary service until their final appointment as lifetime officials were identified by the prefix "a.p." or "ap.", meaning "extraordinary" (ausserplanmässig). An order (LV 41, No.783) dated 4 July 1941 prescribed the abbreviated suffix of the branch (abbreviations as stated with the section "Branches" above) following the title of technical officials.

An official, who had been a soldier and had held a higher soldier's rank than his title as official allowed, was permitted to wear the grade insignia of this rank regardless of his title, as per order (LV 36, No.80) dated 15 January 1936. The higher grade insignia were naturally consumed upon promotion.

The subsequent list of titles mainly follows the order (LV 40, No.1426) "Rank Structure of the Armed Forces Officials of the Luftwaffe" (Rangverhältnisse der Wehrmachtbeamten der Luftwaffe) dated 2 November 1940. It is possibly not complete.

Ranks of Soldiers	Titles of Officials of Equal Rank
	Lower Career
Feldwebel	Ministerialamtsgehilfe, Amtsgehilfe, Amtsobergehilfe, Techn. Gehilfe, Maschinist, Drucker, Bauaufseher, Laborant, Lagermeister, Betriebsassistent, Materialienverwalter, Magazinaufseher, Kastellan, Pförtner, Kassengehilfe, Justizwachtmeister, Heizer, Hauswart, Lagerwart, Wächter, Werkführer, Beamte im Verbereitungs- und Probedienst für den einfachen Dienst
Oberfeldwebel	Maschinenmeister 1), Magazinmeister, Botenmeister, Justizoberwachtmeister
	After 5 years as official: Ministerialamtsgehilfe, Amtsgehilfe, Amtsobergehilfe, Techn. Gehilfe, Maschinist, Drucker, Bauaufseher, Laborant, Lagermeister, Betriebsassistent, Materialienverwalter, Magazinaufseher, Kastellan, Techn. Gehilfe, Pförtner, Kassengehilfe, Justizwachtmeister, Werkführer

| | After 10 years as official: Heizer, Hauswart, Lagermeister, Wächter |
| Oberfeldwebel 2) | Oberbotenmeister, Ministerialhausinspektor |

Official with rank of Oberfeldwebel in the Lower Career as denoted by the lack of collar patch piping.

Medium Career

Oberfeldwebel	Assistent of all branches, Techn. Assistent, Wetterdienstassistent, Flugsicherungsassistent, Amtsmeister, Werkmeister, Prüfmeister, Maschinenmeister 1), Oberlotsenmeister, Beamte on probation for the medium career
Leutnant	Sekretär of all branches, Techn. Sekretär, Wetterdienstsekretär, Justizsekretär, Ministerialkanzleivorsteher, Oberwerkmeister, Oberprüfmeister, Maschinenmeister 1), Betriebsleiter 1), Flugsicherungsbetriebsleiter
Oberleutnant	Obersekretär of all branches, Techn. Obersekretär, Justizobersekretär, Lithograph, Kartograph, Hauptwerkmeister, Hauptprüfmeister, Waffenmeister, Betriebsleiter 1)

Elevated Career

Leutnant	a.p. Inspektor of all branches, a.p. Techn. Inspektor, a.p. Kriegsgerichtsinspektor, a.p. Beamte title of the rank of Oberleutnant
Oberleutnant	Inspektor of all branches, Techn. Inspektor, Regierungsinspektor, Regierungsbauinspektor, Verwaltungsinspektor, Wetterdienstinspektor, Vermessungsinspektor, Justizinspektor, Kartographeninspektor, Waffenrevisor, Ministerialregistrator, Volksschullehrer am Grossen Militärwaisenhaus in Potsdam
Hauptmann	Oberinspektor of all branches, Techn. Oberinspektor, Regierungsoberinspektor, Regierungsbauoberinspektor, Verwaltungsoberinspektor, Wetterdienstoberinspektor, Vermessungsoberinspektor, Justizoberinspektor, Kriegsgerichtsoberinspektor, Kartographenoberinspektor,

	Waffenoberrevisor, Rektor und Konrektor am Grossen Militärwaisenhaus in Potsdam
Major	Amtmann of all branches, Techn. Amtmann, Regierungsamtmann, Verwaltungsamtmann, Justizamtmann, Oberamtmann aller Fachrichtungen, Techn. Oberamtmann, Regierungsoberamtmann, Verwaltungsoberamtmann, Justizoberamtmann, Amtsrat aller Fachrichtungen, Techn. Amtsrat, Ministerialkanzleivorsteher 3)
Oberstleutnant	Oberamtmann and Amtsrat upon personal bestowal, usually after 25 years of service

High Grade Career

Leutnant	Feldapotheker 4)
Oberleutnant	Oberapotheker 4)
Hauptmann	Stabsapotheker 4), Regierungsassessor, Regierungsbauassessor, Wetterdienstassessor, Kriegsrichter, Wissenschaftlicher Hilfsarbeiter, Assessor on probation (im Probedienst)
Major	Regierungsrat, Regierungsbaurat, Regierungsmedizinalrat, Regierungschemiker/Regierungschemierat 5), Kriegsgerichtsrat, Oberstabsapothcker, Archivar
Oberstleutnant	Oberregierungsrat, Oberregierungsbaurat, Oberregierungsmedizinalrat, Oberregierungschemierat, Ministerialbürodirektor, Oberkiegsgerichtsrat, Oberfeldapotheker
Oberst	Ministerialrat, Oberstintendant 6), Oberstkriegsgerichtsrat, Baudirektor, Direktor im Reichswetterdienst, Direktor beim Reichsamt für Wetterdienst, Direktor bei der deutschen Seewarte
Generalmajor	Ministerialdirigent, Präsident des Reichsamts für Wetterdienst, Präsident der deutschen Seewarte, Luftflottenintendant 7), Luftgauintendant/Luftkreisintendant 7), Luftgauintendant/Luftkreisintendant 7), Generalintendant 7)
Generalleutnant	Ministerialdirektor

Annotations:

1) According to pay group

2) These lower career officials wore collar patches and shoulder boards of officials of the medium career of Oberfeldwebel rank, but collar patches without surround, as per order (LV 40, No.1427) dated 2 November 1940.

3) Amtsrat und Oberamtmann: collar patches with two pips (but shoulder boards of Major rank) with immediate effect, as per order (LV 41, No.1978) dated 29 November 1941, to distinguish these from the Amtmann (one pip, also Major rank), except when they were bestowed with the personal rank of Oberstleutnant. This also relates to these ranks of the following lists.

4) Introduction probably at the end of 1939; omitted in the above order of 2 November 1940 about the Rank Structure.
5) Renaming of the title "Regierungschemiker" about 1938
6) Introduction about 1938.
7) By order (LV 40, No.57) dated 22 January 1940 the titles "Luftflottenintendant" and "Luftgauintendant/Luftkreisintendant" were altered to "Generalintendant." The old titles continued to be used as "position designations" (Dienstbezeichnungen) for the chief of the administrative section of a Luftflotte, a Luftgau or Luftkreis.

Supreme Reich Court Martial

The titles of the Luftwaffe officials of the Supreme Reich Court Martial (Reichskriegsgericht) that was constituted per 1 October 1936 were introduced by order dated 14 October 1936, and published on 30 November 1936 (LV 36, No.1625) as follows:

Rank of Soldiers	Titles of Officials of Equal Rank
Lower Career	
Feldwebel	Reichskriegsgerichtswachtmeister
Oberfeldwebel	Oberbotenmeister beim Reichskriegsgericht, Reichskriegsgerichtsoberwachtmeister 1)
Medium Career	
Leutnant	Reichskriegsgerichtssekretär
Oberleutnant	Reichskriegsgerichtsobersekretär 1)
Elevated Career	
Oberleutnant	Reichskriegsgerichtsinspektor 2), Kanzleivorsteher beim Reichskriegsgericht 2)
Hauptmann	Reichskriegsgerichtsoberinspektor
Major	Amtsrat beim Reichskriegsgericht, Amtmann beim Reichskriegsgericht 2)
Oberstleutnant	Bürodirektor beim Reichskriegsgericht 2)
High Grade Career	
Oberstleutnant	Reichskriegsgerichtsrat
Oberst	Oberkriegsgerichtsrat beim Reichskriegsgericht 2)
Generalmajor	Reichskriegsanwalt, Reichskriegsgerichtsrat
Generalleutnant	Oberreichskriegsanwalt, Senatspräsident beim Reichskriegsgericht

Annotations:
1) Introduction probably about 1937/38.
2) Introduction by order (LV 38B, No.227) dated 9 August 1938.

Special School Service

The titles of the officials of the Special School Service (Fachschuldienst) were introduced by an order (LV 38A, No.48) dated 2 February 1939 as follows:

Ranks of Soldier	Titles of Officials of Equal Rank
	Elevated Career
Oberleutnant	a.p. Oberfachschullehrer
Hauptmann	Oberfachschullehrer, Gewerbeoberlehrer, Fachschulkonrektor
Major	Fachschulrektor
	High Grade Career
Hauptmann	Fachstudiensassessor
Major	Fachstudienrat, Fachstudiendirektor
Oberstleutnant	Oberfachstudiendirektor, Oberfachschulrat

By an order (LV 45, No.93) dated 2 January 1945 new titles were introduced to replace the above titles as follows:

Rank of Soldiers	Titles of Officials of Equal Rank
	Elevated Career
Oberleutnant	a.p. Oberlehrer der Luftwaffe
Hauptmann	Gewerbeoberlehrer der Luftwaffe, Konrektor der Luftwaffe
Major	Rektor der Luftwaffe
	High Grade Career
Hauptmann	a.p. Studienassessor der Luftwaffe
Major	Studienrat der Luftwaffe, Studiendirektor der Luftwaffe
Oberstleutnant	Oberstudiendirektor der Luftwaffe
Oberst	Oberschulrat der Luftwaffe

Craftsmen's Service

Some titles of the Craftsmen's Service of the medium career (mittlerer handwerker Dienst) were altered by an order (BLB 39, No.714) as follows:

Ranks of Soldiers	Old Titles	New Titles (all with suffix "der Luftwaffe")
Oberfeldwebel	Werkführer	Werkmeister, Prüfmeister
Leutnant	Oberwerkmeister	Oberwerkmeister, Oberprüfmeister
Hauptmann	Betriebsleiter (Kraftfahrdienst) or (Bekleidung-Maschinenfach), Schneidermeister, Schuhmachermeister	Hauptwerkmeister

Non-technical Administrative Service

The titles of the Non-technical Administrative Service (nichttechnischer Verwaltungsdienst) were altered by an order (LV 40, No.1539) dated 25 November 1940 as follows:

Ranks of Soldiers	Old Titles	New Titles
	Medium Career	
Oberfeldwebel	a.p. Assistent	a.p. Verwaltungsassistent
	Assistent	Verwaltungsassistent
Leutnant	Sekretär	Verwaltungssekretär
Oberleutnant	Obersekretär	Verwaltungsobersekretär
	Elevated Career	
Oberleutnant	Inspektor	Inspektor mit Vorsatz der Fachrichtung, z.B. Verwaltungsinspektor
Major	Amtmann	Regierungsamtmann
	Oberamtmann	Regierungsoberamtmann

A subsequent alteration of titles was introduced by an order (LV 43, No.886) dated 3 May 1943 as follows:

Ranks of Soldiers	Old Titles	New Titles
	Elevated Career	
Leutnant	a.p. Regierungsinspektor	Zahlmeister
Oberleutnant	Regierungsinspektor, Verwaltungsinspektor	Oberzahlmeister
Hauptmann	Regierungsoberinspektor, Verwaltungsoberinspektor	Stabszahlmeister
Major	Regierungsamtmann	Oberstabszahlmeister
Oberstleutnant	Regierungsoberamtmann	Oberfeldzahlmeister
	High Grade Career	
Hauptmann	a.p. Regierungsassessor	a.p. Stabsintendant
Major	Regierungsrat	Oberstabsintendant
Oberstleutnant	Oberregierungsrat	Oberfeldintendant

However, the officials of the Reich Air Ministry and the Luftwaffe officials of the Armed Forces, Army and Navy High Commands retained their titles.

As the titles composed with "Zahlmeister" and "Intendant" were exclusively reserved for the grade designations of the officers of the new Special Troop Service (Truppensonderdienst), the old titles were introduced again by order (LV 44, No.1134) dated 10 August 1944 as follows:

- elevated career: Regierungsinspektor, Regierungsoberin-

spektor, Regierungsamtmann, Regierungsoberamtmann, Amtsrat
- high grade career: Regierungsrat, Oberregierungsrat, Ministerialrat, Ministerialdirigent, Ministerialdirektor

Position Designations: The position designations of the chiefs of the administrative section of higher commands, which were not related to a definite rank, were ordered as follows:

- order (LV 42, No.1184) dated September 1942: "Feldintendant" at all major commands and offices.
- order (LV 43, No.57) dated 9 February 1942: "Korpsintendant" at an Air Corps, Flak Corps, Luftwaffe Field Corps, and "Divisionsintendant" at an Air Division, Flak Division, Luftwaffe Field Division.

Technical Administrative Service

By an order (LV 40, No.57) dated 8 June 1940 the titles of several officials of the Technical Administrative Service (Technischer Verwaltungsdienst) were altered as follows:

Rank of Soldiers	Old Titles	New Titles
Major	Techn. Verwaltungsamtmann	Techn. Amtmann (Pay Group A 3 b)
	Techn. Verwaltungsamtmann Verwaltungsamtmann	Techn. Oberamtmann Verwaltungsoberamtmann (Pay Group A 2 d)

Ordnance Technical Service

As a result of a merger of the elevated careers of the Ordnance Technical Service (waffentechnischer Dienst) and the Weapon and Ammunition Service (Waffen- und Munitionsdienst) as a new branch "elevated Ordnance Technical Service (gehobener waffentechnischer Dienst) it became necessary to alter some titles per order (LV 41, No.880) dated 14 July 1941 as follows:

Ranks of Soldiers	Old Titles ordnance tech. service	weapon & ammo service	New Titles ordnance tech. service
Oberleutnant	Waffenrevisor	Techn. Inspektor	Waffeninspektor
Hauptmann	Waffenoberrevisor	Techn. Oberinspektor	Waffenoberinspektor
Major	Techn. Amtmann*	Techn. Amtmann	Waffenamtmann
Major	Techn. Oberamtmann**	Techn. Oberamtmann	Waffenoberamtmann

*Pay group A3b (comparable to Hauptmann).
**Pay group A2d (comparable to Major).

Surveying Technical Service

By order (LV 42, No.2245) dated 19 August 1942 the titles of the medium and high grade career officials of the Surveying Administrative Service (vermessungstechnischer Dienst) were standardized and renamed as follows:

Rank of Soldiers	Old Titles	New Titles
Elevated Career		
Leutnant	a.p. Vermesungsinspektor	a.p. Regierungsvermessungsinspektor
Oberleutnant	Regierungsbauinspektor, Vermessungsinspektor	Regierungsvermessungsinspektor
Hauptmann	Regierungsoberbauinspektor, Vermessungsoberinspektor	Regierungsvermessungsoberinspektor
Major	Vermessungsamtmann	Regierungsvermessungsamtmann
High Grade Career		
Hauptmann	Regierungsbauassessor, Vermessungsassessor	Regierungsvermessungsassessor
Major	Regierungsrat, Regierungsbaurat, Vermessungsrat	Regierungsvermessungsrat
Oberstleutnant	Oberregierungsbaurat	Oberregierungsvermessungsrat

Technical Aircraft Service

As a result of a sub-division of the Technical Aircraft Service (flugzeugtechnischer Dienst) the medium career officials were renamed according to their sub-branch by an order (LV 42, No.2845) dated 5 November 1942 as follows:

Ranks of Soldiers	Aircraft Examination Ser. (Flugzeugprüfdienst)	Aircraft Maintenance Ser. (Flugzeugwerkstattdienst)
Oberfeldwebel	Prüfmeister	Werkmeister
Leutnant	Oberprüfmeister	Oberwerkmeister
Oberleutnant	Hauptprüfmeister	Hauptwerkmeister

3. Regulations for the Wear of the Uniform: As far as the wear of the uniform was concerned, all officials were classed with one of two groups:

    a. Officials with the obligation to wear the uniform: This group was obligated to wear the uniform as soldiers were. However, the off-duty wear of civilian clothes did not require special permission. The obligation was prescribed by several orders between 6 September 1934 and 10 May 1938, which have not been found. Among others, the following officials were included in this group:

- The Luftwaffe Music Superintendent (Luftwaffenmusikinspizient) by order (Der Reichsminister der Luftfahrt L.D. No.30337/35 g.Kdos. D.IV.2b. Az.64.c. 30.) dated 24 March 1935.
- all officials of Supreme Reich Court Martial (Reichskriegsgericht) by order (LV 36, No.1625) dated 14 October 1936.

New regulations were published by an order (BLB 38, No.348) dated 9 August 1938 that required the wear of the uniform on duty by the following officials

- Officials on service with the Luftwaffe Group Commands (Luftwaffengruppenkommando) and the Air District Commands (Luftgaukommando)
- Air Fleet Commands (Luftflottenkommando) and Luftwaffe Commands (Luftwaffenkommando), and with units under the command of these (except officials with the Air Offices [Luftamt] and the Clothing Depots) of the following branches—non-technical Administrative Service (nichttechnischer Verwaltungsdienst), Judicial Service (Justizdienst), Construction-technical Service (bautechnischer Dienst), Motor Maintenance Service (kraftfahr-technischer Dienst), Photo Service (bildtechnischer Dienst), Signal Service (nachrichtechnischer Dienst), Ordnance Service (Waffendienst), Technical Machine Service (maschinentechnischer Dienst), Weapons and Ammunition Service (Waffen- und Munitionswesen), Cartographic Service (kartographischer Dienst), Lithographic Service (lithographischer Dienst)
- The following officials of the Reich Weather Service (Reichswetterdienst): officials of the high grade career of the Luftwaffe Group Commands and Air Offices, all officials on service at air fields and with Weather Reconnaisance Squadrons.
- Officials of the Administration School (Verwaltungsschule), of the Air Traffic Control School (Reichsschule für Luftaufsicht), and of the Recruiting Service (Wehrersatzstellen).

By order (BLB 39, No.153) dated 17 February 1939 the following officials were also obliged to wear the uniform:

- officials of the Weather Service School (Wetterdienstschule) and on service with Weather Advisory Centers (Wetterberatungszentralen) and Radio Balloon Detachments (Radiosondentrupps).
- officials on service with Clothing Depots (Bekleidungsämter) and high grade career officials of the Psychological

Service (psychologisches Prüfwesen).

b. Officials with the authorization to wear the uniform: All officials without the obligation to wear the uniform had the option of wearing the uniform or civilian clothes on or off duty. However, they had to wear the uniform when on temporary service with units or on maneuvers, or when expressly ordered to wear the uniform. Certain groups of officials had to procure a uniform for the event of mobilization, but only if they had performed the military basic training as required by order (L.D. II 1 No.22306/37) dated 22 March 1937.

The officials of the School Service (Fachschuldienst) were included in this group by order (LV 38A, No.48) dated 2 February 1938.

The above order of 9 August 1938 included all officials in this group, which were not classed with the obligation to wear the uniform by that order.

By an order (LV 40, No.969) dated 4 June 1940 all officials were ordered to wear the uniform for the duration of the war, but only if they had performed the military basic training as soldiers.

Generally, officials during their training and probation period of time did not wear the uniform (with some exceptions, however, for officials of the elevated career of some technical branches. An order (LV 42, No.886) dated 26 March 1942 required the wear of the uniform by all officials of the medium and elevated careers during the training and probation period.

4. Uniform and Insignia of Rank: As a principle, the officials wore the same uniform as the soldiers of equal rank. Naturally, newly introduced clothing and equipment articles were also worn by officials if not ordered otherwise. The dark green branch color was displayed in the same manner as by soldiers. The rank insignia, however, differed in details, as discussed below.

On the dark green collar patches, the rank was determined by the number of three-pointed pips in lieu of the double wings of soldiers. One point of the pips was directed vertically upwards, and the distance between the ends of the points was 10mm. However, embroidered pips were usually slightly larger and came in minor variants due to the kind of embroidery.

The officials of the medium career, and since 1940 also the lower career, wore shoulder boards, which were officially termed "Schulterlitzen" (as opposed "Schulterstücke" of officer ranks). These were made of 3-4mm wide flat cords ("Kantenschnüre") made of V-pattern threads with a slight center indentation. The center braiding had five bends at either side, and ended in a buttonhole sling above, and was surrounded by double flat cords in such a manner that the braiding and the surround at the base made three bends. The double backing was stiffened. The regulation width was 3.4cm, but the boards were frequently wider (up to 4.7cm). The rank pips were aluminum-colored as worn by NCOs. There were two variants regarding the backing:

- The backing reached to the end of the buttonhole sling, and was with a slit for the buttonhole or a metal grommet with a 6-7mm inner diameter to slip the shaft of the button through. At the beginning of the buttonhole sling the edges of the backing were frequently indented in length of approximately 1cm for some unknown reason.

• The backing ended in a half-circle at the beginning of the buttonhole sling, which protruded over the backing.

Shoulder board of medium and later lower career officials.

Three examples of variant backings.

The double backing of the shoulder boards of officers and NCO ranks was dark green below, and of the secondary color above, with the upper underlay extending 1mm beyond the flat cords, and the lower underlay extending 1mm beyond the upper one. A colored 1mm wide web cord was sometimes sewn in between the flat cords and the lower underlay in lieu of the regulation cloth underlay. All shoulder boards with braiding came in pairs, with the higher part of the buttonhole sling rearwards of the shoulder button.

An order (LV 36, No.401) dated 27 March 1936 required the wear of the sword by officials of NCO rank at all occasions where it was prescribed for officer and officials of officer rank. By order (LV 40, No.1083) dated 19 August 1940 the officials with NCO rank were granted the right to wear the officer's dagger in lieu of the flyer's dagger.

a. Officials of the Lower Career: Lower career officials wore the same uniform as senior NCOs. The collars of the tunic and the flyer's blouse were adorned with the aluminum Tresse surround as prescribed for NCOs. Secondary colors were worn when the shoulder straps were exchanged for shoulder boards in 1940.
- Collar Patches: dark green with metal pips, and without piping; those of the greatcoat were with a 5mm wide Tresse along the bottom and outer edges.
- Shoulder Straps (Schulterklappen): as for NCOs, and with dark green piping.

Rank as	Collar Patches	Shoulder Straps:
Feldwebel	3 pips	1 aluminum pip
Oberfeldwebel	4 pips	2 aluminum pips

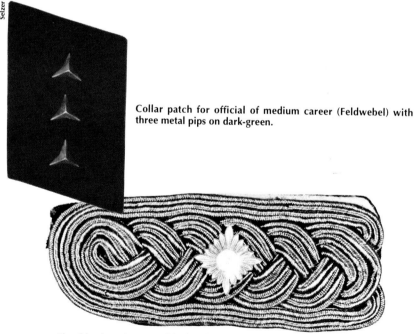

Collar patch for official of medium career (Feldwebel) with three metal pips on dark-green.

Shoulder board worn with the above collar patch. This pattern board was introduced 2 November 1940.

Collar patches for an Oberfeldwebel.

2 November 1940 pattern shoulder board for Oberfeldwebel.

Several alterations were introduced by order (LV 40, No.1427) dated 2 November 1940, to be worn by 1 February 1941 at the latest, as follows:

- Tresse surround of the collars abolished.
- collar patches: pips of matte grey machine-embroidery; number of pips as before; Tresse on collar patches of greatcoats omitted.
- shoulder boards (Schulterlitzen) to replace the shoulder straps: braiding made of double blue-grey flat cords with a surround of double blue-grey cords; double backing; number of pips as before.
- certain groups of officials (such as Oberbotenmeister, etc.) with collar patches and shoulder boards as the medium career officials (as of that order) for distinction, however, with collar patches without a cord piping.

    b. Officials of the Medium Career:

        1) Officials with NCO rank: Uniform as senior NCOs, but without the Tresse surround of the collars of tunics and flyer's blouses. They ranked higher than the Oberfeldwebel.

- Collar Patches: dark green with oak leaves wreath (as for company grade officers) and with one pip; made of aluminum-colored metal, but since the end of 1936 machine-embroidered of matte grey cotton or artificial silk (in many shades); 2mm wide twist cord piping composed of two thin aluminum and two thin blue-grey cords.

- Shoulder Boards: braiding made of double blue-grey flat cords with a center aluminum flat cord between and surrounded by double blue-grey cords; double underlay; without pip.

Official of the Medium Career wearing the 1936 pattern rank insignia.

Alterations by the above order of 2 November 1940, to be worn by 1 February 1941:

- Collar Patches: oakleaf wreath and four pips of matte grey machine-embroidery, surround of a twist cord of thin aluminum and dark green cords.
- Shoulder Boards: as above, with two aluminum-colored pips.

27

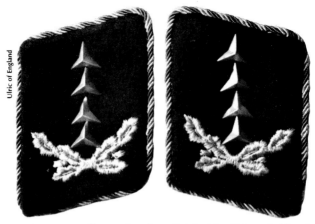

Ulric of England

Pre-November 1940 collar patches for official with NCO rank. The pips are metal, and the piping alternating two cords aluminum and two cords light blue.

Ulric of England

As above, but with embroidered pips.

Ulric of England

Collar patches for the official with NCO rank per the 2 November 1940 change. The piping is alternating aluminum and dark-green whereas previously it was aluminum and light-blue.

Shoulder board for official of the Medium Career with dark-green underlay and red secondary color; without pip.

The official with NCO rank at the right assists in inspecting tropical boots.

Shoulder board for official with NCO rank—dark-green underlay with red secondary and two pips per the 2 November 1940 order.

2) Officials with officer rank: collar patches and shoulder boards as for officials of the elevated career (rank of Leutnant and Oberleutnant), but distinguished from these by the piping of the collar patches that consisted of a twist cord of aluminum and blue-grey cords; since the 2 November 1940 order, of aluminum and dark green cords.   **29**

Rank insignia of Officials with High Grade Career prior to 31 December 1939 had aluminum twist cord piping about the collar patches. After that date the piping was gold. Shown below are the progression of rank insignia from Leutnant to Generalleutnant for officials with High Grade Career for ease of reference.

Halcomb Smith

Pre-31 December 1939 Leutnant.

A standard pattern Flyer's Blouse with rank insignia of an administrative official.

Capparelli

As above, Oberleutnant (left) and Hauptmann (right).

Post-31 December 1939 collar patches with gold twist cord piping for Oberleutnant of a High Grade Career.

As above, but for Hauptmann.

c. Officials of the Elevated Career: The officials of the elevated career wore the uniform of the officers of the ranks of Leutnant through Oberstleutnant. The dark green collar patches were with pips in lieu of wings, and the shoulder boards had a double underlay.

By an order (LV 41, No.1978) dated 29 November 1941 the officials with titles of Amtsrat and Oberamtmann were distinguished by two pips within the oakleaf wreath of the collar patches from the rank of Amtmann whose patches remained unchanged. All three titles held the rank of Major. However, some senior Amtsrat and Oberamtmann officials were bestowed with the personal rank of Oberstleutnant—usually after 25 years of service.

d. Officials of the High Grade Career: The officials of the high grade career wore the uniform of officers of the ranks of Leutnant through Generalleutnant. The dark green collar patches were with pips in lieu of wings, and the shoulder boards had a double underlay.

Originally, the piping of the collar patches of officials with ranks from Leutnant through Oberst was made of a twisted aluminum cord. Because they were not distinguished from the officials of the elevated career of equal ranks by the aluminum cord, the piping was altered to a twist gold cord by an order (LV 39C, No.1086) dated 5 December 1939. Wear of collar patches with aluminum piping was permitted until 31 December 1939 at the latest.

Oberleutnant of High Grade Career. Note the single gold pip on the shoulder board.

Hauptmann of High Grade Career with two pips on the shoulder boards.

Shoulder board for Hauptmann of a High Grade Career. Basic underlay is dark-green with bright red secondary color. The two pips are gold.

Pre-31 December 1939 pattern for Major as denoted by the aluminum piping.

Major of a High Grade Career wearing the collar patches of the post-December 1939 pattern with gold piping.

Shoulder board for Major with High Grade Career.

33

The Luftwaffe Music Superintendent (Luftwaffenmusikinspizient) held the rank of Major, and was on duty with the RLM. By order (LV 35, No.423) dated 26 July 1935 his secondary color was bright red, and he was distinguished by a gold metal lyre on his shoulder boards. By order (LV 35, No.786) dated 23 October 1935 his secondary color as that of all officials of the RLM was altered to black. By order (LV 38A, No.116) dated 12 April 1938 he was transferred to officer status with corresponding officer's collar patches and shoulder boards.

Other alterations prescribed by the above order of 5 December 1939 were the following (with the previous insignia permitted until 31 December 1939):

- Ministerialbürodirektor: gold cord piping on the collar patches
- high grade career judicial officials with collar patches of the secondary color as follows:
- officials of the Supreme Reich Court Martial: crimson (bordorot)
- other judicial officers: wine red

Judicial official with rank of Major with a High Grade Career. The collar patch is wine red with gold piping.

Ulric of England

Pre-31 December 1939 collar patches for rank of Oberstleutnant.

Shoulder board (right side) for Oberstleutnant.

As above. Note the pronounced configuration of the pips.

Korpsintendant (Oberstleutnant) Diecke.

As at left but with post-31 December 1939 gold twist cord piping.

35

Oberst of High Grade Career wearing the post-December 1939 collar patches with gold piping.

By an order (LVB 44, No.1189) dated 19 August 1944 the secondary color of the officials of the Construction-technical Administrative Service of the department of the Chief of the Luftwaffe Construction Service was altered to black (previously bright red), and the collar patches were also ordered to be black.

    e. Officials with General Officer Rank: The officials with general officer ranks wore the uniform and accouterments of general officers.
- Collar Patches: dark green with gold embroidery and twist cord piping. The color of the patches was altered for certain branches as follows:
  - order (LV 39C, No.1086) dated 5 December 1939: officials of the Supreme Reich Court Martial—crimson (bordorot); other judicial officials wine red.

- (LV 44, No.1189) dated 19 August 1944: Construction-technical Administrative Service—black
- Shoulder Boards: lower underlay dark green; upper underlay bright red. Alterations were as follows:
  - Supreme Reich Court Martial: crimson
  - other judicial officials: wine red according to order (LV 40, No.569) dated 10 May 1940 (but probably introduced already in 1938/39).
  - order (LV 40C, No.187) dated 16 February 1940: upper underlay white for all officials except those fo the Supreme Reich Court Martial and of other judicial officials that remained crimson and respectively wine red.
  - order (LV 44, No.561) dated 25 April 1944: upper underlay of the secondary color of the respective branch (white color abolished again!).
  - order of 19 August 1944 (as above): Construction-technical Administrative Service: upper underlay—black

Dr. Ing. e.h. Kurt Knipfer, inspector of the civilian Luftschutz, wears shoulder boards with white secondary underlay, and stripes on his breeches in white.

Trimming and piping of the greatcoat, the undress tunic of general officers, the long trousers, the breeches, the long trousers of the informal evening dress uniform and the cape were dark green, and were worn as prescribed for general officers. Alterations of the color were as follows:

- Greatcoats: Supreme Reich Court Martial and other judicial officials—crimson respectively wine red as per above order of 5 December 1938.
- Long trousers and breeches:
  - order of 5 December 1939: Supreme Reich Court Martial and other judicial officials—crimson respectively wine red.
  - order (LV 40C, No.187) dated 16 February 1940: white for all officials (also for the trousers of the informal evening full dress uniform) except those of the Supreme Reich Court Martial and of the other judicial officer, to be effective immediately.
  - order (LV 44, No.561) dated 25 April 1944: white again replaced by dark green.
  - order (LV 44, No.1189) dated 19 August 1944: Construction-technical Administrative Service—black.

Alterations of trim and piping of the undress tunic, the trousers of the informal evening dress uniform (one exception above) and the cape were not mentioned, probably because new procurement of these garments was prohibited during the war.

Grünberg

Uniform tunic of a Reichskriegsanwalt with rank of Generalmajor. The cut and style of the tunic is identical to those of the Luftwaffe.

Collar patch for official with general officer rank—dark-green patch with gold embroidery and piping.

Director of the Meteorological Department of the Luftwaffe R. Habermehl bears the equivalent rank of Generalmajor. The secondary color of the shoulder board is white per the 16 February 1940 order.

Collar patch and shoulder boards for Luftwaffe Judicial Official with general officer rank. The base color is wine red.

The official's greatcoat carries the equivalent rank of Generalleutnant. The collar patches are gold embroidery and piping on dark green, the shoulder boards have a white and dark green underlay, and the lapels are dark green. The uniform is that of Kurt Knipfer.

Charita

Ministerialdirektor Fisch (right) and NSFK Obergruppenführer Otto von Bülow. Note wear of the white trouser stripes as worn by a general officer. This is the highest rank of official.

As above, but wearing the rarely observed white uniform.

    f. Aspirants and Officials on Preparation Service and On Probation: Aspirants of the medium career which were on service in TO&E positions of officials "by an expressly given order of the RLM" wore the uniform of an official of the medium career of Oberfeldwebel rank with the following deviations:
- Collar Patches: one pip only
- Shoulder Boards: with one aluminum pip

Soldiers of Oberfeldwebel rank as aspirants for the elevated career (administrative branch) were accorded the uniform of Oberfähnrich of their respective soldier's branches after passing the prescribed examination by an order (LV 36, No.498) dated 16 April 1936, to be worn until the final appointment as official.

By order (LV 41, No.269) dated 3 March 1941, soldiers of Oberfeldwebel rank as official aspirants who served in TO&E position of an official of the elevated career were to wear the uniform of an Oberfeldwebel of their respective soldier's branch, but with a dark green piping around the collar patches.

By order (LV 40, No.886) dated 26 March 1940, all officials of the medium and elevated careers during their preparation and probation period were identified by a 1cm wide loop of dark green cloth around the base of the shoulder boards. The aspirants of the medium career wore the uniform of an official of Oberfeldwebel rank, and those of the elevated career the uniform of an official of Leutnant rank, all of their respective career.

Rank Insignia of the Garments of the Special Clothing

Rank insignia of the garments of the special clothing were introduced by an order (LV 37, No.1083) dated 17 August 1937, to be worn on the upper sleeves in the same manner as prescribed for officers. The insignia differed from those of the soldiers in the following manner:

- officials with titles Assistent and Werkführer and aspirants of Oberfeldwebel rank: one white horizontal bar measuring 6cm long and .5cm wide, with white triangular pips above the bar in the number as worn on collar patches.
- all other officials according to their rank: bars of 10cm in length and 1cm in width and triangular pips above in lieu of the wings of soldiers. The color of bars and pips was white, and golden-yellow for officials of general officer rank.

The pips were 2cm high and were sewn on one above the other over the center of the bars, and with one point vertically upwards. The backing was rectangular in the height of the bars and triangular above that. There was no distinction of careers or branches.

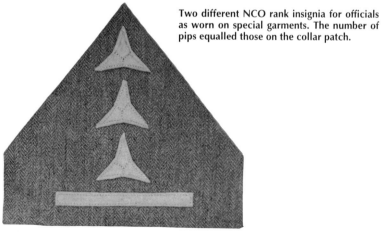

Two different NCO rank insignia for officials as worn on special garments. The number of pips equalled those on the collar patch.

Note the configuration of the rank patch worn on the motorcycle coat.

The same insignia were introduced for the sports training suit, possibly at an earlier date.

The distinction of the sports shirt was the same as prescribed for soldiers of equal rank: one 1cm wide black ribbon around the neck cut-out for NCO rank, and two ribbons for officer ranks.

5. Officials of the Body of Reserves, at Disposal, and Retired Officials: The officials of these groups followed the same regulations as the respective groups of officers. they were recognized by special accouterments. Following the outbreak of the war, and for the duration of the war, all officials of these groups recalled to service were required to wear the uniform of the active officials of their careers and branches without any distinctive insignia, a per order (BLB 40, No.70) dated 123 January 1940. The suffixes d.R., d.L., z.V. and a.D. were also omitted, except when necessary in documents of personnel matters.

   a. Officials of the Body of Reserves: The officials of the body of reserves (des Beurlaubtenstandes—d.B.) were classed in reserve officials (der Reserve—d.R.) and officials of the secondary reserve (der Landwehr—d.L.), with the respective suffix following the titles. By an "order of the Führer" (LV 43, No.142) dated 18 December 1943, the Landwehr status was abolished, and all officials of the secondary reserve were transferred to reserve status, with the suffix d.R.

Since about 1942 the suffix d.R., which was omitted since 1940, was frequently used again, and even required for reserve officials of certain branches open only for reserve personnel.

   • Uniform of the officials of the Body of Reserves: The officials wore the uniform of the active officials of their respective career and branch, and were recognized by a light blue secondary color that was introduced by an order of 1937, which has not been found. The secondary color was displayed by a light blue piping between the edges of the collar patches and the cord piping, and a light blue

43

Collar patches of officials of the Body of Reserves as denoted by the light blue secondary cord piping within the aluminum piping.

upper underlay of the shoulder boards (in lieu of the secondary color of the branch), with the result that the branch was no longer recognized. An outward distinction of officials of the reserve and the secondary reserve was not made.

Officials of officer rank as aspirants for the commission in the body of reserves which were not yet finally accepted, wore the uniform as ordered and with distinctive insignia when they voluntarily served a tour—usually four or eight weeks, to decide about their acceptance. The insignia took the form of two bridles of the pattern of retired officials under each shoulder board. The wear of the uniform was permitted only on duty, on the way to and from duty, and at the officer's mess.

- Uniform of Officials at Disposal: According to an ordinance (RGBl Part I 1938, page 214) dated 22 February 1938, officials of the body of reserves were accorded the status "At disposal" (zur Verfügung—z.V.) if they were accounted for a definite position in the case of mobilization. They had their normal titles with the suffix "z.V.", sometimes written as "d.R.z.V.", and wore the uniform of officials of the body of reserves without any additional insignia.

6. Luftwaffe Chaplains: Unlike the army or the navy, the Luftwaffe had no chaplains or bishops of its own. Rather, the Luftwaffe drew upon the chaplain personnel of the other two services to meet its needs. Thus, no specific uniform for a Luftwaffe chaplain or bishop existed.

7. Wartime Officials: The institution of the wartime officials, Beamte auf Kriegsdauer (officials for the war's duration) was introduced by the "Mobilization Order of the Luftwaffe" of 31 October 1938. Members of the Luftwaffe—NCOs and privates only—without the requirements for appointment as active or reserve officials, but

Army chaplain presiding over a Luftwaffe funeral.

needed for their civilian knowledge, could be appointed as "wartime officials" on a position of the wartime TO&E of units or commands. They were appointed with a rank according to their skills and education level. The wartime officials had the equivalent rank of officers or NCOs. Promotions to a higher rank were not possible.

The longer the war lasted, the more the wartime officials were appointed as reserve officials, usually after additional training. In order to preserve all able-bodied personnel for the fighting forces, admission to the status of wartime officials was restricted by order (LV 41, No.1548) dated 5 August 1941 to the following groups:

- For non-technical branches: only personnel born in 1909 and older; personnel already on duty as wartime officials of the years 1910 - 1927 were retained, however.
- In technical branches and in the Reich Weather Service: also personnel of the birth years 1910 - 1917 under the proviso of a basic military training.
- All branches: personnel of birth years 1910 - 1917 with a medical declaration "unfit for front line service."

An order (LV 42, No.2497) dated 24 September 1942 prohibited all further appointments of wartime officials. Wartime officials with the prescribed requirements were appointed reserve officials. Wartime officials without the requirements had to undergo an additional military training in order to be appointed as reserve officials until 1 October 1943 at the latest. All other wartime officials were renounced, and returned to their former soldier's status as NCOs or privates. By order (LV 43, NO.1755) dated 22 September 1943 some exceptions were permitted, but only until 31 March 1944 at the latest.

- Titles: The wartime officials had the title of their career and branch according to their duty position, with the suffix **45** "auf Kriegsdauer—a.Kr., a.K." by order (LV 41, No.1875) dated 24 November 1944.

- Uniform: The uniform of the wartime officials was introduced by the "Mobilization Order," Annex 12. They wore the uniform of equivalent active officials, but with special collar patches and with "shoulder cords" (Schulterschnüre) instead of shoulder boards. However, wartime officials in duty positions with the Reich Air Ministry and its immediately subordinated units were required to wear civilian clothes when on duty.
- Collar Patches: The dark green collar patches were without pips, but with the piping according to the career, to include the alterations for the medium and high grade careers (as discussed with the uniform of active officials) respectively without piping for the lower career. The "Mobilization Order" did not mention the oakleaf embroidery, which was actually worn.
- Shoulder Cords: The shoulder cords were of the same pattern as prescribed for Specialist Leaders (Sonderführer), and were without any underlay so that the branch was not identified. Apparently, irregular shoulder cords were frequently worn, and prohibited by several orders, but without much success. An order (BLB 40, No.1223) dated 8 October 1940 expressly stated that shoulder cords with 1.8cm, and of these of Leutnant rank with 1.4cm. Shoulder cords with backing or wider than prescribed were again prohibited by order (LV 42, No.639) dated 3 March 1942.

Rank of Soldiers	Shoulder Cords	Collar Patches
Oberfeldwebel	braided dark green flat cord of artificial silk with a 1mm wide center aluminum cord, 1 braided slide of aluminum threads	without pips and piping
Medium Career		
Oberfeldwebel	same, two slides	matte grey oakleaf wreath embroidery
Leutnant	parallel aluminum flat cord with a bend above	aluminum oakleaf wreath embroidery
Elevated Career		
Oberleutnant	same as Leutnant, with one slide braided of golden yellow artificial silk	aluminum oakleaf wreath embroidery

High Grade Career

Major

braided aluminum flat cord
with 8 - 11 lateral bends
and two bends at the base

aluminum oakleaf
wreath embroidery

Insignia for wartime Official with equivalent rank of Ober-feldwebel. The dark-green collar patch for the einfachen Dienstes was without adornment.

Two Oberfeldwebels of the Medium Career.

As above, but for Oberfeldwebel of the Medium Career.

Wartime official of Oberfeldwebel rank performing duties as a parachute rigger. He is of the Medium Career.

Wartime official of the Medium Career as denoted by the aluminum wreath and twist cord piping (left) and for the High Grade Career (right) denoted by the gold twist cord piping.

Wartime official of Medium Career. Note the unauthorized shoulder cord with underlay.

Fritz Otto Dreesen.

Wartime officials of various ranks.

49

Shoulder cords with backings, in these cases dark-green with bright red secondary, were prohibited by regulations, but still manufactured and worn.

Wartime official of Officer Rank but without any wreath in the collar patches.

Collar patch as worn on the greatcoat at right.

Collar patch with gold piping and unofficial shoulder cord for Oberleutnant with Elevated Career. The slide is yellow, and the underlay dark-greek with red secondary.

Wartime official with rank of Ober-leutnant as denoted by the single yellow slide on the aluminum shoulder cords.

Below: Two wartime officials with Oberleutnant rank wear the regulation rank insignia.

Mesturini

51

Wartime official with rank of Major wearing the regulation rank insignia. Note what appears to be the lack of piping about the collar patches.

Selzer

Elevated (left) and High Grade (right) careers. The wreath is aluminum hand-embroidery with either aluminum or gold twist cord piping.

Unauthorized shoulder cord for Major equivalent with pink underlay. There are ten bends.

Authorized shoulder cords without underlay.

52

Heitzer

Major of Elevated Career wearing unauthorized shoulder cords with underlay. Note the lack of wreath on the visor cap.

Wartime official wearing the white-topped visor cap and 1938 pattern Luftwaffe dagger.

The rank insignia of the garments of the protective clothing were the same as worn by active officials of equal rank as prescribed by an order (BLB 41, No.158) dated 6 February 1941.

Wear of dark green cords interwoven with aluminum threads on the visor caps, a habit apparently quite frequent with wartime officials of NCO rank, was prohibited by an order (BLB 40, No.1524) dated 17 December 1940.

By order (LV 40, No.1983) dated 19 August 1940 the wartime officials of NCO rank were granted the right to wear the officer's dagger in lieu of the flyer's dagger.

8. War Correspondents (Kriegsberichter): While one would think that war correspondents might fall into the category of wartime officials, they were NOT, in fact, officials at all, but rather drawn from professional photographers drafted into the general body of the Luftwaffe for the duration of the war. Unlike the army, the navy and the Luftwaffe did not have a "Propagandatruppen" in which to incorporate the war correspondents, while it can be assumed that separate units were formed after 1943. The status of the war correspondents was as officer or Sonderführer (later converted to soldier status).

Personnel of the propaganda units did not wear any special uniforms, but were identified by a sleeveband bearing the title "Kriegsberichter der Luftwaffe"* on the lower right sleeve. Enlisted patterns were without the top and bottom aluminum stripe, while those of officers were.

Enlisted Kriegsberichter typing his story. Note wear of the sleeveband without the top and bottom border stripes.

---

*Introduced by order (LV40, No. 1518) dated 20 November 1940.

Sleeveband for "Kriegsberichter der Luftwaffe" officer at the top, and enlisted personnel at the bottom.

Kriegsberichter officer recording his story on tape.

Taugourdeau

CHAPTER • 22
OFFICIALS WITH SPECIAL UNIFORMS

The uniforms of the Air Base Fire Departments and of the Forestry Officials were officially classified as "service clothing" (Dienstkleidung or Dienstbekleidung) rather than as "uniform". However, to simplify matters, the term "uniform" will be used.

A. Air Base Fire Departments and Officials of the Fire Protection Branch:

The Air Base Fire Departments (Fliegerhorstfeuerwehr) performed the fire protection and fire control duties at air bases and air fields, and at technical installations of the Luftwaffe such as depots, firing ranges, POL depots, ammunition depots and plants, etc. At the air bases, etc., the Fire Departments were organized in "Extinguishing Groups" (Löschgruppe) made up of 14 - 18 "civilian cadre personnel" (ziviles Stammpersonal) with the status of salaried employees (Angestellte) or hourly wage workers (Arbeiter). Officials of the fire protection branch of the medium career were in positions of leaders of the local Fire Departments, but also in administrative positions at the RLM and at major commands as were the officials of the high grade career. The director of the section "Fire Protection" of the RLM was an official with the title of "Ministerialrat".

During the early years of the Luftwaffe, the main portion of the cadre personnel and also of the officials was enlisted from the civilian professional and voluntary fire departments.

The earliest document found about the uniform of the Air Base Fire Departments was dated 22 March 1937. In later orders, references about uniforms are contained in two early orders (not yet found), which are dated 10 December 1934 and 29 April 1935.

The pre-1937 uniform most probably was that of the Prussian civilian fire departments, which deviated from the 1937 pattern uniform in minor details only. An order (LV 35, No.770) dated 21 October 1935 mentioned (but did not describe) a visor cap, tunic, long trousers and boots.

    1. Soldiers of the Extinguishing Groups: The extinguishing groups were reinforced by four to eight soldiers—usually one junior NCO

and privates—on a daily roster. The prescribed kind of dress was the drill dress. By order (LV 35, No.217) dated 13 May 1935 a light blue armband was prescribed to be worn on both upper sleeves. The 13cm wide and 39cm long armband was to be stamped on the inside by the issuing unit. The fire fighting equipment was the same as worn by the civilian cadre personnel—special helmet, belt with hook and hatchet.

Fire extinguishing group at the Luftwaffe airfield at Fürth, circa 1936/37.

2. Civilian Cadre Personnel: The civilian cadre personnel comprised the ranks of Feuerwehrmann, Oberfeuerwehrmann and Löschmeister. The latter had the status of employees, and the other personnel that of workers. They were neither soldiers nor officials, but rather "members of the Luftwaffe" (Angehörige der Luftwaffe).

Uniform, insignia and special equipment were introduced by order (LV 37, No.407) dated 22 March 1937. Off-duty wear of the uniform was prohibited except on the way to and from duty. If necessary, additional garments such as woolen pullovers or oil coats were issued from the stocks of the units.

- Rank Insignia: The ranks were recognized by collar patches and shoulder straps. The aluminum-colored rank pips and gulls were of the pattern as worn by Luftwaffe NCOs. The piping was made of crimson cloth or a woven Litze.
- Collar patches: The collar patches were made of black cloth with crimson piping, and took the form of the rhomboid measuring approximately 7.5 x 4cm. A metal wing was horizontally (to the long edge) affixed at the center. The addition and placement of the pip(s) distinguished the higher ranks.
- Shoulder straps: The straps were made of the basic cloth of the tunic, ended in a triangular point with a buttonhole near the end, and were with crimson piping and a centered metal wing. As with the collar patches, the addition and placement of the pip(s) distinguished the higher ranks.

Rank	Collar Patches	Shoulder Straps
Feuerwehrmann	gull, but no pip	gull, but no pip
Oberfeuerwehrmann	gull, with one pip positioned at the lower front corner	gull, with one pip below
Löschmeister	gull with one pip at the lower front and upper rear corners	gull, with one pip below and one above

Feuerwehrmann

The collar patches of the Feuerwehrmann were worn as a mirror image as shown here.

Lautenschläger

Oberfeuerwehrmann

Löschmeister

- Uniform:
  - Visor Cap: The style and design was identical to that of the standard Luftwaffe visor cap. It was made, however, of dark blue cloth with a cap band of black cloth, and with crimson piping around the top and at either edge of the cap band. The visor and chip strap were made of black lacquered leather, with the strap secured by two small (12mm) black smooth buttons. The Reich pattern national emblem was affixed to the upper front portion. The eagle, with head facing to its right wing, measured 4.4cm (wingspan) and 3cm high. The enlarged civilian badge of employees and workers of the Luftwaffe was affixed to the front center of the cap band. The badge was a swastika standing on its point surrounded by a circular oakleaf wreath, and with wings projecting horizontally at each side. An order (LV

38A, No.34) dated 3 February 1939 prescribed the wingspan to be 11cm, and the wreath diameter 2.9cm. Both national emblem and civilian badge were stamped aluminum-colored metal.

Period photos indicate the wear of the following non-regulation aluminum metal insignia instead of those prescribed:

    a. Luftwaffe pattern national emblem

    b. Luftwaffe pattern winged oakleaf wreath with cockade

    c. Winged oakleaf wreath with cockade resembling the DLV—a rather narrow wreath with short wings

Apparently, any combination of regulation and non-regulation insignia was worn.

Enlisted visor cap of the Luftwaffe Fire Defense Service—course dark blue top and cap band with crimson piping at the top and bottom of the cap band, and about the cap top. Metal insignia are either aluminum or silver-colored. The black leather chinstrap is of the army pattern, and retained by black enamel buttons. The interior is lined with a brownish cotton. The underside of the black vulcan-fiber visor is of the same brownish color.

Note the three variations of insignia being worn on the visor caps at the same time.

- Tunic: The tunic was termed "Rockbluse" ("tunic-blouse"). It was made of dark blue cloth, and buttoned by eight 2cm aluminum-colored buttons. Two breast pockets were of the patch-type variety with center pleats. The hip pockets were diagonally inserted slash types. All pockets had scalloped flaps with 1.6cm diameter buttons, which were replaced by 2cm diameter buttons in November 1938. An inside pocket was at the left breast. The stand-up-lay-down collar was made of basic cloth, and was with a sewn-in black neckliner. The collar patches were sewn on at a distance of approximately .8cm from the front and lower edges. A belt hook was positioned at either side seam in the waistline. The back was with a center seam, which opened as a slash from the waistline downwards, and with two seams which curved from the sleeve cut-out downwards. A 2cm diameter button was positioned a the crossing points of the curved seams with the waistline seam. At either side of the slash was an inside pocket. The sleeves ended with open turn-up cuffs. The shoulder straps were sewn into the sleeve seam.

The national emblem of the Reich pattern was positioned at the center of the upper left sleeve. It was machine-embroidered of matte grey threads on a backing of basic cloth. The head of the eagle was turned to its right wing. **61**

Oberfeuerwehrmann instructs in fighting incindiary bombs. He wears the dark blue uniform of the Luftwaffe air base fire department.

National emblem as worn on the upper left sleeve—machine-embroidered white eagle on a round 55mm black backing.

The eagle clutched a wreath with a swastika standing on one point. The measurements were approximately 9.5 x 3.8cm (without backing). However, there is photographic evidence that tunics were frequently worn without the national emblem.

Long Trousers: Cut and design of the black trousers were identical to the standard Luftwaffe trousers. The 2mm side seam piping was crimson. When worn with boots the trousers were tucked into the boots.

Greatcoat: The greatcoat was made of black cloth, and was buttoned by two rows of six 2cm diameter aluminum-colored buttons each. The sleeves ended in 16cm high open cuffs. Both sides of the collar were made of the dark blue cloth of the tunic. The collar piping was 2mm crimson. Collar patches were not worn. The inserted hip pockets were with slanted openings, and with a non-buttoned flap with a rounded lower front corner. The back was with a center pleat that opened to a slash from the waistline downwards. The slash was buttoned by three small aluminum buttons. The two-part back belt was buttoned at the center. A patch (Faltenleiste) that was twice scalloped at the inner edge was sewn on below the ends of the belt and downwards in a length of approximately 18cm, and with the straight outward edge of the patches sewn into the side seams. Three 2cm diameter buttons were positioned on each patch, one on the belt, and one each at the center and bottom points. A short slash was positioned at either side seam to put through the belt hooks of the tunic. The greatcoat was worn buttoned up to the collar.

The sewn-in shoulder straps and the national sleeve emblem were as worn on the tunic.

Footwear: Boots and lace-up shoes were the standard Luftwaffe models.

Leather belt and cross strap: These were made of black leather and of the pattern generally worn by the civilian fire departments. The belt buckle and the metal parts of the cross strap were made of aluminum-colored light-metal alloy. The distinctive belt buckle had a slightly curved pebbled face. A circular stamped shield measuring about 4.2cm in diameter featured a center swastika standing on its point, and on a finely pebbled center field surrounded by a 1cm wide border edged by two narrow rope-like rims. Within the border, on a finely grained background, was the inscription of Gothic letters above

Police pattern aluminum belt buckle worn with a black leather belt with or without the cross strap.

"Gott mit uns" (God with us), and in the lower half were oakleaf branches bound by a vertical ribbon.

Wear of the belt and cross strap, with a bayonet and tassel, was permitted on the way to and from work only. However, there is photographic evidence that these accouterments were also worn at ceremonial occasions. Belt and cross strap and the bayonet were not issue articles, but had to be privately procured.

Bayonet and Tassel: The bayonet was termed "Faschinenmesser" (literally "knife to cut fascines," a side arm peculiar to the civilian fire departments). The basic design was that of the standard Luftwaffe bayonet. the cross guard curved upwards at the front and downwards at the rear. Grip and cross guard were nickel-plated, and the grip plates were black plastic. The scabbard was matte black. The usual bayonets had either a 20cm long blade, frequently with a saw at the top edge, or a 25cm long blade, which also could be with the saw back. The black bayonet frog was the standard Luftwaffe model.

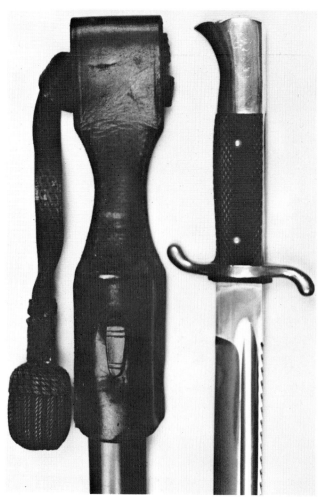

Distinctive fire department dress sidearm with recurve guard. Specimen is with a sawtooth top edge, which was an optional feature. The ball of the tassel is aluminum and crimson.

The tassel took the form of the army pattern portepee, and was with a flat ball of an oval cross-section. Slide, crown and ball were made of aluminum and crimson thin cords. The tassel was wound around the bayonet frog.

Protective Garments and Equipment: Work suits and work caps were the standard Luftwaffe models, and were issued from Luftwaffe stocks. The other articles were of the pattern worn by civilian fire fighting units, both professional and volunteer.

Work Suit: The one-piece work suit (Arbeitsschutzanzug) was made of black drill fabric. Grade insignia were not worn. By order (LV 40, No.708) dated 4 June 1940 the color was altered to dark blue.

Charita

One and two-piece protective garments being worn.

Black work cap made of drill cloth, and with the national emblem of the pattern as worn on the left sleeve. The cap was produced with and without the air vent grommets.

Work Cap: The work cap was made of black drill fabric (dark blue drill since 4 June 1940). The national emblem was sewn to the upper front above the flap. It was of the pattern of the tunic, but reduced in size and was matte grey machine-embroidered.

65

Helmet: The matte black lacquered helmet was made of a light-metal alloy (1.3mm thick) or of steel (.8mm thick). The form was similar to the M1935 steel helmet. However, the neck guard was shorter, and the slanted transition from the visor to the neck guard was not rounded but angular. Two 1.5cm diameter washer rings, which allowed for ventilation, were positioned at either side and in height of the rounded top and with a distance of 5cm between their centers. The rings were covered by a black wire net. Since about 1938 the wire nets were replaced by a circular piece of metal with seven small holes—one in the center and six around it. Finally, the washer rings were omitted, and the seven holes were drilled into the body of the helmet.

The liner unit consisted of a lining with cushion and a black buckled chinstrap, and was connected with the body of the helmet by three or four rivets. The cushion at the inside top was usually affixed by a cross made of stripes of vulcanfibre. The detachable black leather neck protective guard was slanted toward the back at the sides and rounded at the rear bottom edge. It was affixed to the liner unit by short narrow leather bands secured in slits of the leather neck guard.

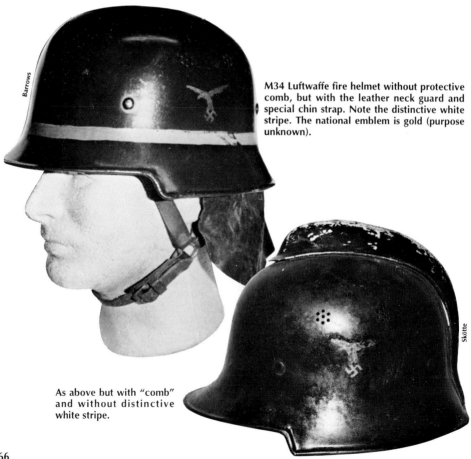

Barrows

M34 Luftwaffe fire helmet without protective comb, but with the leather neck guard and special chin strap. Note the distinctive white stripe. The national emblem is gold (purpose unknown).

Skötte

As above but with "comb" and without distinctive white stripe.

Standard pattern M34 helmet—black with white stripe and standard pattern luftwaffe insignia.

Halcomb Smith

Instructor wears the helmet without comb, but with protective neck guard. Also shown is the wide leather utility belt with hook.

A nickel-plated "comb" (Kamm) with a triangular cross-section reached longitudinally from the rounded top towards the rear edge of the neck guard, and was affixed by two internal screws in holes at the top and one screw at the neck guard. Its height continually decreased to the rear edge of the helmet. When the comb was abolished in about 1939, the holes of the helmet were covered by small metal or leather patches. New helmets were manufactured without these holes. Since about 1940, a 1cm wide white stripe was painted around the base of the helmet above the visor and the neck guard.

The insignia were the same as on the M1935 steel helmet of the Luftwaffe—national emblem at left, and national tri-color shield on the right.

During the war standard Luftwaffe steel helmets were also issued, and were with or without the white stripe.

Borowicz

Black fire protection helmet with white painted designation "Fliegerhorstfeuerwehr" (air field fire protection) on the side, and the number "138" on the front.

Another example of the black fire protection helmet with comb.

Skötte

Belt with Hook (Hakengurt): The approximately 8.5cm wide belt of strong black leather was buckled by two leather straps right and two metal buckles left or by a two-pronged buckle affixed to the left end of the belt. A strong carbine hook of nickel-plated steel was secured to the left side of the belt by a slit of its flat rear through which the belt was passed. The height of the hook was about 12cm. At the right front a strong steel D-ring was riveted to the belt by means of a metal plate. Ring and hook served the purpose to secure the wearer of the belt to ropes, etc.

Hatchet (Beil): The head of the hatchet was covered by a black leather carrying case that was buckled or looped onto the left side of the belt.

Axe used by fire protection personnel. The black leather carrying case is marked with the Luftwaffe control stamp under the flap. The small pouch is probably for a sharpening stone.

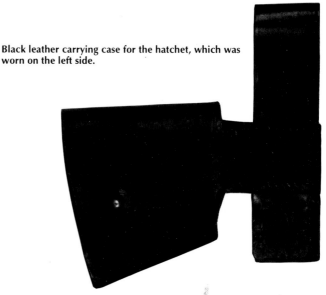

Black leather carrying case for the hatchet, which was worn on the left side.

Rope (Fangleine): The rope was 20m long, and had a gadget to affix the water hose.

Whistle (Signalpfeife): The whistle was made of black horn, and was secured by a nickel-plated chain, which usually was hooked to a button of the tunic or work suit.

Gas Mask: Normally the standard gas mask was issued, but with a special filter canister that protected against smoke gases.

3. Officials of the Fire Protection Branch: The officials of the fire protection branch (Feuerschutzbeamte) belonged to the medium and high grade careers. In 1940/41, the introduction of the elevated career, too, was under consideration, but this was not executed. The officials were obliged to wear the uniform.

a. Officials of the Medium Career:

1) Uniform of 1937: Uniform, ranks and insignia were introduced by an order (LV 37, No.407) dated 22 March 1937. The branch color was determined as dark green, and the secondary color as golden brown, to be worn on the shoulder boards only. Except for the insignia, the garments were identical with the uniform of the civilian cadre personnel. Black breeches with high boots were also worn. If necessary, protective garments and equipment were issued as for the civilian cadre personnel.

The ranks of Brandmeister and higher were accorded some accouterments of officers, but did not possess the full officer's prerogatives and insignia.

• Collar Patches: The dark green collar patches had oakleaves (as Leutnant) and triangular pips in matte light grey machine-embroidery and a 2mm wide twist aluminum and blue-grey cord piping.

Personnel wearing the 1937 pattern uniform. Note the wide variety of cap wreaths and national emblems.

- Shoulder Boards: Shoulder boards were termed "Schulterlitzen" (vice "Schulterstücke" of officers). The center braiding with five bends at either side was made of two blue-grey flat cords and a center aluminum flat cord, and was surrounded by two blue-grey flat cords. The backing was dark green with an upper (inner) underlay of golden brown. The aluminum rank pips were of the NCO pattern. The general make of the shoulder boards was the same as previously discussed with the other officials of Oberfeldwebel rank. Rank insignia were as follows:

Title	collar patches	shoulder boards
Unterbrandmeister	1 pip	none
Brandmeister	2 pips	1 pip
Hauptbrandmeister	3 pips	2 pips

Aspirants of the medium career on probational service wore the uniform and rank insignia of a Löschmeister, and were recognized by a 5mm thick twisted aluminum and blue-grey cord around the base of the shoulder straps. After passing an examination they were appointed as a.p. (a.p.= außerplanmäßig = supernumerary) Unterbrandmeister with the respective uniform.

71

Hauptbrandmeister wears the saber sidearm.

Shoulder board of the Hauptbrandmeister.

- National Emblem: The national emblem was matte grey machine-embroidery for Unterbrandmeister, and aluminum hand-embroidery for Brandmeister and Hauptbrandmeister. It was sewn on above the right breast pocket of the tunic.
- Tunic: At times the tunic was adorned by crimson piping around the collar and on the left front edge. However, this was against regulations, and was expressly forbidden by several orders. Wear of an "office tunic" (Bürorock) made of dark blue gabardine and in cut and style of the cloth tunic was permitted for office duties.
- Visor Cap: Dark blue with crimson piping, and with the metal national emblem and winged wreath of the Luftwaffe NCOs and privates. Ranks of Brandmeister and Hauptbrandmeister were with aluminum officer's cord, and wear of aluminum hand-embroidered insignia was permitted.
- Leather Coat: A black leather coat of the cut and style of the officers' leather coat was introduced about the end of 1937, to be worn with the shoulder boards. A variant coat was made of black artificial leather.

- Side Arms: The side arms were worn with the standard Luftwaffe portepee. When on duty, wear of the M84/98 bayonet was required, to be worn with the bayonet frog corresponding in color with the leather belt.

The saber of the civilian fire departments was permitted for optional off-duty wear. The general design of the saber was that of the army officer's saber. The metal parts of the hilt were gold-colored and polished but undecorated. The regulations required the war of the saber by a carrying sling of army pattern which was looped onto the leather belt and hooked to the ring of the scabbard. The leather sling was black or brown corresponding to the color of the belt, and the hooked chain was nickel-plated. However, the saber was usually hooked to a special saber frog that was worn through a slit beneath the flap of the left hip pocket.

Special Accouterments:
- Unterbrandmeister: Leather belt and belt buckle as for Luftwaffe NCOs and privates.
- Brandmeister and Hauptbrandmeister: Leather belt and cross strap as for officers (cross strap abolished as for officers in the early war).
- Hauptbrandmeister: Wear of a cape was permitted. The cape was made of the black cloth of the greatcoat. Both sides of the collar were made of the dark blue cloth of the tunic, and the front and bottom edges were with crimson piping.

By an order (LV 37, No.1139) dated 1 September 1937 the new rank of Oberbrandmeister was introduced. All existing Hauptbrandmeister were re-designated Oberbrandmeister effective by the end of 1937. The grade designation Hauptbrandmeister was retained as the new senior rank of the medium career. The grade insignia were determined by an order (LV 38B, No.18) dated 27 January 1938 as follows:
- Unterbrandmeister: Insignia as before
- Brandmeister: Insignia as before
- Oberbrandmeister: As Hauptbrandmeister before
- Hauptbrandmeister: Collar patches with four pips; shoulder boards as before, but with the outer cord of the surround with 4mm wide aluminum V-threads spaced 8mm apart; 2 rank pips

The officer-pattern accouterments of the ranks of Brandmeister through Hauptbrandmeister were retained as before. The cape, however, was permitted for the "new" Hauptbrandmeister rank exclusively.

Grade Insignia of the Special Clothing: These consisted of a 6cm long and .5cm wide white bar with white triangular pips above. Manner of construction and wear were as prescribed for soldiers.

2) Uniform of 1940: By order (LV 40, No.569) dated 10 May 1940 the secondary color was altered to bright red. The dark green branch color was retained.

By order (LV 40, No.1426) dated 2 November 1940 the ranks of Brandmeister through Hauptbrandmeister were equaled in every aspect with

Official in the rank of Brandmeister.

Pre-September 1939 pattern collar patch for Hauptbrandmeister.

Collar patch (right side) for the 1 September 1939 Hauptbrandmeister.

officials with the rank of Leutnant and Oberleutnant respectively. They now wore the blue-grey standard uniform of officials. The side arms were replaced by the officer's dagger and the sword. Details about the blue-grey uniform and the insignia were proclaimed by an order (LV 40, No.1427) of the same day. Garments of the dark blue fire fighting uniform were to be worn out "until completely unfit for wear." Certainly, these garments were soon considered "unfit for wear," and the blue-grey uniform was adopted shortly afterwards. By the same order the piping of collar patches was altered to an aluminum and dark green. The grade insignia were as follows:

Title	Grade Insignia	Rank Equivalent
Unterbrandmeister	collar patches with oakleaf and 3 pips in matte grey machine-embroidery; piping	Oberfeldwebel

Brandmeister	officer-pattern collar patches with oakleaf and one gull; piping as above; shoulder boards as officials with the rank of Leutnant—double backing of dark green and bright red	Leutnant
Oberbrandmeister	collar patches as Brandmeister with two gulls; shoulder boards as Brandmeister, with one pip	Oberleutnant
Hauptbrandmeister	as Oberbrandmeister (difference in pay only)	Oberleutnant

During a transition period the dark blue tunic was worn with the new collar patches and shoulder boards, and the black greatcoat with the new shoulder boards.

- Grade Insignia of the Special Clothing: In consequence of the new ranking system the ranks of Brandmeister through Hauptbrandmeister now wore the grade insignia of officials with company grade rank, i.e. a 10cm long and 1cm wide white bar with one respectively two pips above. The Unterbrandmeister retained the 6cm long bar, but with three pips above.

b. Officials of the High Grade Career: The officials of the high grade career were incorporated in the "general construction administrative branch" (allgemeiner Bauverwaltungsdienst), and wore the standard official's uniform with dark green branch color and bright red secondary color. The aluminum collar patch piping was altered to a gold twist cord by order (LV 39C, No.1096) dated 5 December 1939. The grade insignia, including these of the special clothing, were the same as worn by other officials of equal rank as follows:

(a.p.) Regierungsbauassessor: as officials equal in rank to Hauptmann
Regierungsbaurat: Major
Oberregierungsbaurat: Oberstleutnant
Ministerialrat: Oberst

c. Wartime Officials: When, during the early phases of the war, the demand for fire department units vastly increased, wartime officials (Beamte auf Kriegsdauer) were employed to fill the duty positions. Löschmeister personnel could rise to the rank of Unterbrandmeister a.K. As it seems, an elevated career for wartime officials was constituted for experienced officials of the medium career. The grade insignia and uniform of the wartime officials was the same as worn by other wartime officials. Titles and the equivalent ranks were as follows:

- Medium Career: Unterbrandmeister a.K.   Oberfeldwebel
                      Brandmeister a.K.   Leutnant
- Elevated Career: Regierungsbauinspektor a.K.   Oberleutnant

4. Air Base Fire Departments during the War: At the beginning of the war, able-bodied personnel were mobilized as soldiers. The peacetime fire departments had to form the cadre personnel for the ever-increasing demand of fire fighting units when the war widened throughout Europe and North Africa. To meet the demand "auxiliary personnel" (Hilfsfeuerwehrmänner) were drafted in accordance with the War Service Laws (Notdienstverpflichtung).

Wartime air base fire leader (Hauptbrandmeister) in 1944 wearing the later issued standard Luftwaffe blue-grey uniform, but with the earlier pattern rank insignia.

Personnel of the Brandmeister candidate course in 1941. Most wear the insignia of a Unterbrandmeister a.K.

The personnel of the fire fighting detachments (Einsatzkommando) at air fields outside the Reich was apparently issued standard Luftwaffe uniforms, which were worn with the peacetime collar patches and shoulder straps. Since about 1940/41 the personnel was ultimately transferred to the status of soldier. These wore the standard Luftwaffe uniform with the golden-yellow branch color. In the occupied countries, the detachments were also reinforced by non-German personnel. For defense, the detachments in the occupied countries and in the war zones were equipped with light arms.

In the home war zone (Heimatkriegsgebiet) personnel medically unfit for front-line duty were drafted as "fire protection soldiers" (Feuerschutzsoldaten).

Official documents about the uniform of the air base fire departments at air fields outside of the Reich have not been located. An order (LV 43, No.1163) dated 27 May 1943 would indicate that the dark blue peacetime uniform continued to be worn by the civilian cadre personnel. The order required "if necessary" the issue of standard Luftwaffe flyer's caps, work suits, boots and greatcoats, with the requirement that the national emblem and the cockade of the flyer's cap and the shoulder straps of the greatcoat had to be removed. When on duty, German personnel were required to wear the white armband with the black inscription "Im Dienst der Deutschen Wehrmacht," and the citizens of "allied or befriended countries" on service outside of their home state had to wear an armband of the colors of the respective state with the same inscription.

By order (LV 44, page 406) dated 1 June 1944 the fire fighting departments were reorganized as military units.

- Specialist Leaders (Sonderführer): When parts of the air base fire departments were transferred to a soldier's status it became necessary to accord the grades of Oberfeuerwehrmann and Löschmeister with a military rank, if they did not already possess a suitable rank as soldier of the reserve. They were collectively termed "Sonderführer F" (F = Feuerwehr), and were given the specialist leader's ranks of "Sonderführer G" (equivalent to

Unteroffizier) or "Sonderführer O" (equivalent to Oberfeldwebel). The rank insignia were the same as worn by other specialist leaders. The branch color was golden-yellow.

- Female Auxiliaries: Since mid-1944 when more personnel of the fire departments were transferred to front-line duties, the units were re-filled by female auxiliaries (Feuerschutzhelferinnen—fire protection auxiliaries) who either voluntarily enlisted or were drafted according to the Emergency War Service Laws. The auxiliaries wore the standard uniform of the Luftwaffe signal auxiliaries, and were issued the protective garments and equipment necessary for fire fighting duties.

A special insigne was worn on the upper left sleeve—a machine-embroidered red Gothic "F" on a round underlay of basic cloth. The rank of "Vorhelferin" was recognized by a chevron made of NCO Tresse below the "F" insigne, with 10cm, angle of about 140°, point downwards.

B. Luftwaffe Forestry Service: The task of the Luftwaffe Forestry Administration or Service (Forstverwaltung der Luftwaffe) was the supervision and direction of the forestry administration, economical utilization and hunting service of all forestry properties of the Luftwaffe, such as training areas, etc. As far as forestry matters were concerned, it was directed by the regulations of the Reich Forestry Service.

The uniform of the officials of the Luftwaffe Forestry Administration was quite different from that of the soldiers, and marks an important departure from the uniform worn by other officials. Basically, the uniform was that of the State or Reich forestry officials, but with the insignia and accouterments of the Luftwaffe.

The forestry officials had the general NCO or officer rank as documented by their grade insignia, but they did not have any determined NCO or officer rank. A distinction was made between operational officials (Forstbetriebsbeamte) belonging to the medium and elevated careers, and administrative officials (Forstverwaltungsbeamte) of the high grade career.

1. Uniform of 1936: By an order (LV 36, No.376) dated 18 March 1936 the uniform of the Army Forestry Officials was adopted by the Luftwaffe Forestry Officials, but worn with standard Luftwaffe insignia and accouterments. The army manual H.Dv.120 "Uniform Regulations for Army Forestry Officials" (Dienstkleidungsvorschrift für die Heeresforstverwaltung) published on 28 February 1935 was also valid for Luftwaffe Forestry administration.

The kinds of dress were as follows—forest dress (Walddienstanzug), office dress (Innendienstanzug), and dress uniform (Gesellschaftsanzug). For off-duty wear the officials had the option of the office dress (with tunic A) or the forest dress. The parade dress was the forest dress with tunic B and aiguillette.

The M1936 pattern uniform consisted of the following articles:

a. Tunic A (Rock A): A single-breasted grey-green cloth tunic, with an open collar, and closed with four buttons at the front. The collar was made of dark green cloth, and with a cord trimming in length of the embroidery on the collar of the tunic B. Two patch breast pockets with pleats, and two slanted inserted side pockets were with scalloped buttoned flaps. The sleeves were with 16cm long turn-back open cuffs. The cut of the back was with a center seam ending in a back slash, two curved seams from the sleeve cut-out down, and with two buttons in the waistline at the crossing point with the curved seams. The back slash reached 2.5cm beyond the center line to the right side, and was with an inside pocket at either edge. At the left waist was a slit for the frog of the hunting cutlass. Buttons were 1.9mm (1.6mm for shoulder boards) dark green pebbled horn. A dark green piping along the left front edge, around the lapels, on the edges of the pocket flaps, around the cuffs, and on the edge of the back slash adorned the tunic.

b. Tunic B (Rock B): This was in the same design and color as tunic A, but with the following deviations—collar was made of dark green velvet with an oakleaf embroidery (without patches i.e. directly into the collar), and a trimming of cord or a woven Litze on the corners in the length of the embroidery. Buttons were of the bright pebbled aluminum variety. The embroidery consisted of two oakleaves and four acorns as follows:

- operational officials: Leaves and lower part of the acorns green; stems, ribs of the leaves and upper part of the acorns in aluminum embroidery.
- administrative officials: Leaves and lower part of the acorns in aluminum embroidery; stems, ribs of the leaves and upper part of the acorns in green embroidery.

National emblem of both tunics was of the Luftwaffe pattern, and positioned above the right breast pocket with the bottom point of the swastika immediately above the button, and covering the buttonhole. The embroidery was made of dark green silk mixed with aluminum threads and on a base of grey-green basic cloth.

c. Trousers and Breeches: Cut and design of the trousers were of the standard Luftwaffe pattern, and were grey-green with dark green piping along the outer seams. The leather strap at the cuffs were secured around the soles, and were prescribed when the elastic-sided black boots were worn. The straps were prohibited for wear with the lace-up shoes. Breeches (Stiefelhose) were of mouse-grey cloth.

d. Footwear: Brown or black lace-up shoes or low-quarter shoes were optional with tunic A. Only black shoes were permitted with tunic B. Breeches were worn with high boots, or with lace-up shoes with knee-length leather leggings (Leder-

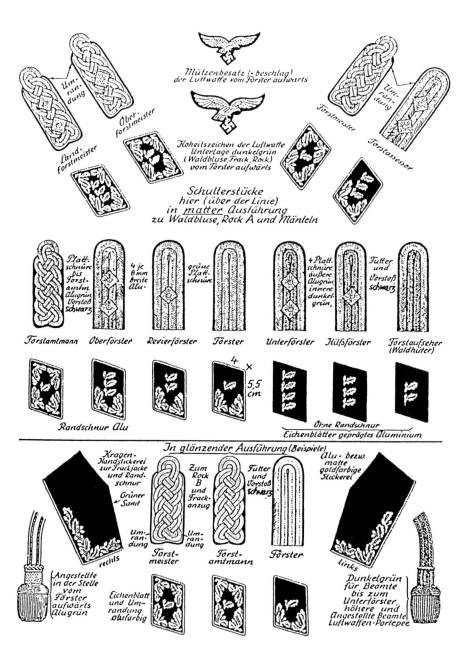

gamaschen) of the same color as the shoes, or with grey-green knee-length wrap-around puttees (Wickelgamaschen), or with grey or grey-green knee-length wool stockings (Strumpfgamaschen).

e. Greatcoat (Mantel): Made of grey-green cloth in the design of the officer's greatcoat. It had a dark green collar with isosceles trimming on the corners of the collar as on the tunic B. The open cuffs measured 18cm long. The dark green pebbled but-

Revierförster wears the standard uniform with greatcoat.

tons measured 1.9cm in diameter. A dark green piping was around the cuffs and the back belt. A slit for the frog of the hunting cutlass was positioned below the flap of the left side pocket. The greatcoat was normally worn with the uppermost three buttons unbuttoned and the lapels turned outwards.

Coats of a civilian design made of grey-green coarse woolen waterproof cloth (Loden coat) were permitted for wear at forest duties. The usual design was with short lapels and buttoned at the front by a hidden buttonhole tape, with two side pockets with unbuttoned flaps, and frequently with a muff-pocket above the side pockets. The back was with a center pleat from the collar downwards, and was without a back belt. Shoulder boards were not worn.

f. Overjacket (Überziehjoppe): Made of grey-green, water-repellent fabric, of similar design as the windjacket of the army mountain troops, double-breasted with two rows of three buttons each. Reaching nearly down to the knees, it had two large patch side pockets with center pleats, and two slanted, inserted muff-pockets. The buttoned flaps of the side pockets were scalloped. The back was without a pleat, and with a 6cm wide belt in two parts, buttoned by two buttons. There was a dark green piping around the collar and the back belt, and along the edges of the flaps and the muff-pocket tapes. The front edge of the collar was trimmed by a cord as on tunic B. The 2.5cm diameter buttons were made of dark green leather. Shoulder boards were not worn.

g. Windjacket (Windjacke): Grey-green windjackets of any civilian design were permitted for optional wear with the forest uniform in lieu of the overjacket. Shoulder boards were not worn.

h. Cape (Umhang): The cape was of the Luftwaffe officer's design, and made of grey-green cloth with a dark green collar.

i. Headgear: The Luftwaffe national emblem pressed of aluminum-colored metal was worn on all hats and caps except the field cap. Administrative officials had the option to wear aluminum-embroidered emblems.

- Hat (Hut): The hat, worn with the forest uniform, was made of grey-green felt, with a high head part with a shallow, longitudinal crease, and with a 6-7cm wide brim bordered by a narrow band of dark green rep. Around the base of the head part was a 5cm wide band of dark green rep with a bow on the left side. The national emblem was affixed on the front, immediately over the hat-band. On the bow of the hat-band was a tuft of hair made of wild boar bristle, or of chamois beard, or of hair of badgers or red deer. The hair tuft was fastened by a circular black-white-red cockade measuring 3cm in diameter.

Forestry hat of the type worn by the Luftwaffe Forestry Service, whose hats would have the Luftwaffe national emblem and a black/white/red cocade at the brush.

- Visor cap (Schirmmütze): The visor cap was prescribed for wear with the tunic B, and optionally permitted with the tunic A, except on forest duties. It was made of grey-green cloth in the design of the Luftwaffe visor cap. It had a dark green cap-band and a dark green piping around the crown, with a black patent leather visor. Centered on the front of the cap band was the embroidered winged oakleaf wreath of the Luftwaffe pattern with cockade. The national emblem was affixed above. Embroideries (on dark green backing) and cap cords/chin straps were as follows:
  1) Forstanwärter, Hilfsförder and Forstaufseher: Winged wreath embroidered of green silk. Black patent leather chin strap buttoned by two 1.2cm diameter smooth black buttons.
  2) Operational officials (Förster, Revierförster, Oberförster): Winged wreath embroidered of green silk interwoven with aluminum threads. Officer pattern cord was made of green silk interwoven with aluminum threads, and buttoned by two 1.2cm diameter pebbled aluminum-colored buttons.
  3) Administrative officials (Forstassessor and higher): Winged wreath embroidered of aluminum threads interwoven with green silk. Officer pattern cord made of aluminum interwoven with green silk, buttons as b) above.
- Field cap (Feldmütze): This was made of the soft design of the army officer's old style field cap i.e. a visor cap without stiffening devices and without cord or strap. It was made of grey-green cloth or lightweight fabric, with a dark green cap band and dark green piping around the crown, and with a black flexible leather visor. The embroidered winged wreath with cockade was as worn on the visor cap. The field cap was worn without the national emblem. Wear of the field cap was optional with all forest duties in lieu of the hat.
- Winter field cap (Baschlikmütze): This was permitted for wear during the winter months instead of the hat or the field cap on forest duties. It was made of grey-green cloth, and of the design of the mountain cap as worn by the army mountain troops. The visor was cloth-covered on both sides. The flap was secured by two small 1.6cm diameter dark green pebbled horn buttons. A metal tri-colored rosette and above it the aluminum Luftwaffe pattern national emblem were affixed to the upper front of the cap.

j. Shirts (Hemden): A dark mignonette green (resedagrün) "hunting shirt" (Jagdhemd) with a dark green tie was worn with tunic A. For office duties and for off-duty wear white shirts

Winter field cap of the type worn by the Luftwaffe Forestry Service, but with the Luftwaffe national emblem.

with a dark green tie were optionally permitted. White shirts with a starched collar and with a black tie were prescribed for wear with the tunic B. All shirts were with a detachable collar with was buttoned to the shirt.

k. Summer uniforms: Summer uniforms made of lightweight fabrics—woolen cloth, linen or drill fabric—in color, cut and accouterments of the tunic A and the trousers were permitted during the summer months.

l. Belt (Koppel): The belt was 4.5cm wide dark green leather with a double-claw buckle—burnished for wear with tunic A, and aluminum-colored for wear with tunic B. The belt was prescribed for wear with tunic B at all occasions (without pistol), and with tunic A on forest duties when wear of a pistol was necessary, and otherwise at special semi-formal events. When the pistol was worn, the holster was made of dark green leather.

Dark green leather 4.5cm wide leather belt with aluminum-colored pebbled double open-claw buckle as worn with the tunic B.

m. Dress Aiguillette (Fangschnur): This was worn with tunic B at ceremonial events, and always with the belt and hunting cutlass. The design and manner of wear was the same as the Luftwaffe dress aiguillette for officers up to the rank of Oberst. The dress aiguillettes were made as follows:

- Operational officials (Förster, Revierförster, Oberförster): Dark green silk interwoven with aluminum threads.
- Administrative officials (Forstassessor and higher): Aluminum threads interwoven with dark green silk.

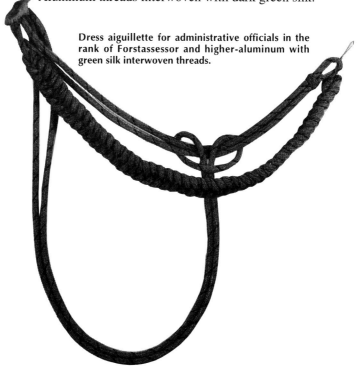

Dress aiguillette for administrative officials in the rank of Forstassessor and higher-aluminum with green silk interwoven threads.

n. Hunting Knife (Hirschfänger—also commonly referred to as cutlass): The Luftwaffe Forestry Officials wore the hunting knife adopted by State Forestry Officials. The knife was offered by manufacturers in large numbers of variations. The commonly accepted pattern was with gold-colored metal fittings, with a knuckle bow, and a clamshell crossguard ending in a deer hove. The grip was made of staghorn for operational officials, or white celluloid or genuine ivory for administrative officials, and adorned with three gold-colored metal acorns with or without two small oakleaves each. The black leather scabbard was with gold-colored metal fittings, with the top fitting with a protruding acorn pattern lug to secure it to the dark green leather frog. Brown or black frogs were also used. The knife was worn suspended by a narrow green web waistbelt worn underneath the tunic, with the frog coming through the

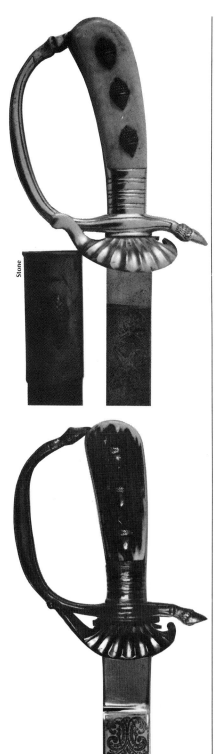

Forestry sidearm as worn by members of the Luftwaffe Forestry officials. At left, with the ivory grip, is the sidearm worn by administrative officials, and at bottom left the sidearm worn by operational officials with the staghorn grip. A portepee with a dark green leather strap and two rows of aluminum threads was worn by the ranks of Förster and above, while officials up to Unterförster wore the same portepee, but with dark green silk threads instead of aluminum. More elaborate patterns of the sidearm could be purchased and worn.

Above: Dress sidearm presumed to have been worn by enlisted members of the Luftwaffe Forestry Service. The blade is marked "Waffen-Loesche/Berlin."

Stone

side slit of the tunic or the greatcoat. An inside shoulder hanger was also sometimes used for suspension. Wear of the cutlass was prescribed when participating in public events. Wear of inherited or honorary hunting knives was permitted.

The knot (Portepee) was in the design and style as the army officer's portepee, but with a dark green leather strap with two rows of aluminum threads. The slide was braided of dark green leather with a thin aluminum cord. The flat ball with crown was of an oval cross-section. Former officers and senior NCOs and those of the body of reserves were permitted to wear the Luftwaffe portepee. Personnel holding the rank of Forstanwärter and Forstaufseher wore the portepee with dark green silk threads, and of the same design.

o. Medals and decorations were worn according to the regulations of the Luftwaffe.

Titles and Rank Insignia

Shoulder boards: These were with a backing of dark green velvet, and sewn into the sleeve headseam. The distance from the button end of the shoulder board and the collar was 2 - 3cm. The gold-colored pips measured 11mm (lateral length). For descriptions, see below.

Collar trim: A 2mm diameter twist cord, or, usually on tunic B, a 2mm woven Litze was affixed in the following manner—on tunics A and B around the corners of the collar in the length of the embroidery of tunic B; on the greatcoat as an isosceles in the length of the front edge of the collar; on the overjacket on the front edge only. Colors of the cord were as follows:
- Operational officials (Forstgehilfe to Oberförster): green interwoven with aluminum
- Administrative officials: aluminum-colored cord

Embroidery of tunic B: On collars as discussed with tunic B.

Titles and ranks were as follows:

Titles	Shoulder Boards	Equivalent Rank :
Operational Officials		
Medium Career		
Forstanwärter	None	
Hilfsförster	Five double-laid dark green 7mm flat cords	Feldwebel
Forstaufseher	As above, but with one centered gold pip	Oberfeldwebel
Elevated Career		
Förster	Two dark green 5mm wide flat braided cords with five lateral bends	Leutnant
Revierförster	As above, but with one gold pip	Oberleutnant

Revierförster Operational Official.

Forstmeister Administrative Official.

| Oberförster | As above, but with two gold pips | Hauptmann |

Administrative Officials—High Grade Career

Forstassessor	As with Förster, but surrounded by a 3mm wide gold woven Litze	Hauptmann
Forstmeister	As above, but with one gold pip	Major
Oberforstmeister	As above, but with two gold pips	Oberstleutnant
Dienstaufsichts- führender Oberforstmeister (senior Forestry official)	As Oberforstmeister, but with additional (unknown) accouterments	Oberst

Manion-Foxhole Col.

Forstmeister Administrative Official in retired status as denoted by the gold on green litzen.

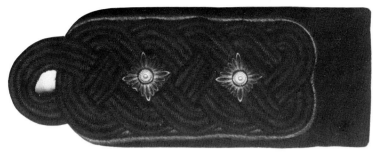

Oberforstmeister Administrative Official.

2. Uniform of 1939: A new uniform, new rank insignia and several new uniform garments were introduced by an order dated 22 April 1938, to be in effect on 1 June 1938, for wear by the Reich Forestry Officials. Subsequently, the new uniform was also ordered for all Luftwaffe Forestry Officials by the new L.Dv.84 "Uniform Regulations for the Luftwaffe Forestry Officials" dated 1 June 1939. It is possible, if not even probable, that the new rank insignia were already in wear before that date.

The following descriptions are relevant only to alterations as compared with the uniform of 1936:

a. Tunics A and B: The addition of collar patches denoting rank, with embroidery of the collar of tunic B omitted; a twist cord surrounding the entire collar.

Halcomb Smith

1939 pattern type A tunic for Forstamtmann.

Aluminum wire on green breast eagle for the Type A tunic.

b. Forest blouse (Waldbluse): This was worn with the informal forest dress. It was in cut and style as the Luftwaffe officer's flyer's blouse, but made of grey-green cloth, and with a dark green collar without collar patches and trimming. The green buttons were smooth. The blouse was worn with shoulder boards and the national emblem on the right breast. For sum-

Luftwaffe Forestry Service Waldbluse for Unterförster—similar in cut to the standard pattern Fliegerbluse. The blouse is forestry green with a green velvet collar.

mer wear, a blouse made of grey-green linen or drill fabrics was permitted.

c. National emblems: The emblems of tunics A and B and the forest blouse were silver-grey machine-embroidered for officials of the medium career, and aluminum hand-embroidered for rank of Förster and above. The backing was made of basic cloth.

d. Summer tunic (Sommerrock or Sommerjacke): The tunic was in cut and style as tunic A, but made of white cotton ticking or similar fabrics, with a white collar without piping, and with detachable collar patches. The buttons were detachable pebbled aluminum. A slit for the frog of the hunting knife was beneath the flap of the left side pocket. The shoulder boards were placed through the opening of the shoulder head seam from the interior of the tunic, and secured by screw-on buttons. A metal national emblem of the pattern prescribed for the white tunic worn by Luftwaffe officers was worn over the right breast pocket.

e. Trousers and Breeches: Breeches made of linen or drill fabrics and of the prescribed color were permitted for summer wear. Ski trousers made of mouse-grey cloth and either of the tapered style or bloused over the shoes were permitted for winter wear. In alpine districts and with the informal forest dress wear of leather shorts (Lederhosen) of civilian models or of mouse-grey shorts was permitted during the summer months, to be worn with grey knee-length stockings.

f. Greatcoat: Now worn with collar patches as worn with tunic A. The grey-green weather coat of the army officers was optionally permitted for the ranks of Förster and higher, to be worn with shoulder boards, but without collar patches. Cut and style of the weather coat was identical to that of the Luftwaffe officers.

g. Overjacket: This was without insignia and collar trim.

h. Cape: Secured by an aluminum chain buckle and the addition of the national emblem on the left side, as prescribed for Luftwaffe officers. The measurements of the national emblem were stated as having a wingspan of approximately 17.5cm, a height of 9.2cm and the swastika measuring 3.4cm from point to point.

i. Headgear: The materials of the national emblems and the winged oakleaf wreath were altered as follows:
  • Visor cap: Officials of the medium career were with aluminum metal, while those of the elevated and high career were of aluminum hand-embroidery on a dark green backing. Officials of the rank of Förster and higher had the aluminum officer pattern chin cord. The aluminum piping around the crown and at the top and bottom of the cap band

was occasionally observed, but these were against regulations, as mentioned in an order (LV 41, No.1139) dated 18 August 1941.

Luftwaffe Forestry visored cap with metal insignia for the medium career.

Luftwaffe Forestry visor cap with green velvet cap band, green piping and green backing to the hand-embroidered aluminum insignia.

- Field cap: Silver-grey machine-embroidered insignia for officials of the medium career, and aluminum hand-embroidery for ranks of Förster and above, all on a dark green backing; now worn with the national emblem.
- Winter field cap: An embroidered national emblem—silver-grey or aluminum according to rank groups—of the size as on the flyer's cap was worn above a woven or embroidered cockade.

Field cap of the Luftwaffe Forestry. Also shown is the interior markings.

Neal

j. Shirts: The dark green shirt was worn with the dark green tie with the forest dress, while the light green shirt with dark green tie worn with the reporting dress, the parade dress and white tunic. However, during the war shirts of other, similar colors were also worn.

k. Belt: The belt was new termed "Leibriemen." It was made of dark green leather with a burnished pebbled double-claw buckle. The width of the belt was 4.5cm for ranks up to and including Unterförster, and 6cm for Förster and above. The latter also wore a dark green strap of the Luftwaffe officer's pattern with burnished metal fittings. The pistol holster was also made of dark green leather. When Förster and higher wore the brocade dress belt, officials of the medium career had to wear their dark green belt with a bright aluminum buckle.

The cross strap was eventually omitted as prescribed for officers. An order (LV 41, No.791) dated 10 July 1941 prescribed belts and holster of "light havanna brown" leather for the ranks of Förster and higher, but only if they had to procure new ones.

The brocade dress belt was of the pattern of Luftwaffe officers, and worn by ranks of Förster and above.

l. Dress Aiguillette: This was now termed "Achselband," and was of the pattern and aluminum cords as worn by Luftwaffe officers. It was worn by Förster and above with the parade dress, the formal evening dress uniform, and the dress-suit uniform.

93

m. Officer's dagger: An order (LV 41, No.791) dated 10 July 1942 prescribed optional wear of the Luftwaffe officer's dagger (instead of the hunting knife) by all ranks when on office duty, with the formal forest dress, the informal dress uniform and when traveling and when off duty. Wear of the dagger was prohibited when the hat, the overjacket, or the "Lodenmantel" were worn. Wear of the hunting knife was prescribed when officially reporting to superiors, and at all occasions where officers had to wear the sword.

Portepee was as follows: Officials up to the rank of Unterförster—portepee of army pattern with a dark green leather band with two rows of aluminum threads and with a dark green flat ball. Förster and above—the Luftwaffe dagger portepee. The portepee was wound around the hunting knife in the same way as on the flyer's dagger.

n. Frock-coat dress (Frackanzug): The elegant evening dress was introduced for optional wear by officials of the rank of Förster and above instead of the formal dress uniform at special occasions. Cut, design and accouterments were identical to the formal evening dress uniform of the Luftwaffe officers. Jacket

Frock coat dress.

and trousers were made of fine dark green cloth. The frock-coat dress was worn with a white vest, and a stiff white dress shirt with a high collar and with a white bow tie. The trousers were trimmed along the outside lateral seams by a 4cm wide aluminum Tresse, and were worn with black patent leather low-quarter shoes and black socks.

Short jacket: There were several deviations from the Luftwaffe model jacket as follows—the collar was made of dark green velvet with a 2mm twist aluminum cord piping, and an oakleaf aluminum embroidery. The embroidery consisted of four leaves and three acorns on the front edge of the collar, and of five leaves and five acorns on the outer edge. The sleeves ended in a 9cm wide sewn-on cuff of dark green velvet with a cord piping (as on the collar) along the upper edge and the vertical rear edge. The national emblem and the sewn-in shoulder boards were as on the tunic B. The jacket was worn with the dress aiguillette.

o. Cape: A cape made of the cloth as on the frock-coat dress, and with collar of the same cloth optionally permitted. Cut and accouterments were as the officer's cape.

p. Other items: For winter forest duties, wear of a green woolen scarf, a muff and grey fur-lined gloves was permitted. Wear of a can (Waldstock) was permitted with forest duties. Wear of spurs was restricted to riding.

The Oberlandforstmeister wore the embroideries, buttons, collar and cuff surround, dress aiguillette, national emblems, chained buckle of the cape, and lateral trim of the trousers in gold-colored material.

Titles and Rank Insignia

Shoulder boards: The make of the shoulder boards was of the officer pattern. The flat cords were "aluminum-green" (aluminiumgrün—aluminum colored, but in a distinct hue of dark green). Since about 1940, these were eventually replaced by aluminum flat cords—probably to standardize production. The shoulder boards of the tunic A, the forest blouse and the greatcoats were in matte finish, and those of the tunic B, the white tunic and the jacket of the frock-coat dress were in bright finish. The backing was made of dark green velvet. The officials of the high grade career were distinguished by an inner (upper) surround of 3mm wide bright aluminum web Litze. On the weather coat shoulder boards were of the button-on variety, while all other garments (with the exception of the summer tunic) they were sewn-in. The gold-colored rank pips had a lateral length of 14mm.

Collar patches: The collar patches of tunic A and the cloth greatcoat were made of black cloth, while those of tunic B and the white tunic were of black velvet. They took the shape of a rhomboid measuring 4x5.5cm and with angles of approximately 70° and 110°, and came in pairs of a mirror image. A stiffening inlay of a suitable material served as the backing. The patches were sewn onto the corners of the collar at a distance of approximately 8mm from the front and outer edges. The ornaments were as follows:

- Medium career: Oakleaves of aluminum-colored metal; without piping.
- Elevated and high grade careers: Aluminum hand-embroidery; 2mm wide twist aluminum piping.

Collar piping: Officials with the rank of Förster and above wore a 3mm wide twist aluminum collar piping on tunics A and B, the cloth greatcoat, and the jacket of the frock-coat dress. Officials of the medium career did not wear a collar piping.

Titles (with suffix "der Luftwaffe")	Shoulder Boards	Collar Patches	Rank Equivalent
Operational Officials **Medium Career**			
Forstanwärter	4 dark green flat cords	1 centered metal oakleaf	Feldwebel
Forstaufseher (Waldhüter)	2 outer aluminum-green flat cords and two inner dark green cords, of 8mm width each	2 oakleaves, one above the other	Oberfeldwebel
Hilfsförster	as above, but 1 pip	3 oakleaves	?
Unterförster	as above, but 2 pips	4 oakleaves	?

Forstanwärter

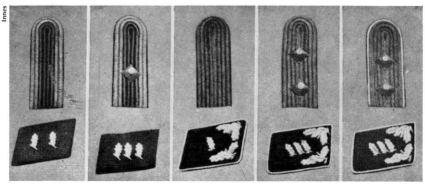

Innes

Forstaufseher   Hilfsförster   Förster   Oberförster   Forstassessor

Left Forstaufseher while right is Hilfsförster.

Top is Forstaufseher while bottom is Hilfsförster. Both are for high grade career as denoted by aluminum upper base.

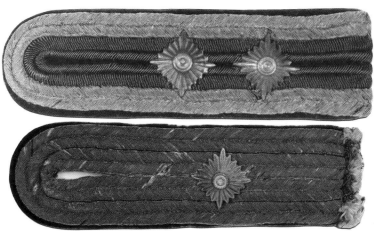

Top is Unterförster, while bottom is Revierförster.

Elevated Career

Förster	4 aluminum-green flat cords, each 8mm wide	3 oakleaves in each of the two lower corners; one oakleaf in the center	Leutnant
Revierförster	as above, but with 1 pip	as above, but with 2 oakleaves	Oberleutnant
Oberförster	as above, but with 2 pips	as above, but with 3 oakleaves	Hauptmann

Left is Förster, while right is Revierförster.

Luftwaffe combat veteran wears the uniform of a Luftwaffe Förster.

Halcomb-Smith

Luftwaffe Revierförster.

Administrative Officials
Elevated Career

Forstamtmann	braiding as for Major, but made of 2 aluminum-green flat cords of 5mm width each	3 oakleaves in each corner, one oakleaf in the center	Major

 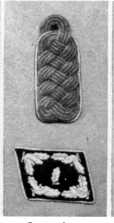  

| Forstamtmann | Forstmeister | Landforstmeister | Oberlandforstmeister |

High Grade Career

Forstassessor	as Oberförster	as Oberförster	Hauptmann
Forstmeister	as Forstamtmann	as Forstamtmann	Major
Oberforstmeister	as above, but with 1 pip	as above, but with 2 oakleaves in the center	Oberstleutnant
Landforstmeister	as above, but with 2 pips	as above, but with 3 oakleaves in the center	Oberst
Oberlandforst-meister	braiding as Generalmajor with a bright aluminum-green cords between two bright gold round cords; without the inner aluminum surround of the high grade career	as Forstamtmann, but embroidery and piping gold-colored	Generalmajor

> Note: High grade careers identified by inner aluminum surround on shoulder boards (not for Oberlandforstmeister).

The Oberlandforstmeister was the head of the Luftwaffe Forestry Service, and was distinguished by the general accouterments of general officers. Buttons, embroideries, national emblems, cord piping of the collar, collar patches and cuffs, cap cords, buckle and fittings of the leather belt and cross strap, buckle of the brocade dress belt, dress aiguillette, and the chained

Oberförster of the High Grade Career.

Forstamtmann Administrative Official of Elevated Career
(without inner aluminum surround).
Forstmeister Administrative Official of High Grade Career.

Shoulder board and collar patch for Oberforstmeister.

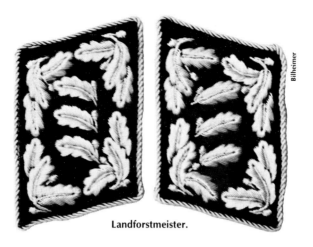

Landforstmeister.

Oberlandforstmeister—embroidery is gold.

Reichsforstmeister
Fredrick Alpers (photo
taken of him as a
Landforstmeister).

101

M1939 Rank Insignia

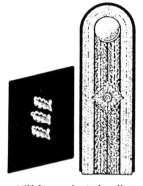
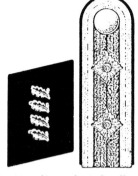

Forstaufseher der Luftwaffe   Hilfsförster der Luftwaffe   Unterförster der Luftwaffe

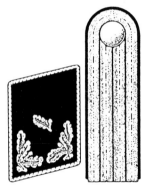

a.p. Revierförster der Luftwaffe   Revierförster der Luftwaffe   Oberförster der Luftwaffe

Forstamtmann der Luftwaffe

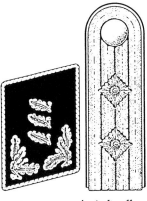

Forstassessor der Luftwaffe

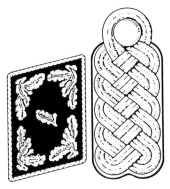

Forstmeister der Luftwaffe

Oberförstmeister der Luftwaffe

Landforstmeister der Luftwaffe

Oberlandforstmeister der Luftwaffe

buckle of the cape were of gold-colored material. The lapels of the cloth greatcoat and the piping and stripes of the trousers were made of dark green badge cloth, and the trim of the trousers of the frock-coat dress was a gold Tresse. He had the right to wear spurs. The section chief of the Forestry Section of the RLM who ranked as a Ministerialrat was accorded the right to wear the uniform of the Oberlandforstmeister instead of the standard uniform of officials.

3. Kinds of Dress: The composition of the various kinds of dress allowed a wide range of variations. In order to achieve a certain degree of uniformity of dress, the composition, especially of the forest dress and the service dress, was prescribed for the various events.

- Informal forest dress (kleiner Walddienstanzug): Forest blouse, breeches or knee-length trousers, dark green shirt with green tie, black boots, black or brown lace-up shoes, leather leggings, wrap-around puttees or knee-length stockings, hat or field cap, leather belt with pistol, cross strap; when suitable—greatcoat, overjacket, "loden" coat, winter field cap. The light green shirt was permitted since mid-1941.

- Formal forest dress (grosser Walddienstanzug): Tunic A, breeches, light green shirt with green tie, black boots, visor cap (hat at special occasions), leather belt, cross strap, grey leather gloves, ribbon bar, hunting knife, greatcoat or weather coat; permitted at suitable occasions—lace-up shoes with wrap-around puttees, over jacket, "Loden" coat.

- Service dress (Dienstanzug): Tunic A, long trousers or breeches, light green shirt with green tie, black boots, black lace-up shoes or low-quarter shoes with black socks, visor cap, grey leather gloves, ribbon bar; when suitable—leather belt, cross strap, greatcoat, weather coat, cape, pistol. White tunic for office duties optional.

The service dress with long trousers or breeches was permitted for off-duty wear, thus serving as a walking-out dress.

- Reporting dress (Meldeanzug): Tunic B, white shirt with black tie, breeches, black boots, visor cap, brocade dress belt or leather belt with aluminum buckle for officials up to Unterförster, grey leather gloves, hunting knife and ribbon bar.

- Parade dress (Paradeanzug): As reporting dress; additionally with dress aiguillette, medal bar; greatcoat when so ordered.

- Informal dress uniform (kleiner Gesellschaftsanzug): Tunic B, white shirt with black tie, black lace-up shoes or low-quarter shoes (patent leather shoes permitted), visor cap, grey gloves, hunting knife, ribbon bar, greatcoat or cape.

- Formal dress uniform (grosser Gesellschaftsanzug): As the informal dress uniform; additionally with dress aiguillette, brocade dress belt or leather belt with aluminum buckle, white leather gloves, medal bar. The visor cap, greatcoat or cape and hunting knife was worn on the street.

Wear of the frock-coat dress was permitted at social events and receptions of a more official nature, at weddings, formal dances, etc.

- Summer dress (Sommeranzug): White tunic, long grey-green trousers, white shirt with black tie, black lace-up or low-quarter shoes with black socks, visor cap, hunting knife, white gloves, ribbon bar; if suitable greatcoat or cape.

Wear of the summer dress was permitted off duty and instead of the informal dress uniform at social events.

When the wear of the officer's dagger was introduced for wear by forestry officials in 1941, the dagger could be optionally worn instead of the hunting knife, except with the reporting dress and parade dress.

To better utilize the garments, wear of the tunic B with the formal forest dress and the service dress was permitted since mid-1941, to be worn with the light green shirts and green ties. In this case the velvet collar could be replaced by a collar of dark green cloth.

4. Retired Officials: Retired officials who were granted the right to wear the uniform at retirement were recognized by a 1cm wide aluminum Tresse (Oberlandforstmeister a.D. in gold) with a zig-zag design. The Tresse was sewn onto the double-laid 1.5cm wide tape of basic cloth, which was sewn with the ends crosswise and centered beneath the shoulder boards to be visible for .5cm at either side. The titles had the suffix "a.D." (ausser Dienst—retired).

The uniform had to be in conformity with the dress regulations at the time of retirement or with later regulations. Wear of long trousers in lieu of breeches was permitted with all kinds of dress.

5. Employees of the Luftwaffe Forestry Service: Besides officials there were Forestry Employees (Forstangestellte), which were predominantly utilized for administrative duties. They were employed on the basis of voluntary individual agreements. Some, if not all, were obliged to wear the uniform.

By order (LV 37, No.1214) dated 13 September 1937 they continued to wear the uniform of the Forestry Administration (State, Reich or private forests) they were employed before transfer to the Luftwaffe Forestry Service. As the wear of the national emblem was denied, this was how they were discerned from the officials.

The L.Dv.84 dated 1 June 1939 granted the employees, if obliged to wear the uniform, the same uniform was worn by officials of comparable rank, but without the national emblem on the breast of the tunics and forest blouses. The portepee also served for distinction:

- Employees of comparable rank up to Unterförster: Dark green portepee with leather band and flat ball.
- Employees with the rank of Förster and above: Portepee of the same pattern, but aluminum-green.

If employees held the status of a NCO or officer of the body of reserves, they had the right to wear the officer's portepee.

When a brown leather belt was prescribed for officials with officer rank by order (LV 41, No.791) dated 10 July 1941, the wear of dark green belt was continued for employees as expressly stated.

C. Reich Air Traffic Control:

The Reich Air Traffic Control was termed Reichsluftaufsichtsdienst, but commonly referred to as Reichsluftaufsicht or Luftaufsicht (Air Control). While it was composed of soldiers (officers, NCOs and privates), it was predominantly made up of officials. Its duties were the control of the air traffic of civilian airports and airfields.

1. Soldiers: The uniform of the soldiers of the Reich Air Traffic Control was determined by the order about the "Uniform of the Luftwaffe after its De-camouflage" (Der Reichsminister der Luftfahrt L.D. No.30575/35 geh.Kdos. D IV, 3 Az.64.e.10.) dated 1 March 1935 as follows:
   - introduction of military shoulder straps and boards
   - branch color: light green
   - NCOs: Tresse surround on two edges of the collar patches of the tunic and the flyer's blouse (as worn with the uniform of the Fliegerschaft) abolished, but retained on collar patches of the greatcoat, introduction of the Tresse surround of the collar of tunics and blouses.
   - Supplementary officers: light grey secondary color as an inner (upper) underlay of shoulder boards (abolished as described with the section "Supplementary Officer").

2. Officials: Most of the officials belonged to the medium career. Officials of the elevated and high grade careers served with the administrative section of the Air Traffic Control at the RLM and major commands.

By an order of 1 September 1934 (HM 34, No.57, dated 23 October 1934) a "special uniform" was introduced for officials of the Reich Air Traffic Control, which "closely resembled the uniform of the DLV in color, cut, insignia, etc.,", but with light green collar patches. This uniform was that of the Fliegerschaft. The light green backing of the shoulder boards was not mentioned by the order. The collar patches were with metal double wings.

The alterations by the above order of 1 March 1935 were as follows:
   - light green branch color also for officials
   - collar patches with triangular pips in lieu of double wings
   - Air Control officials with NCO rank up to and including the rank of Flughauptwachtmeister: uniform as NCOs with light green branch color (but shoulder straps without secondary color); abolishment of the Tresse piping of collar patches and introduction of the Tresse surround of collars as stated above with NCOs.

NOTE: The grade designations were those of NCO ranks of the Fliegerschaft. As there wasn't any further mention of this group of officials, it must be assumed that all were upgraded to the rank of Untermeister by mid-1935 at the latest.

    a. Officials with the rank of Meister and Obermeister: The Meister and Obermeister ranks were officials of the medium career who were distinguished by the officer's cap cord. Wear of the officer pattern belt and cross strap and of other officers' insignia were not mentioned (but introduced shortly afterwards). The insignia of the collar patches were also not mentioned. Probably only triangular pips without an oakleaf were worn.

      • Shoulder boards (Schulterlitzen) "of the pattern of the hitherto worn shoulder cords (Achsellitzen), but of a wider design and with aluminum-colored pips replacing the slides"; double backing of the shoulder boards: light green below and bright red above. The wording used in the order would indicate that the previously worn shoulder cords were retained, but with a surround of double blue-grey cords, thus making them wider.

      • Visor cap: With the officer pattern aluminum chin cord; light green piping; aluminum metal insignia.

      • Officials of the elevated and high grade careers: Not mentioned by the order.

Branch color and secondary color: By order (LV 35, No.423) dated 23 July 1935 the light green branch color and bright red secondary color were introduced for all officials of the Reich Air Traffic Control. By an order (LV 40, No.569) dated 10 May 1940 this was altered to a dark green branch color (as for the other officials) with the secondary color light green.

    b. Officials of the Medium Career: Insignia and accouterments were described in detail in the L.Dv.422 A "Dress Regulations" of 27 November 1935. This leads to the conclusion that they were introduced at some unknown date in mid-1935.

The Untermeister ranked above the Oberfeldwebel rank of senior NCOs while the Meister and Obermeister did possess officer's rank, but were not granted all accouterments of officers. Applicants on probation (Versorgungsanwärter zur Probedienstleistung) wore the uniform of an Untermeister.

      • Collar patches: These were of the appropriate branch color and with an oakleaf wreath with triangular pips centered above. The wreath and pips were made of aluminum-colored metal, but this was altered to matte grey machine-embroidery by an order (LV 37, No.14) dated 28 December 1936, with the new pattern patches to be worn after 1 October 1937 at the latest. The piping consisted of a 2mm wide twist cord of alternating aluminum and blue-grey.

- Shoulder boards: These were officially termed "Schulterlitzen" (as opposed to "Schulterstücke" of officers). A center braiding with five bends at either side was made of two blue-grey flat cords and a center aluminum flat cord, and was surrounded by two blue-grey flat cords. Double underlay of branch color and inner (upper) secondary color; NCO pattern aluminum pips. The design of the shoulder cords was identical to those of other officials with Oberfeldwebel rank.

Title (with suffix "im Reichsluftaufsichtsdienst"	Rank Pips	
	Collar Patches	Shoulder Boards
Untermeister	1	none
(since mid-1935)Meister	2	1
Obermeister	3	2

1st Pattern rank insignia for Meister with pressed aluminum wreath and metal pips.

Obermeister with embroidered insignia.

Meister of the Luftwaffe Air Traffic Control.

Untermeister.

Obermeister.

All ranks wore a 3mm wide twist cord of the branch color as a collar piping on tunics and flyer's blouses in lieu of the NCO Tresse surround. The NCO pattern flyer's cap was also worn by Meister and Obermeister.

The officer pattern accouterments of Meister and Obermeister ranks were as follows:

- Visor caps: With aluminum chin cord, but with piping of the branch color; embroidered insignia were permitted.
- National emblems of aluminum hand-embroidery on tunics and blouses
- Leather belt and shoulder strap (with shoulder strap abolished during the early war as for officers)
- Cape of officers: Only permitted for Obermeister

By an order (LV 37, No.1083) dated 17 August 1937 rank insignia of special garments and of the jacket of the sports suit were introduced. They consisted of a white horizontal bar measuring 6cm long and .5cm in wide, and of white triangular pips centered above the bar positioned vertically one above the other. Otherwise the design and manner of wear were as prescribed for soldiers. The backing, however, was rectangular at the base and triangular above. The number of pips corresponded with the collar patches.

By an order about "Rank System of the Armed Forces Officials" of 2 November 1940 (LV 40, No.1426) the Meister and Obermeister were ranked as Leutnant and Oberleutnant respectively, with the full officer's uniform. The embroidery of the dark green collar patches was now aluminum-colored. The officer pattern shoulder boards were with a dark green underlay below, and a light green secondary above.

By order (LV 40, No.1427) dated 2 November 1940 the cord piping of the collar patches of Untermeister, Meister and Obermeister ranks was prescribed as a twist cord of alternating aluminum and dark green.

    c. Officials of the Elevated and High Grade Careers: These had the titles of the officials of the general administrative branch with the suffix "im Reichsluftaufsichtsdienst," and wore the standard uniform of officials according to their careers. Branch and secondary colors were light green and bright red or dark green and light green by the above order of 10 May 1940. The grade insignia of the garments of the special clothing were as prescribed for other officials.

3. Other Insignia and Garments:
- Gorget: By the above order of 1 September 1934 (in HM 34, No.57) a gorget with a stylized national emblem and the inscription "Reichsluftaufsicht" was introduced for wear by officials on duty (i.e., at airports). By order (LV 35, No.80) dated 8 November 1935 the wear of the gorget was prescribed for NCOs and officials when on controlling duty at airports and airfields.

The gorget was a kidney-shaped back-plate with raised perimeter rim. The national emblem took the form of a gold-colored swastika standing on its point inside a winged circle. The wings curved upwards, following the top portion of the shield. Below the emblem was the underlined inscription in Latin capital letters "REICHS-LUFT-AUFSICHT" that were curved parallel to the bottom edge of the plate. There were two patterns of the gorget differing in the material used as follows:

- First Pattern: The center plate was stamped of polished German silver (Neusilber), and emblem and inscription were made of polished brass. The plate measured approximately 16cm wide and 9cm high. The reverse was covered by blue-grey cloth. The chain was made of intertwined links of nickel-plated rings, and was affixed at one corner of the reverse and hooked onto the other corner.

Anconetani

1st Pattern Reichsluftaufsicht gorget.

- Second Pattern: This was probably introduced in 1939. The basic design remained the same, but had the addition of a 2cm diameter button with ribbed bordering ring in each corner. The plate was slightly smaller, and was stamped of matte grey light-metal. The swastika was polished, and the circle and wings were matte. The inscription was either matte or polished. Brass was replaced by a gold-colored light-metal alloy. The reverse was usually covered by a glued-on patch of dark green artificial leather. In lieu of the suspension chain of the first pattern, the gorget was most commonly fitted with a chain made of approximately oval rings connected by rectangular sheet metal links.

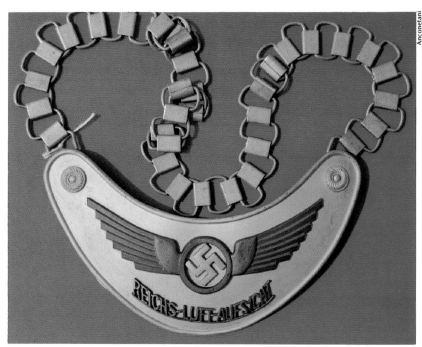

2nd Pattern gorget—note the bosses and change in the chain.

- Bayonet: An order (LV 36, No.965) dated 23 July 1936 prescribed wear of the M84/98 bayonet by senior NCOs and officials when on duty at the landing field.
- Portepee and tassel: By an order (LV 35, No.77) dated 21 March 1935 the standard Luftwaffe pattern portepee and tassel (Faustriemen) were introduced for wear by NCOs and officials of the Reich Air Traffic Control according to their respective ranks. The previously worn portepee was abolished. This model was described by the order as "silver mixed with green." It probably was a portepee with a leather band with silver stripes, and with stem, crown and ball made of silver and green alternating cords.
- Armband: Start Directors at the landing field were recognized by a white armband measuring 13cm wide and 39cm long, and worn on the left upper sleeve. The seal of the unit was to be placed on the inner side near the seam.
- White coat and cap: By an order (LV 39B, No.205) dated 13 June 1939 a coat (Startmantel) and a wide-brimmed cap (Südwester) were introduced for personnel on duty at the landing field in order to better identify them by landing aircraft. Coat and cap were made of white water-repellent fabric. The coat was buttoned at the front by one row of white buttons. The rectangular patch-type hip pockets were with or without flaps. The coat came in two sizes: for sum-

mer wear over the service dress, and for winter wear over the surcoat.

D. Corps of Engineers of the Luftwaffe:

The Corps of Engineers of the Luftwaffe (Ingenieurkorps der Luftwaffe) was constituted by a "Decree of the Führer and Reichskanzler" dated 20 April 1935 (LV 35, No.161). Details of the new branch were ordered by the "Law about the Corps of Engineers of the Luftwaffe" dated 18 October 1935 (LV 36, No.11). The members of the corps were not soldiers but "members of the Luftwaffe" with a status comparable to that of officials. They were subjected to all service and legal obligations in the same way as officials. They were mainly differentiated from officials by a uniform career (i.e., not divided into careers as officials were) and by a separate order of pay.

The conditions of acceptance into the Corps of Engineers were altered several times. Basically, personnel with a university or college degree in engineering were admitted. Engineers with a university degree were enlisted with the rank of Fliegerhauptingenieur, and those with a college degree with the rank of Fliegeringenieur.

All members of the Corps of Engineers possessed a defined military rank according to their rank insignia.

After constitution of the Corps of Engineer Officers by an order (LV 40, No.577) dated 11 May 1940 the eventual disbanding of the Corps of Engineers was intended. A subsequent order (LV 40, No.577) dated 16 May 1940 provided for the transfer of members of the Corps of Engineers as officers to the new Corps of Engineer Officers, and for the disbanding of the Corps of Engineers at a later, yet to be fixed date. However, it was expressly proclaimed by the same order that all was postponed "until further notice." Actually, the Corps of Engineers was never disbanded, and both corps co-existed for the duration of the war.

NOTE: The uniform of the Corps of Engineers and of the engineer officers was identical except for the collar patches: members of the Corps of Engineers had propellers on the collar patches, while the engineer officers had gulls, and utilized the standard officer grade designations with the suffix "Ing.—."

1. Uniform, Titles and Insignia: Uniform, titles and insignia were introduced by the "Execution Order" (LV 35, No.12) dated 18 October 1935. The members of the Corps of Engineers were accorded the pink branch color. They wore the uniform of officers of comparable ranks, and were obliged to wear the uniform.

The prefix "Flieger-..." of the titles was usually abbreviated as "Fl." e.g. Fliegeringenieur = Fl.Ingenieur.

- Collar patches: The pink collar patches had a oakleaf wreath (short resp. full) in aluminum for ranks from Fl.Ingenieur to Fl.Hauptingenieur or gold hand-embroidery for the two highest ranks. The piping was an aluminum or gold twist cord according to the rank embroidery. Embroidered propellers ("Luftschrauben") designated the rank corresponding to the color of the embroidery. A two-bladed propeller was positioned vertically, a three-bladed propeller had one blade directed upwards, and two spread below, while the blades of the four- bladed propeller were set diagonally.

- Shoulder boards: These were of the officer pattern, and with a pink underlay. Pips for ranks up to and including Fl.Hauptstabsingenieur were in gold, while those above were in silver.

Titles	Equivalent Rank	Collar Patches
Fl.Ingenieur	Leutnant	Short alum. oakleaf wreath with two-bladed propeller
Fl.Oberingenieur	Oberleutnant	Same, three-bladed prop.
Fl.Hauptingenieur	Hauptmann	Same, four-bladed propeller
Fl.Stabsingenieur	Major	Full oakleaf wreath with two-bladed propeller
Fl.Oberstabsingenieur	Oberstleutnant	Same, three-bladed prop.
Fl.Hauptstabsingenieur	Oberst	Same, four-bladed propeller
Fl.Chefingenieur	Generalmajor	Same, two-bladed propeller (gold)
Leitender Fl.Chef-ingenieur	Generalleutnant	Same, three-bladed propeller (gold)

Left to right—Fl. Ingenieur, Fl. Oberingenieur, and Fl. Hauptingenieur. Because these pieces were hand-embroidered, some variations in the propeller and wreath patterns exist.

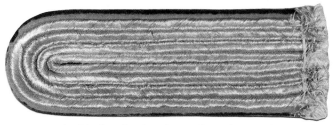

Fl. Ingenieur shoulder board with pink secondary color over the green base.

As above, but for Fl. Oberingenieur.

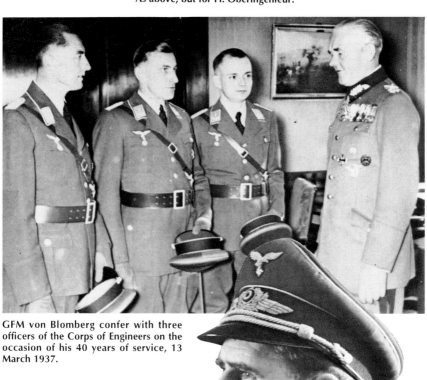

GFM von Blomberg confer with three officers of the Corps of Engineers on the occasion of his 40 years of service, 13 March 1937.

Flieger-Stabsingenieur Horst Hädrich.

Bender

Jim Plante

Fl. Stabsingenieur.

Selzer

Minor variation of the Fl. Stabsingenieur at left, while at right is an unexplained pattern, probably representing the Fl. Oberstabsingenieur.

Fl. Hauptstabsingenieur shoulder board with pink underlay.

Fl. Oberstabsingenieur.

Unidentified Fl. Hauptstabsingenieur.

Fl. Hauptstabsingenieur shoulder board with pink underlay.

The ranks of Fl.Chefingenieur and Leitender Fl.Chefingenieur had general officer rank, and were distinguished by the general accouterments of that rank. However, where the color was white for other general officers, the color of these officers was pink. Wear of the pink piping and stripes on breeches became optional by an order (LV 39C, No.875) dated 21 September 1939, also the wear of pink stripes on long trousers by order (LV 43, No.2084) dated 2 November 1943 (with pink piping retained, however).

Collar patches and shoulder board of a Fl. Chefingenieur. Embroidery of the collar patches is gold on pink.

Unidentified Fl. Chefingenieur.

Flyer's blouse of a Fl. Chefingenieur.

Blouse of a Fl. Chefingenieur.

Petroni

Rank insignia of a Leitender Fl. Chefingenieur. This was the highest rank of the Corps of Engineers.

As a result of order LV 35, No.13, dated 29 November 1935, titles and ranks insignia were split up, probably because the age ranges within the ranks were over-extended. This splitting was unique in the armed forces. The order mentioned only shoulder boards. The conclusion that the collar patches according to the respective titles were retained is certainly wrong as the order of 27 May 1938 (as below) mentioned "grade insignia," i.e. shoulder boards and collar patches. The pay according to the original titles was retained, however. In consequence of the splitting the proper titles were no longer recognized by the grade.

Order of 29 November 1935:

Titles	Age Range	Grade Insignia of
Fl.Stabsingenieur	to the end of the 39th year	Fl.Hauptingenieur
Fl.Oberstabsingenieur	to the end of the 36th year	Fl.Hauptingenieur
	from 36th to the end of the 41st year	Fl.Stabsingenieur
Fl.Hauptstabsingenieur	to the end of the 41st year	Fl.Stabsingenieur
	from 41st to end of the 45th year	Fl.Oberstabsingenieur
Fl.Chefingenieur, Leitender Fl.Chefingenieur	to the end of the 45th year	Fl.Hauptstabsingenieur

NOTE: It has not been found if these last two ranks, whose titles indicated general officer rank, wore the general accouterments of general officers with the grade insignia of the equivalent rank of Oberst. This would have been unique in the entire Armed Forces. It is therefore assumed that these ranks wore the general accouterments of field grade officers as Oberst equivalent rank.

The grading was altered and somewhat simplified as a result of an order (LV 38B, No.147) dated 27 May 1938 as follows:

Titles	Age Range	Grade Insignia of
Fl.Stabsingenieur	to the end of the 35th year	Fl.Hauptingenieur
Fl.Oberstabsingenieur	to the end of the 39th year	Fl.Stabsingenieur
Fl.Hauptstabsingenieur	to the end of the 39th year	Fl.Oberstabsingenieur
Fl.Chefingenieur, Leitender Fl.Chefingenieur	to the end of the 45th year	Fl.Hauptstabsingenieur

By order (LV 40, No.139) dated 5 February 1940 the splitting between titles and grade insignia was abolished, and the grade insignia now corresponded with the titles (as listed by the above order of 18 October 1935).

Several titles were renamed by order (LV 40, No.790) dated 8 June 1940 (to be effective immediately) as follows:

Fl.Hauptstabsingenieur	renamed as:	Oberstingenieur
Fl.Chefingenieur	renamed as:	Generalingenieur
Leitender Fl.Chefingenieur	renamed as	Generalstabsingenieur

Engineers on probational service wore the uniform of a Fl.Ingenieur and were identified by a 1cm wide loop of pink cloth around the base of the shoulder boards, as per order (LV 43, No.191) dated 15 January 1943.

By an order (LV 37, No.1571) dated 1 December 1937 rank insignia were introduced for wear on the garments of the special clothing and on the jacket of the sports suit as follows:

Titles	Bars	Propeller	Color
Fl.Ingenieur	1	Two-bladed	white
Fl.Oberingenieur	1	Three-bladed	white
Fl.Hauptingenieur	1	Four-bladed	white
Fl.Stabsingenieur	2	Two-bladed	white

Fl.Oberstabsingenieur	2	Three-bladed	white
Fl.Hauptstabsingenieur	2	Four-bladed	white
Fl.Chefingenieur	1	Two-bladed	golden-yellow
Leitender Fl.Chefingenieur	1	Three-bladed	golden-yellow

The direction of the blades of the propellers was identical with those of the collar patches. The measurements were as follows:

bars	10cm long, 1cm high
two-bladed propellers	7cm high
three-bladed propellers	4.5cm high and 5.5cm wide
four-bladed propellers	6cm high and 6cm wide

The underlays were rectangular at the base, and pointed above. The insignia were worn on the upper sleeves following the regulations as prescribed for soldiers.

2. Members of the Corps of Engineers of the Body of Reserves: Those had the suffix "d.R." (der Reserve—of the reserve) with the titles, and were identified by a light blue secondary color that appears as a piping of the collar patch (inside the twist cord piping) and as an inner (upper) underlay of the shoulder boards. Suffix and secondary color were omitted during the early war as prescribed for officials of the body of reserves.

Halcomb Smith

Selzer

Examples of collar patches of members of the Corps of Engineers of the Body of Reserves as indicated by the blue secondary color—left—Fl. Oberingenieur, right—Leitender Fl. Chefingenieur.

Fl. Hauptstabsingenieur.

3. Wartime Members of the Corps of Engineers: The institution of wartime members of the Corps of Engineers (Angehörige des Ingenieurkorps auf Kriegsdauer) was introduced by the "Mobilization Order of the Luftwaffe." All regulations related to wartime officials were also valid. The titles had the suffix "a.Kr." or later "a.K." (auf Kriegsdauer—for the duration of the war). The pink collar patches were decorated with a short open oakleaf wreath or full closed oakleaf wreath only, and were with a twist aluminum cord piping. The shoulder cords were of the pattern of wartime officials, and were without backing.

Titles	Shoulder Cords	Collar Patches
Fl.Ingenieur a.K.	Parallel cord of aluminum	short oakleaf wreath
Fl.Oberingenieur a.K.	same, with one golden-yellow artificial silk braided slide	same
Fl.Hauptingenieur a.K.	same, but two slides	same
Fl.Stabsingenieur a.K.	braiding of one aluminum cord	full oakleaf wreath

The rank insignia of the garments of the special clothing were the same as those worn by active members of the Corps of Engineers, as prescribed by an order (LV 43, No.191) dated 15 January 1943.

Collar patch for Wartime Members of the Corps of Engineers for ranks Fl. Ingenieur a.K. thru Fl. Hauptingenieur a.K. The patch is pink with aluminum embroidery and twist cord piping.

Fl. Ingenieur a.K. (left) confers with a Fl. Stabsingenieur a.K. Note the lack of the breast eagle.

Heckler

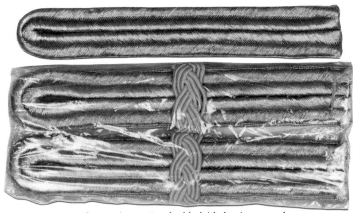

Top: Fl. Ingenieur a.K.—double-laid aluminum cord.
Bottom: Fl. Oberingenieur a.K.—as above, but one golden-yellow braided slide.

Top: Fl. Hauptingenieur a.K.—as above, but two slides.
Bottom: Fl. Stabsingenieur a.K. —interwoven aluminum cord.

Fl. Stabsingenieur a.K.

As above, but minor variation to the collar patch.

E. Navigation Corps of the Luftwaffe:

The Navigation Corps (Nautikerkorps der Luftwaffe) was constituted in late 1938 or early 1939. The constitution order has not been located. All members of the corps belonged to the elevated career. By order (BLB 39, No.153) dated 17 February 1939 the members of the corps were obliged to wear the uniform.

The basic rank insignia—collar patches, shoulder boards and sleeve insignia of the special clothing—were the same as those of members of the Corps of Engineers.

Originally, the branch color was dark green and the secondary color was golden-yellow. This was altered as follows:

- branch color dark green; secondary color lemon yellow: order (LV 40, No. 569) dated 10 May 1940.
- branch color pink; secondary color light blue: order (LV 41, No.1562) dated 8 October 1941.

Collar patches: These were of the branch color, and with propellers (of the pattern of members of the Corps of Engineers) in lieu of pips.

Shoulder boards: double backing with branch color and upper secondary color

Titles	Rank Insignia as:
Fl.Obernautiker	Fl.Oberingenieur
Fl.Hauptnautiker	Fl.Hauptingenieur
Fl.Stabsnautiker	Fl.Stabsingenieur

Fl. Obernautiker conducts instrument training.

Fl. Obernautiker—aluminum hand-embroidery on dark green.

Fl. Hauptnautiker.

By order (LV 41, No.1940) dated 29 November 1941 the Navigation Corps was disbanded. Most of its members were transferred to the status of line officers of the flying branch. Those who did not meet the conditions for transfer, or did not consent to a status as officer were transferred to the Corps of Engineers as navigation personnel. After the end of the transfers the Navigation Corps ceased to exist.

F. Flying Leaders Corps:

A special branch termed "Flying Leaders" (Flugführer)—also known as "Flying Leaders Corps" (Flugführerkorps) or "Pilot's Corps" (Flugzeugführerkorps)—was constituted in the spring of 1940. By order (LV 40, No.1152) dated 5 September 1940 the conditions of acceptance were published. Only NCOs after their 10th year of service were accepted who had held a pilot's license for at least four years. There was only the elevated career. These experienced pilots were utilized on very specialized fields, e.g. as flight instructors, test pilots, controlling pilots at aircraft plants, on weather reconnaissance flights, etc.

The dark green branch color and golden-yellow secondary color were introduced by order (LV 40, No.569) dated 10 May 1940. Uniform and rank insignia were those of the other officials of the elevated career, to include triangular pips on the collar patches. The backing of the shoulder boards was dark green and golden-yellow above. The order determined the titles as follows:

Titles	Equivalent Rank of
Flugführer	Leutnant
Oberflugführer	Oberleutnant
Hauptflugführer	Hauptmann
Stabsflugführer, Stabsflugführer I. Klasse	Major

By order (LV 41, No.1562) dated 8 October 1941 the branch color was altered to pink. The golden-yellow secondary color was retained. The pink collar patches were now with propellers in lieu of pips (of the pattern of the Corps of Engineers).

Titles	Collar Patches
Flugführer	short oakleaf wreath, two-bladed propeller
Oberflugführer	same, three-bladed propeller
Hauptflugführer	same, four-bladed propeller
Stabsflugführer, Stabsflugführer I.Klasse	Full oakleaf wreath, two-bladed propeller

The grade insignia of the special clothing had one bar and pips or propellers as displayed on the collar patches.

G. Secret Field Police:

By an order (LV 43, No.2083) dated 5 November 1943 the Secret Field Police (Geheime Feldpolizei) of the Luftwaffe was constituted. Its members were officials of the Reich Security Police (Sicherheitspolizei) or of the Secret Field Police branch of the army who were transferred to the Luftwaffe.

The officials wore the standard uniform of officials of the respective career. The branch color was dark green and the secondary color wine red. The shoulder boards were with a double backing of dark green and wine red, and had the pressed gold-colored metal capitals "GFP" in the center.

The titles were introduced by the above order as follows:

Career	Titles	Equivalent Rank of
Medium Career	Feldpolizeisekretär	Leutnant
Elevated Career	Feldpolizeiinspektor	Oberleutnant
	Feldpolizeikommissar	Hauptmann
High Grade Career	Feldpolizeidirektor	Major
	Oberfeldpolizeidirektor	Oberstleutnant

Feldpolizeikommissar

Feldpolizeidirektor

There were also soldiers with agencies of the Secret Field Police in such functions as clerical personnel, drivers, guards, etc. Nothing has been found about any special uniform insignia worn by those soldiers.

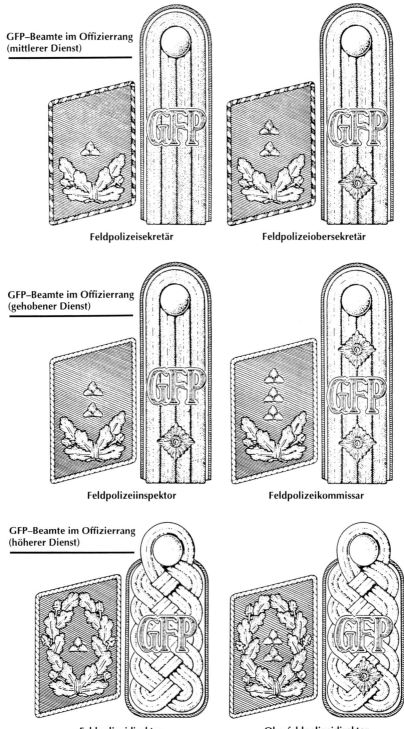

GFP–Beamte im Offizierrang
(mittlerer Dienst)

Feldpolizeisekretär

Feldpolizeiobersekretär

GFP–Beamte im Offizierrang
(gehobener Dienst)

Feldpolizeiinspektor

Feldpolizeikommissar

GFP–Beamte im Offizierrang
(höherer Dienst)

Feldpolizeidirektor

Oberfeldpolizeidirektor

CHAPTER • 23
MISCELLANEOUS CIVILIAN ORGANIZATIONS OF THE LUFTWAFFE

T here existed units that were removed from the main body of the Luftwaffe, and were considered either under the operational control or attached to the Luftwaffe for administration, pay and general support. It is possible that not all such units will be addressed here due to lack of information. Those that are are sorely lacking in published regulations, and most data was derived from period photographs.

When not in uniform, civilian personnel were usually identified by an armband or lapel pin.

1. **Civilian Flying Employees of the Luftwaffe** (Fliegerisch tätige Angestellte der Luftwaffe): These civilian employees with flying duties were largely test pilots, mechanics and instructors within the Luftwaffe structure. It is presumed that many came from the German airline Lufthansa.

There were several Air Service Units (Luftdienstverband; later renamed Luftdienst-Abteilung) manned by civilian flying employees who had been called into service after the outbreak of war. Their main duty was as pilots for towed targets at manouvers and training of anti-aircraft units. An Air Service Unit was composed of several Air Service Commands (Luftdienstkommando; later renamed Luftdienststaffel). At the end of 1943 there was an Air Target Division (Flieger-Zieldivision) with Air Target Wings No. 1-3.

A uniform was introduced for wear by the civilian members by order (LV 36, No.488) dated 3 April 1936. The resultant uniform closely resembled that of the German Lufthansa. The navy blue service uniform consisted of the following:

a. Jacket (Jackett): Double-breasted jacket with two rows of three black buttons each, and secured on the right side by two of the three buttons. The lapels were with buttonholes (either actual or false). At each hip was a concealed pocket with or without unbuttoned straight-edge flap. A slightly angled concealed pocket was at the left breast. Two black buttons were at the rear front edge of the cuff end of the sleeve. The rear of the jacket skirt was without slit.

b. Trousers (Lange Hose): The long trousers were with cuffs, and a hip pocket right and left side.

c. Visor Cap (Schirmmütze): The top was normally of doeskin, and void of any insigne. The cap band was black mohair with distinctive insigne, chin cord and side buttons (for details, see below), and black vulcan fiber visor.

d. Shoes: Black low-quarter or optional black other with black socks.

e. Shirt and Tie: Blue-grey shirt with fall-down collar, and a black four-in-hand tie. The dress version of the uniform was worn with a white dress shirt with black bow tie.

f. Greatcoat (Mantel): The waterproof fabric double-breasted greatcoat (of trenchcoat style) was with two rows of four buttons each, and secured by four buttons on the right side. At each hip was an angled slash pocket without flap. A cloth waistbelt with black plastic buckle secured the waist. A buttoned strap with pointed end was at each sleeve cuff. A black leather greatcoat of the same cut and style as the fabric coat, and one to include that of the Luftwaffe style, was also permitted.

g. Gloves (Handschuhe): Brown leather.

131

The visor cap insigne for all established ranks took the form of a gold hand-embroidered metallic wire wing, and a sprig of four leaves projecting to the right and left of a silver hand-embroidered metallic wire swastika standing on its point. Total length of the wings was 14.5cm, while the swastika was 14mm square. A grouping classified as Other Civilian Flying Personel (sonstige fliegerische Angestellte) wore an identical insigne, but with reversed colors (aluminum wings and leaves with gold swastika). Period photos show the insigne also centered at the juncture seam between the top and cap band as well as centered on the top.

While there was a rank structure, there were no specific rank insignia, but rather a rank grouping distinguished by the color of the cap cord. The cap cord was of the standard pattern double-laid twist cord secured by a metal button at each end.

Civilian flying employee of the Luftwaffe. His rank is determined by the cap cord.

Ranks were not ranks as such, but rather a grouping of service or trade positions (Dienststellung). Service positions with the respective cap cords were as follows:

Service Position	Cap Cord	Cap Insigne
Flugbetriebsleiter	Gold with black interwoven	Gold(Flight Leader)
Stellvertr. Flugbetriebsleiter	Same	Gold (Deputy Flight Leader)
Flugkapitän	Same	Gold (Flight Captain)
Flugzeugführer	Black with gold interwoven	Gold (Pilot)
Hauptfluglehrer	Same	Gold (Senior Pilot Instructor)
Fluglehrer	Same	Gold (Pilot Instructor)
Hilfsfluglehrer	Same	Gold (Pilot Co-Instructor)
Orterlehrer	Same	Gold (Navigator Instructor)
Navigationslehrer	Same	Gold (Navigation Instructor)
Nachrichtenlehrer	Same	Gold (Signal Instructor)
Bordfunker	Aluminum with black interwoven	Gold (Communications)
Other Flying Personnel	Medium-blue	Silver (alum)

Visor cap of a civilian flying member of the Luftwaffe. Period photographs would indicate that the insigne was positioned either at the top or centered.

Visor cap insigne of the civilian flying employee—gold wings with aluminum swastika.

Visor cap insigne for "other civilian flying personnel"—aluminum wings with gold swastika.

Two forms of the greatcoat being worn by civilian flying employees of the Luftwaffe—At left is the cloth greatcoat, while at right is the leather.

NOTE: Cap cords were specifically addressed in an order (LV 37, No.231) dated 17 Feburary 1937.

No insignia was worn with the work coveralls or flying suits, which were of the same design as those of the Luftwaffe.

2. **Maritime Personnel** (Seemännisches Personal): At the outbreak of the war, the Luftwaffe included 14 Coastal Air Squadrons (Küstenfliegerstaffeln) and two Naval Air Squadrons (Bordfliegerstaffeln), all under the command of the Commander of Naval Air Units and Inspector General of Naval Aviation (Befehlshaber der Marinefliegerverbände und Inspekteur der Seeflieger). Air-traffic control ships and boats (Flugbetriebsboote) and supply ships and boats (Versorgungsschiffe, Versorgungsboote) were used for air safety control, the service within seaplane bases (Seefliegerhorst) and for the Sea Rescue Service (Seenotdienst). The crews were civilian personnel with the status of employees (Angestellte) or workers (Arbeiter). Employees served in functions comparable to officers and NCOs, and workers in enlisted functions. During the war, the civilian personnel were included in the Armed Forces Train.

The Air Rescue Service within the areas of the North Sea and the Baltic was constituted at the end of 1935. During the war the service was enlarged, and operated in all theaters of war.

Since about 1940, anti-aircraft weapons were installed on board larger ships and vessels, and manned by soldiers. Soldiers in the function of radio operators and medical personnel were also on board ships. This resulted in a mix of civilian and military personnel and uniforms. Some ships were under the command of military officers, and smaller vessels by senior NCOs.

So-called Siebel crafts (Siebelfähren—named after their designer) were built to transport material across the English Channel when the invasion of Great Britain was planned in 1940. Later they served as transports from Italy to North Africa or as anti-aircraft crafts (Flakkampffähren) with a number of AA weapons on board. These crafts were manned by soldiers.

A Naval School of the Luftwaffe (Seefahrtschule der Luftwaffe) was constituted about mid-1940 for training of military and civilian personnel. The necessary specialists—radio operators, signal personnel, mechanics, etc.—were transferred from the navy until sufficient Luftwaffe personnel could replace them.

Flags on Vessels and Boats: An order (LV 36, No.1145) dated 3 September 1936 presceibed the Reich service flag for air security vessels with military or non-military crews, and the Reich war flag for air-traffic control ships and boats and smaller vessels whenever an officer or an official with officer rank was on board.

An order (LV 38A, No.337) dated 4 November 1938 abolished the above order and mentioned a special order concerning display of flags of vessels, etc., of the Luftwaffe. This special order has not been found, however.

The manual L.Dv.1805 "Wartime Orders for Leaders of Maritime Vessels of the Luftwaffe" dated 12 February 1943 prescribed the Reich war flag on all vessels with a soldier commanding, and the Reich service flag for all other vessels.

Uniforms: Protective and special clothing for duties on board were the same as issued to Luftwaffe soldiers or navy personnel. Crews of ships and vessels in the Mediterranean were issued standard tropical uniforms.

Protective clothing (Schutzbekleidung) for duties on board ship were individually issued: leather clothing for engine personnel, work uniforms made of khaki-colored twill for employees and made of off-white or grey twill for sailors and selected technical enlisted personnel.

The special clothing (Sonderbekleidung) was equipment of the ships and vessels, and was issued only if necessary: oil clothing, rubber boots, leather clothing, winter clothing, furs, etc.

- Military Personnel: soldiers wore the standard uniforms with the golden-yellow or red branch colors. Trade and specialist insignia of enlisted personnel were as follows:
- Nautical Military Personnel (seemännisches militärisches Bootspersonal): The insigne was introduced by order (LV 36, No.1501) dated 7 January 1936. It was a fouled anchor with two horizontal wings, measuring 9.5 x 3.2cm, and in matte grey or off-white machine embroidery on a base of blue-grey uniform cloth cut out in the design of the insigne. The insigne was worn on the left lower sleeve 1cm above the cuff of the tunic or in a corresponding place on the blouse.

Radio operators, AA crews and medical personnel wore their trade insignia as described previously.

A group of personnel (probably civilian) wearing a dark coverall. It is believed these men are assigned to the nautical branch for civilians. Some significant aspects of the uniforms are: 1) Mixture of insignia worn on the visor cap. Note the two that have the winged anchor, the one with the winged propeller and the mixture of wreaths; 2) Note the three leaders as denoted by a single or three pips on each collar; 3) Note the variation buckles being worn.

- Civilian Personnel: Only one manual relating to uniforms has been located, L.Dv.2901/1, part 3 Administration (Verwaltung) of June 1943. It prescribed the number of garments issued to individuals of the crews. The design of the garments was not mentioned. The uniform was always worn on duty, off duty only in the area of operations, and in the home area on the way to and from duty. Discussion relative to the uniform is based primarily on a study of period photos.

Information concerning ranks and rank insignia has not been found. The above mentioned regulation includes only the sentence "Orders related to service and rank insignia are to be obeyed." Based on photos, it would appear that officers wore a system of sleeve stripes (of the navy style) on both lower sleeves.

All ranks wore an oval insigne consisting of a golden-yellow or silver-grey (depending on the color of the uniform buttons) embroidered 20mm swastika standing on its point. The insigne was worn on both sleeves. In the case of the officer ranks, above the sleeve stripe(s).

The garments were in cut and style of the navy uniform, and were made of navy blue cloth. Known uniforms were as follows:
- Tunic: The tunic was double-breasted in the cut and style of the navy, made of navy blue fabric, and with two rows

Two variations of the gold sleeve insigne worn by officers. At left is hand-embroidered, while at right is machine-embroidered.

Uniform of Maritime Civilian Personnel. Note the wear of the swastika sleeve insignia worn on each lower sleeve.

Machine-embroidered specimen of the enlisted sliver-grey sleeve insigne.

Embre

Radio operator of an air-sea rescue craft. Note the positioning of the swastika insigne above the sleeve rating stripe.

of four gold or silver buttons each. Speculation is that the gold was for employees, and silver for workers, or, gold for nautical personnel, and silver for technical personnel. The hip pockets were of the concealed variety, and with straight-edged flaps without button. There was no breast pocket.

- Trousers: Long trousers were with cuffs.
- Shirt and tie: The shirt was a light color, and the tie black.
- Visor Cap: NCO and officer equivalents wore a navy blue visor cap in the cut and style of their respective rank. The NCO visor cap was with black leather chin strap, while those of officers were either totally gold or gold or silver with interwoven dark color. Centered on the front of the mohair cap band was an insigne depicting crossed unfouled anchors with a wing projecting right and left, and with a large swastika standing on its point over the anchors. The insigne was either gold or silver-grey, corresponding with the color of the tunic buttons. It has been encountered in the following forms:
  - stamped metal measuring 11.6 x 4.9cm. The swastika was finely grained with a narrow smooth border. It was affixed by two prongs on the reverse.

Gold metal visor cap insigne of Maritime Civilian Personnel.

Officer visor cap worn by a maritime civilian employee, probably air-sea rescue, with metal insigne. The basic pattern of the cap is that of the navy.

White-topped visor cap at left, and blue-topped at right. Note the different chin cords being worn.

Hand-embroidered gold visor cap insigne.

Standard pattern golden-yellow machine-embroidered visor cap insigne.

Two variations of the golden-yellow machine-embroidered visor cap insigne.

As above, but silver-grey for enlisted personnel.

- machine-embroidered measuring 10.8 x 4.5 - 4.9cm (with some variations differing) and backed by a navy blue cloth.
- machine-woven and backed by a navy blue cloth
- hand-embroidered and backed by a navy blue cloth

- Greatcoat: of naval design for employees of officer and NCO rank.
- Short Coat (halblanger Mantel): double-breasted, length to the knees, two inserted side pockets with horizontal opening, and with rectangular unbuttoned flaps.
- Shoes and socks: Black leather low-quarters or ankle-high boots with black socks.

A pullover knitted of dark blue wool and black boots as for soldiers were issued for duty on board ship.

A one-piece coverall with belted waist, and with front button closure. It was worn with the Deutsche Wehrmacht armband on the left sleeve.

Crews rescued from the sea from downed aircraft were issued with sea rescue clothing (Seenotbekleidung): consisting of a blanket, sports suit, sports shoes, under-wear, and towel. Each set of items was enclosed in a package of strong paper or canvas fabric, and with the stenciled inscription of contents.

According to the publication *Uniformen-Markt,* issue 21, dated 1 November 1940 an insigne for divers was introduced in the autumn of 1940. It was an oval navy blue cloth for the jacket or of grey twill for the grey work jacket, and measuring 9x7cm. It depicted a golden-yellow diver's helmet in a pattern as that of the navy, but without the chevrons below the helmet. It was worn on the lower left sleeve.

3. **Personnel of the Chief of Supply and Procurement Service** (Generalluftzeugmeister—GL): Civil technicians of the General-luftzeugmeister were assigned largely as controllers, etc., of armament factories in the Reich and in the occupied countries. No regulations have been encountered, thus information is restricted to the rare items observed or from period photos. Insignia for the GL, termed GL-Industrial Insignia (GL-Industrie-Abzeichen) was introduced by an order (LV 41, No.661) dated 27 May 1941.

Metal "GL-Industrial Insigne" confirmed being worn on the right breast, but not the officer's visor cap.

Uniforms observed in wear from period photos are as follows:

    a. Enlisted Luftwaffe pattern blue-grey Fliegerbluse worn with the collar open at the neck, and with detachable shoulder straps with branch piping (probably red). Affixed directly to each collar without backing, and worn in the vertical position were large white metal GL devices in Latin capitals. On the right breast was a stamped metal emblem depicting a Luftwaffe eagle flying to the viewer's right, and superimposed on a cogged gear. The device, measuring 65mm wide x 50mm high, was affixed by means of three prongs. NOTE: This same insigne has been observed on Luftwaffe pattern officer visor caps in collections, but there is no period photograph or regulation to support such a cap being worn by officer's of the Generalluftzeugmeister.

The cap was of the standard blue-grey enlisted visorless field cap with Luftwaffe insignia.

The black leather enlisted belt was with the enlisted Luftwaffe buckle.

What is presumed to be the basic pattern uniform of the "GL."

Skötte

What appears to be a standard pattern Fliegerbluse, but with variant insignia to the above.

b. As 3.a. above but with the machine-embroidered enlisted Luftwaffe eagle in place of the metal GL insigne. Collar patches were different in that the letter device was on a patch backing (color undetermined). On the right collar patch was the letter G, and on the left a L, both in the vertical position.

Ulric of England

Commercially produced collar patches worn by "GL" personnel. The blue-grey patch is embroidered with silver-grey "GL," and piped in red.

    c. As 3.a. above but without any insignia on the collar. However, the enlisted style shoulder straps depicts a large metal GL at the base, and a metal rank pip centered above, indicating some for of rank structure.

    d. A tunic of undetermined color with two pleated breast pockets, a five button front closure buttoned to the neck, and shoulder straps. On the right breast was the metal GL insigne. On the right collar was the letter G, and on the left a L—both without collar patches, and worn in the horizontal position.

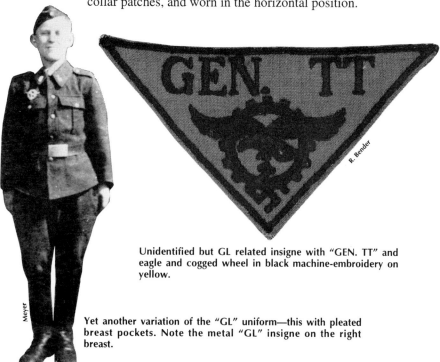

R. Bender

Meyer

Unidentified but GL related insigne with "GEN. TT" and eagle and cogged wheel in black machine-embroidery on yellow.

Yet another variation of the "GL" uniform—this with pleated breast pockets. Note the metal "GL" insigne on the right breast.

Dark colored tunic without breast pockets or breast insigne.

e. A dark colored tunic without breast pockets, but with a concealed hip pocket at each side, and without buttoned flap. The
front closure was five closed at the collar. Sew-in shoulder
straps were with piping (color unknown). On the collar was a
metal G (right) and L (left) affixed directly to the collar without backing, and facing the collar points. Back from each collar vertical edge was a single piping bar.

The visorless field cap was of the Luftwaffe variety as was the black
enlisted leather belt.

A cloth insigne exists that was presumably worn over the right breast of
the black work coverall and work suit. The insigne, black machine-embroi-

Two variation sizes of
the machine-embroi-
dered "GL" insigne exist,
presumable worn on the
work uniform or coverall. The
large example measures 110mm
across the top line, and 85mm for
the smaller.

dery on a yellow field, takes the form of the Luftwaffe eagle flying to the viewer's left superimposed on a cog-wheel, with the letter G in the left corner, and L in the right. The entire insigne was bordered in black. Two distinct sizes exist, and measured by the top border were 85mm and 110mm.

A metal lapel pin depicting a Luftwaffe eagle flying to its right (wingspan measuring 35mm), and clutching a swastika in a cogwheel was worn on the left lapel of the civilian jacket.

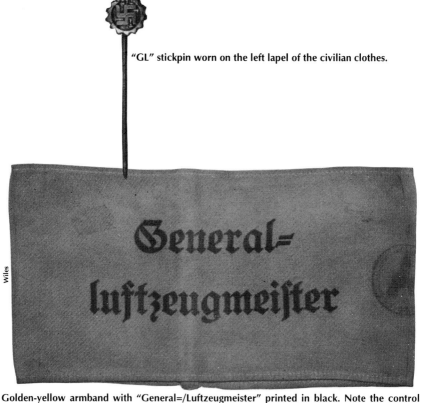

"GL" stickpin worn on the left lapel of the civilian clothes.

Wiles

Golden-yellow armband with "General=/Luftzeugmeister" printed in black. Note the control stamp to the right.

An 11cm wide golden-yellow armband bearing the black Gothic inscription General=/Luftzeugmeister in two lines was probably worn by personnel in factories wearing civilian clothing.

4. **Air Force Construction** (Luftwaffe Bau—L.Bau): Civilian construction employees were also outfitted in Luftwaffe style uniforms. Again, no regulations have been found, thus reliance on period photos was necessary. Uniforms observed were as follows:

a. A service tunic with four pleated patch pockets with four button front closure, and with sleeves with turned-back cuffs. No shoulder straps/boards were worn, but there appear to have been unadorned collar patches closely similiar in color as the tunic. Worn with either breeches and black leather boots or straight pants. There was a distinctive insigne of the L.Bau worn on the left sleeve just below the elbow. It depicted the Wehrmacht Gefolge—WG insigne in white on red with an outer white border, and on a black field with L.BAU in Latin captials below. The outer border was white/red/white. The base of the red border measured 85mm wide and 110mm high.

Service uniform of the "L.Bau." While not clearly shown, there are collar patches being worn, and buttons on the shoulders, but no straps or boards.

Note the position of the "L.Bau" insigne on the left sleeve and the right side of the M43 visored field cap.

The standard pattern Luftwaffe M43 with Luftwaffe eagle (no national tri-colors) worn on the front, and possibly a smaller version of the L.Bau insigne on the right side.

Printed version of the "L.Bau" insigne. The larger version was worn on the left sleeve, while a smaller version was worn on the right side of the M43 cap.

Variation uniforms being worn by personnel of the "L.Bau." Their only insignia appears to be the "L.Bau" insigne on the left sleeve, and the Luftwaffe national emblem on the cap.

    b. As 4.a. above, but without collar patches.

    c. Unadorned tunic with five button front closure to the neck, and without pockets.

    d. Unadorned tunic with four button front closure to the neck, and with concealed hip pockets with angled unbuttoned flaps.

e. As d. above, but with concealed hip pockets with straight-edge unbuttoned flaps, and with four buttons open at the neck.
f. The standard pattern Fliegerbluse.
g. Black HBT tunic with five black pebbled front button closure open at the neck, and with four unpleated patch pockets. Yet another distinctive L.Bau insigne was worn over the right breast pocket. The insigne was white machine-embroidery on a black triangle bordered in white, and took the form of a Luftwaffe eagle flying to the viewer's left, with L.BAU overhead. This insigne was also produced in two sizes. Using the upper border, one measured 110mm, while the other was 80mm.

Dietz

Black HBT tunic with "L.Bau" breast insigne.

Breast insigne of the "L.Bau"—off-white machine-embroidery on black. It was produced in two sizes.

5. **L G:** Exact organization is not known. The only reference comes from an insigne similar to the L.Bau. It was golden-yellow machine-embroiderey on black, and depicted a Luftwaffe eagle flying to it's right and with a Latin capital L on the left, and G on the right. This, too, had a triangular border with the top measuring approximately 85mm. Considering the G L and the L.BAU, it can be presumed this insigne also came in two sizes.

"LG" insigne—golden-yellow machine-embroidery on a black field.

6. **Doormen, Guards and Elevator Operators** (Pförtner, Wächter and Fahrstuhlführer): Civilian doormen, guards and elevator operators of the Reichsluftfahrtministerium (RLM) were permitted wear of a uniform by an order dated 23 April 1936, while doormen of headquarters of Air District Commands were permitted a uniform per order (LV 37, No.753) dated 11 June 1937. The description that follows pertains to the 1937 uniform even though the 1936 uniform was probably identical.

Garments were made of blue-grey uniform cloth. Shirts, tie and shoes were as those of soldiers.

a. Tunic: The double-breasted tunic was of civilian style with two rows each of three flat riffled silver-colored buttons. The collar was made of bordeaux-red badge cloth. The center seam of the back ended in a 20cm long slash. The sleeves ended in a 20cm long cuff. There were two hip pockets with unbuttoned rectangular flaps. The lining was black. A miniature (26mm inclusive of the 9mm wreath) version of the cap badge was positioned parallel to the short edge of each collar. Rank pip(s) in aluminum on each collar if appropriate as follows:

1) Hilfspförtner and Fahrstuhlführer: No pip
2) Pförtner: One pip centered below the wreath
3) Oberpförtner: One pip above and one pip below the wreath

Doormen and Guard Personnel of other headquarters.

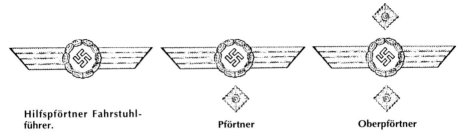

Hilfspförtner Fahrstuhl-
führer.

Pförtner

Oberpförtner

    b. Trousers: Cut and style as the long trousers of soldiers, but with a bordeaux red piping along the outer seam.

    c. Visor Cap: The design of the visor cap was that of soldiers. The piping around the top and the edges of the cap band and the cap band proper were made of bordeaux red badge cloth. The officer-style chin cord was made of black artificial silk affixed by two small metal buttons lacquered in black. The visor was black vulcan fiber.

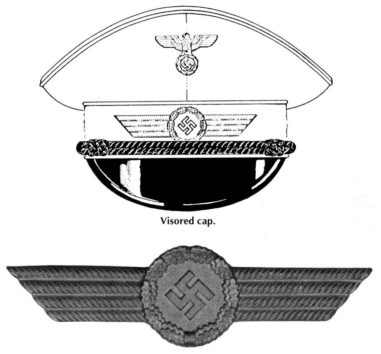

Visored cap.

    The national emblem of the NSDAP was centered at the front peak. However, by an order (LV 37, No.1149) dated 30 August 1937 it was replaced by the national emblem of the Reich with short straight wings. Centered on the cap band was a stamped aluminum metal insigne depicting a swastika standing on its point surrounded by an oakleaf wreath, and wings projecting right and left. Overall length was 11cm.

    There were regulation caps with the insigne on the cap band pressed of gold-colored metal, but the purpose is unknown.

d. Greatcoat: In cut and style as the surcoat of soldiers, with a bordeaux red collar and pebbled aluminum-colored buttons.

e. Rain Coat: As the oiled greatcoat of the special clothing of the Luftwaffe. A light-weight rain coat similar to the rain coats of officers was introduced at a later date.

f. Armbands: Armbands were made of bordeaux red badge cloth, and measured 10cm wide. Centered on the armband was a sewn-on 53mm circular blue-grey cloth backing with the national emblem of the NSDAP (with head turned to its right wing). By the above order dated 30 August 1937 this was substituted by the national emblem of the Reich. The armband was worn on the upper left sleeve of tunics and greatcoats. Rank designations were as follows:

   1) Pförtner and Wächter: No Tresse added to armband
   2) Wachhabender (Leader of Guard): One 1cm aluminum Tresse positioned at the base of the armband 2mm above the edge.
   3) Wachleiter (Head of Guard Detachment): One 1cm aluminum Tresse position at the top and bottom of the armband.

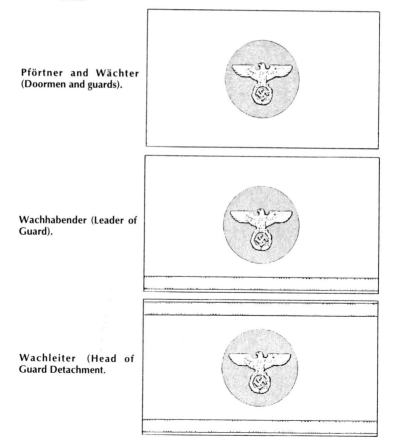

Pförtner and Wächter (Doormen and guards).

Wachhabender (Leader of Guard).

Wachleiter (Head of Guard Detachment.

Armband for Wachhabender (leader of guard).

An order (LV41, No.714) dated 24 June 1941 was a repetition of the 11 June 1937 order. However, it prescribed mignonette green (resedagrün) for piping and cap band of caps, collars of tunics and greatcoats, piping of trousers and armbands for personnel of the RLM. It is highly probable that these were already worn much earlier.

7. **Doormen and Guards of other Commands:** An order (LV 36, No.882) dated 8 July 1937 specified that doormen and guards of other commands, as well as those listed under 6. above, were identified by a cap and an armband worn with the civilian clothing.
   a. Visor cap: As 6.c. above, but with wine-red cap band and piping.
   b. Armband: The 13cm wide armband was made of blue-grey uniform cloth, and with the grey machine-embroidered inscription Luftfahrtverwaltung in Latin or Gothic letters. The edges of the armband were piped in a 2mm wide wine-red badge

Wachmann armband for Doorman and Guards—blue-grey field with red piping (other colors did exist), and with Machine-embroidered "Luftfahrtverwaltung" in off-white.

As above, but with one aluminum Tresse on the lower edge denoting rank of Wachhabender.

As above, but with two aluminum Tresse denoting rank of Wachleiter.

Unknown rank with one aluminum Tresse on the upper edge.

cloth. The armband was worn on the left upper sleeve. A distinctive 1cm wide aluminum Tresse was addressed in an order (LV37, No.1216) dated 13 September 1939 to be positioned 2mm from the piping as follows:

1) Wachmann: No Tresse
2) Wachhabender: One Tresse at the lower edge.
3) Wachleiter: One Tresse top and one Tresse bottom edges

Some institutions were guarded by civilian guards. While no specific orders have been found, order (LV 37, No.1166) dated 6 September 1937 directed that these guards were to be issued surcoats with woolen lining and overshoes if necessary—both as those issued soldiers.

8. Civilian Drivers (Zivilkraftfahrer): Civilian personnel were employed mainly as drivers of staff cars of high commands.

The drivers of the Fliegerschaft probably wore a grey uniform of civilian cut. Per order (Der Reichsminister der Luftfahrt L.D. No. 30087/34 g.Kdos. DIV, 26, Az.64.c.20) dated 10 May 1934 the national emblem was prescribed for wear centered on the crown of the visor cap. The emblem was the same as worn by the enlisted personnel of the Fliegerschaft, i.e. the national emblem of the organizations of the NSDAP in pressed silver-colored metal. The head of the eagle was turned to its left wing, with short horizontal wings, and the swastika in a rather large oakleaf wreath. It measured approximately 3.6x2.7cm.

By an order (LV35, No.545) dated 30 August 1935 a uniform was introduced. It consisted of a visored cap, tunic, long trousers or breeches, greatcoat, black knee-long leather gaiters (worn with the breeches), black lace-up shoes, and gauntlets. The garments were made of grey cloth, but the order did not specify details.

The cap was dark grey with black cap band, with dark grey piping top, center and bottom. The chinstrap was black leather. A silver-colored NSDAP pattern national emblem was affixed to the front center of the peak, and a Reich cockade centered at the front of the cap band. The order specified that these insignia were to be removed for drives of a secret purpose. At a later date the cockade was replaced with the insigne of the doorman.

An order (LV 38C, No.78) dated 26 January 1938 a new uniform and a summer uniform was introduced. The earlier 1935 pattern uniform was to be worn out. The new uniform retained the dark grey color. An order (LV 40C, No.78) dated 19 January 1940 restricted its wear to civilian drivers of staff cars.

a. Tunic and Greatcoat: These were of the civilian design. Open wear (i.e. non-buttoned) was permitted. The tunic was double-breasted with two rows of three black buttons each, with only the lower two being buttoned. The winter greatcoat was lined with woolen cloth or fur.
b. Trousers: the trouser legs ended in a cuff.
c. Visor Cap: The insigne on the cap band was abolished, and the Reich national emblem was worn on the front of the peak.

d. Gauntlets: These were replaced by gloves of the pattern of flyer's gloves.

e. Summer Uniform: The summer uniform was made of light-weight grey-mettled fabric, and consisted of a summer cap, summer tunic, summer trousers and a summer coat in raglan style. No further details were provided.

9. **Insignia of Civilian Retinue of the Luftwaffe and of the Armed Forces Train:** By an order (LV 41, No.1742) dated 30 October 1941 two insignia were introduced for member of the Civilian Retinue of the Armed Forces (Gefolgschaftsmitglieder) and of the Armed Forces Train (Wehrmachtgefolge) for wear in the occupied countries, and in friendly countries providing they were not allotted a uniform. Wear of an armband by non-German personnel was also introduced. This was a white armband worn on the left upper sleeve, and with the inscription Im Dienst der Deutschen Wehrmacht in black Latin or Gothic letters in one or two lines.

a. Members of the Civilian Retinue: Civilian Retinue was the term for all male and female non-military members of the Armed Forces.

The insigne was the M1938 badge for employees and workers taking the form of a silver swastika standing on its point with wings right and left superimposed on an oakleaf wreath open at the top and bound at the bottom. The wingspan was 21mm. It was affixed by either a button or a safety or stick pin to the left lapel of jackets both on and off duty.

The insigne was issued with an authorization document.

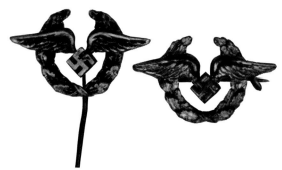

M1938 badge for members of the civilian retinue. At left is the stick pin, while at right is the pin back version.

The order further mentioned that uniforms or clothing similar to a uniform already in wear were to be worn out, but did not mention the kind of these uniforms.

b. Armed Forces Train: An order (LV 42, No.2949) dated 26 November 1942 defined the Armed Forces Train as all male or female persons who were in the service of the Armed Forces or were following or with the Armed Forces out of the area of the Reich. German nationality was not a required supposition.

The bronze-colored badge took the form of an eagle's head turned to its right, and below were the letters WG with a swastika below these. The badge was encircled by a round plain border. The badge came in two sizes—one 2.3cm diameter with a vertical needle pin on the reverse, and the other 3.5cm diameter with a horizontal fastening pin. A subsequent order (OTB 42, No.4 VII) dated 12 December 1942 prescribed wear of the smaller badge by female personnel, and wear of the larger pin by male personnel. It was worn on the left lapel of jackets.

Stick pin and badge worn by male and female members of the Armed Forces Train.

10. **NSKK Transportation Units:** At the end of 1939 or early 1940 transportation units were formed and manned by members of the National Socialist Motor Corps (Nationalsozialistisches Kraftfahr-

Personnel of NSKK-Luftwaffe 7. Note wear of the "Deutsche Wehrmacht" armband at top center.

korps—NSKK). The were under the tactical control of the Armed Forces, and were part of the Armed Forces Train.

Five NSKK-Regiment (Speer) Luftwaffe were in existence in 1941, and were transformed into the NSKK-Transportbrigade Speer, with four more added in 1943/44. There was also two NSKK-Brigade Luftwaffe, which was renamed NSKK-Gruppe Luftwaffe at the end of 1943.

Personnel came from the NSKK and other organizations, and wore uniforms and protective garments of the Luftwaffe, but with NSKK insignia, to include rank collar patches.

There probably existed cuff titles for all the Luftwaffe-related NSKK regiments and brigades, worn on the lower left sleeve of the service jacket or tunic. Known examples are 1.N.S.K.K. Transport-Regiment Luftwaffe and NSKK-Brigade Luftwaffe.

11. Technical Emergency Corps: Some units of the Technical Emergency Corps (Technische Nothilfe—TeNo or TN) were assigned to the Luftwaffe during the war.

TeNo personnel wore the Luftwaffe uniform with TeNo or a combination of TeNo and Luftwaffe insignia. Characteristic, however, was the Technische Nothilfe sleeve band in grey on black with top and bottom border stripes.

CHAPTER •24
AIR PROTECTION ORGANIZATIONS

For purposes of this discussion the term Air Protection will be used, since Air Defense would suggest the military arms of Flak, fighters, etc. Obviously, air protection organizations were a part of air defense. To further confuse the matter, the term Air Defense (Luftverteidigung) was also used as a general collective term for the military air defense and the civilian air protection organizations.

The Air Protection Organizations were under the command of the Reich Air Ministry (RLM). There were several organizations already partially constituted prior to the outbreak of the war. These consisted of the following:

- Air Warning Service (Luftschutz-Warndienst—LSW)
- Security and Assistance Service (Sicherheits- und Hilfsdienst—SHD)
- Air Protection Police (Luftschutzpolizei), which eventually came under control of the police.

The National Air Protection League (Reichsluftschutzbund—RLB) was a separate organization whose main purpose was to instruct the population in awareness of air raids. During the war it lost its importance almost to the degree of non-existence.

To augment any short-fall of volunteers, personnel were drafted under the Air Protection Service Obligation, which was a Reich law.

A.   Uniforms of the Air Protection Organizations:
Pertinent regulation of the period was the manual L.Dv.788 Manual about Uniform of the SHD Ist Grade and the LSW (Vorschrift über die Dienstbekleidung für den SHD I.Ordnung und den LSW), dated 1 August 1941. However, an order (BLB 40, No. 454) dated 27 March 1940 indicates that uniform and insignia were already introduced in the spring of 1940.

Male members of the LSW and SHD wore the basic Luftwaffe uniform with special insignia, etc. Uniform, equipment, protective clothing and clothing for special duties were provided for by the Luftwaffe. The garments were termed LS-Rock (tunic), LS-Bluse (blouse), and LS-Mantel (greatcoat). Grades (Rangstufen) 1 - 3 were enlisted personnel (Mannschaften), and grades 4 and 5 NCOs (Unterführer). Leader personnel (führer) of grades 6 - 10 were subjected to the dress regulations of officers. As a result, the collars of the tunic was piped in aluminum twist cord.

Service tunic of a SHD Stabsgruppenführer in the position of the company sergeant as denoted by the aluminum Tresse about each sleeve. Note position of wear of the SHD armband.

An array of SHD enlisted and officer uniforms.

Enlisted flyer's jacket modified for wear by SHD officer with the addition of the collar cord. Note the wear of the M1943 flyer's cap and the lack of collar patches.

Basic cloth blouse uniform, but with the trousers worn inside the high boots. Note the pattern of the field cap and its insignia.

Tuchbluse being worn with breeches and boots, the latter not addressed in regulations.

Linder

SHD officer at the right, denoted by the piping about the field cap, oversees a group of SHD personnel in work uniforms working with a raft.

163

By order (LV 42, No.2949) dated 26 November 1942 male members of the LSW were subjected to the Military Penal Laws (Militärstrafgesetzbuch) and the Armed Forces Disciplinary Laws (Wehrmacht-Disziplinarordnung). Certainly this was also valid for male members of the SHD as well.

Insignia common to the LSW and SHD were as follows:

1. Headgear:
   a. Flyers Cap: Of the Luftwaffe pattern in fabric and style, but with the Luftschutz national emblem and Reich cockade. The officers cap was with aluminum piping or thin cord around the upper edge of the turn-up.
   b. Visored Flyers Cap: As above, but with the piping or cord about the perimeter of the top.
   c. Visor Cap: Of the Luftwaffe pattern in fabric and style. Grades 1 - 5 were piped in green, while those of 6 - 10 were in aluminum. The Luftschutz national emblem on the front at the top, and the cockade (without winged wreath) at the front of the cap band. Caps of officers were with the aluminum chin cord, and with hand-embroidered emblem.
   d. Helmets: The standard air protection helmet (Luftschutzhelm) was introduced by an order dated 26 September 1938 (der Reichsminister der Luftfahrt und Oberbefehlshaber der Luftwaffe-ZLI 2a No. 3438/38). Steel helmets of army stocks could be used up if they could be distinguished from army helmets by color or distinctive insignia. It was made of steel or of a light metal alloy, and was painted matte blue-grey or black. It took the general form of the M35 helmet with a raised rim of about 8mm in width around the base of the crown. The rim connected the crown with the long visor and the elongated

M1935 beaded Luftschutz helmet worn by SHD and LSW personnel.

M1938 Luftschutz "gladiator" style helmet.

neck guard, with a cut-out for the ears at either side. The helmets were pressed as one-part helmets or two-part helmets. The two parts of the latter, crown and visor with neck guard, were connected by the raised rim around the crown. At either side were two circular ventilation areas spaced 4cm apart and with multiple holes. The bottom edge was with a raised rim.

The liner was a simplified version of the liner of the M35 helmet. The chin strap was made of 2cm wide black leather (later of ersatz material). The manufacturers logo, size, etc., were usually impressed or as a decal on the inside of the neck guard.

SHD fire personnel wearing the standard pattern cloth blouse (Tuchbluse) and trousers with the M1935 pattern helmet. Note that the specialty insignia are worn on the lower left sleeve. 165

Charita

Civilian SHD fire personnel wearing the M1938 pattern Luftschutz helmet.

The national emblem of the Luftschutz pattern was a silver-colored decal, sometimes with a black base, and was applied onto the front of the helmet 2.2cm above the raised rim of the crown. It was introduced by the above order dated 26 September 1938. The insigne featured two wings with a center oakleaf wreath, which was made of one row of leaves and two horizontal leaves and two stalks at the bottom. Superimposed at the bottom was a swastika standing on its point, and above a scroll slightly bent upwards and with the inscription LUFTSCHUTZ in Latin capitals within the frame. The interior design of the wings and leaves, the border of the swastika and the scroll proper were black. The decal measured 13 x 3.3cm.

Other helmets were also utilized—models M16, M18, M35, of the civil pattern, and of various captured stock. There were also M35 helmets with a raised 1cm wide rim between the crown and the visor/neck guard, commonly referred to as the Luftschutz Flak helmet.

Helmets of SHD groups of larger firms of the armaments, etc., industry frequently had the logo of their firm applied to the left or right side of the helmet.

M34 "Square Dip" helmet with satin black finish.

M16 Austrian helmet with 1938 winged decal and medium green finish.

2. Collar Patches: The green parallelogram collar patches measured 4-4.6 x 5.5-5.8, and with a 2cm high off-white letters SHD or LSW machine-embroidered for enlisted Grades 1-5, in aluminum machine-embroidery or aluminum hand-embroidery for officer Grades 6-10. Those of enlisted personnel were piped with a 2mm wide green and white twist cord, while those of officers were in aluminum twist cord. Collar patches were prescribed for wear with the tunic, the blouse and the greatcoat. It was not uncommon to find no collar patches worn with the blouse. No collar patches were worn on the drill uniform.

SHD collar patches for Grades 1-5. The piping is green and white alternating twist cord.

As above, but for LSW.

Machine-embroidered SHD in aluminum thread with twist aluminum cord for grades 6-10.

Variation to the above.

As above, but for LSW.

Specimen of the Luftschutz-Warndienst (LSW) officer collar insigne-silver embroidery on dark green with twist silver cord piping.

Hand-embroidered version of the officer ranks.

Unexplained version of the hand-embroidered LSW officer collar patch.

3. National Emblems: The basic insigne featured a wing projecting to the right and left of a wreath with a swastika standing on its point. Centered on the wreath was a black scroll with the inscription in Latin capitals LUFTSCHUTZ with its frame. Grades 1 - 5 were in grey or off-white, while those of 6 - 10 were hand-embroidered aluminum wire. The national emblems were worn as follows:

- Visor Cap
- Flyers Cap
- Visored Flyers Cap
- Blouse and Tunic
- Helmet
- Belt Buckle

Field cap insigne, 6cm version, grade 1-5.

Field cap insigne, 9cm version, grade 1-5. Also worn over the right breast pocket.

Visor cap insigne, 9cm version, grade 6-10. Silver bullion with printed "Luftschutz."

Visor cap insigne for LSW, 9cm version, grade 6-9. Silver bullion on black.

Visor cap insigne for SHD, 11.5cm version, grade 1-5 in thread; grade 6-10 in aluminum wire. Sometimes also worn on left upper sleeve of leaders grade 6-10.

11.5cm hand-embroidered insigne for grade 6-10.

4. Trade Insignia and Armbands: Trade insignia were worn on the lower left sleeve, while armbands were worn on the upper left sleeve. Each grouping will be discussed in detail with the specific organization.

5. Belt and Buckle: Belts were of the standard Luftwaffe pattern—black with rectangular box buckle for enlisted personnel, and brown with double open-claw aluminum colored buckle for officers. Until the end of 1939 or early 1940 a black or brown leather cross strap was worn.

   a. Enlisted Buckle (Koppelschloss): The buckle was of the RLB rectangular box 2nd pattern stamped with the RLB national emblem with a 5.5cm wide total wing-span and 1.8cm high at the center point. Buckle colors ranged from grey to blue. During the war the standard pattern enlisted Luftwaffe buckle was frequently worn.

   b. Officers Buckle: The officers buckle was the standard double open-claw buckle worn with either the 50mm or 55mm belt.

Standard pattern 5.5cm wide buckle worn by enlisted personnel of the SHD and LSW.

Enlisted member of the SHD undergoes gasmask drill. Clearly shown is the enlisted belt buckle as well as the collar patch and breast insignia.

B. Air Warning Service (Luftschutz-Warndienst—LSW):

The Air Warning Service was established in 1935. Its purpose was to warn the population of air raids. Its members were volunteers or, during the war, drafted according to the War Emergency Laws. The female personnel were the Auxiliaries of the Air Warning Service (L.S.-Warndienst-Helferinnenschaft). Their uniform, etc., will be described in an independent chapter entitled The Female Auxiliaries.

1. Ranks and Rank Insignia: Ranks and insignia before 1941 are not known, but they probably were the same as those introduced later. New rank insignia were introduced by order L.Dv.788 dated 1 August 1941. These were a series of shoulder straps (Schulterschnüre) worn on both shoulders, made of a flat cord, which formed a sling for buttoning. The backing was dark green cloth. The rank insignia were as follows (the numbers indicate the grades, rank equivalent of soldiers in parenthesis):

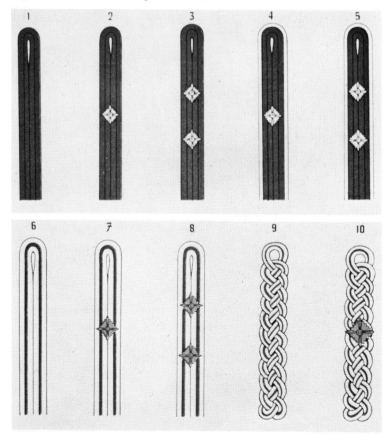

- 1. LSW.-Mann (Private) — 2 cords of dark green artificial silk, 1.5cm wide
- 2. LSW.-Truppführer (Gefreiter) — Same, 1 silver pip
- 3. LSW.-Gruppenführer — Same, 2 silver pips (Feldwebel)

- 4. LSW.-Hauptgruppenführer — Same, with a narrow silver/ aluminum border, (Feldwebel) 2cm wide; 1 silver pip
- 5. LSW.-Stabsgruppenführer — Same, 2 silver pips (Oberfeldwebel)
- 6. LSW.-Zugführer (Leutnant) — 2 silver/aluminum cords with interwoven dark green silk threads, 2cm wide
- 7. LSW.-Oberzugführer — Same, 1 gold pip (Oberleutnant)
- 8. LSW.-Warnzentraleführer — Same, 2 gold pips (Hauptmann)
- 9. LSW.-Warnzentrale- Oberführer (Major) — Braiding of a 7mm wide silver/aluminum cord with inter- woven dark green silk threads, 2.5cm wide

An order (LV 43, No.932) dated 7 May 1943 prescribed pips, later slides. The slides (Knebel) were probably made of thin aluminum or gold cords, similar to those of special leaders (Sonderführer) and were looped onto the shoulder straps.

An order (LV 43, No.2282) dated 21 December 1943 that relates to the Military Penalty Laws of the Retinue of the Lufwaffe included the following ranks without stating further details:

(1.) Luftschutzwarner
(2.) Luftschutzwarntruppführer
(3.) Luftschutzwarndienstgruppenführer
(4.) Luftschutzwarndiensthauptgruppenführer
(5.) Luftschutzwarndienststabsgruppenführer
(6.) Luftschutzwarndienstzugführer
(7.) Luftschutzwarndienstoberzugführer
(8.) Luftschutzwarndiensthauptführer
(9.) Luftschutzwarndienststabsführer

NOTE: The numbers in parentheses probably are consistent with the above 1941 system of ranks.

Other Insignia:
- LSW.-Stabsgruppenführer in the position of company sergeant (Hauptfeldwebel) were identified by one silver/aluminum Tresse around the right lower sleeve of blouse, tunic and greatcoat, posi- tioned 15cm above the edge of the sleeves, per order (LV 43, No.1739) dated 14 September 1943.
- LSW.-Replacement and Training Battalions (LSW.-Ersatz- und Ausbildungsabteilungen): An order (LV 43, No.932) dated 7 May 1943 specified that the cadre personnel were to be identified by the metal Latin letter L centered on the shoulder straps—silver/alu- minum for grades 1 - 5, and gold for grades 6 - 9.
- Collar Patches: See A.2. above for details. The Gothic letters LSW were in white-grey machine-embroidery for enlisted personnel, and silver/aluminum hand-embroidery for officers.

- Cuff Title: A 5cm wide green band bearing the machine-woven off-white inscription L.S. Warndienst (in Gothic letters) was worn on the lower left sleeve. It must be presumed that a hand-embroidered version would be worn by officers.

Cuff title for the Luftschutz Warning Service (L.S. Warndienst) in silver-grey machine-embroidery on a wide green field.

- Armband: The green armband bearing the inscription L.S.-Warndienst was worn by the Female Auxiliaries of the LSW only. Additionally, the manual L.Dv.788 illustrates a Grade Insigne for female members of the LSW—a green armband with white inscription LS-Warndienst in Gothic letters, and with white stripes or Tresse along both borders. No further explanation was provided.
- Trade Badges: A badge, worn on the upper left sleeve of signals personnel, was a 63-65mm high and 52-53mm wide green oval with two crossed silver-grey machine-embroidered lightning bolts with points at each end, and above them the Latin letters LSW measuring 10mm high. Introduction of the badge is not known.

Other sleeve insignia and armbands prescribed for the SHD may also have been worn by the LSW.

- National Emblem: In addition to the national emblems bearing the Luftschutz designation, there also existed a variant (purpose unknown) in aluminum hand-embroidery and bearing the letters L.S.W. in the scroll. It is possible that this was an intended design that gave way to the standard Luftschutz pattern.
- Civil Badge: By an order dated 2 June 1936* a civil badge was introduced to be worn by male and female personnel of the Aircraft Reporting Service and the Air Protection Warning Service.**

---

*(Der Reichsminister der Luftfahrt und Oberbefehlshaber der Luftwaffe Flak D5 Nr. 3787/36 Nr. 21/32.)

**It was identical with the civil badge as described for female Aircraft Reporting Service (see there).

C. Security and Assistance Service (Sicherheits- und Hilfsdienst—SHD):

The SHD was organized at the beginning of the war or shortly before. Its duties were to assist at bomb damage areas, with emphasis towards persons and buildings, and maintaining order and security during air raids.

Cities and villages were classified as communities of Ist, IInd or IIIrd order according to the estimated degree of danger. Accordingly, the SHD organization was organized in SHD Ist Grade (I.Ordnung, under central control of the Reich), SHD IInd and IIIrd Grade (II.Ordnung and III.Ordnung, under control of the communities). An order dated 24 November 1943 abolished the classification of communities, and probably also the according classification of the SHD.

1. SHD Insignia of 1939:
    a. Ranks and Rank Insignia: The ranks (Rangstufen instead of the usual Dienstgrade) were presumably introduced in mid-1939. There were six grades, but soon the system was enlarged to nine. All grades had a dark green, 10cm wide armband on the left upper sleeve. The woven armband had the off-white Gothic inscription Sicherheits- u./Hilfsdienst in two lines. The grades were recognized by aluminum Tresse sewn onto the armband, 7mm wide for narrow Tresse and 1.5cm wide for wider Tresse. Ranks depicted by armbands were as follows:

Basic armband of the SHD—white print on dark green.

Red Cross volunteer member of the SHD. Note that the edge of the armband has been folded under, and worn on the lower sleeve.

Grade	Armband
1	Basic green armband with SHD designation
2	As above, but with 8cm long narrow Tresse on the upper edge above the inscription.
3	As Grade 1, with narrow Tresse around the upper edge.
4	As Grade 1, with an 8cm long narrow Tresse between the Tresse around the edge and the inscription
5	As Grade 1, with narrow Tresse around both edges
6	As Grade 1, with 1.5cm wide Tresse around the upper edge
7	As Grade 1, with wide Tresse around both edges
8	As Grade 7, but with a narrow Tresse around the center of the armband and open between the two lines of inscription
9	As Grade 8, but with a 1.5cm wide center Tresse

(NOTE: Grade 9 was probably intended, but not introduced as no designation was given.) The ranks were the same as with the 1940 order (next page) but with the prefix "LS" instead of "SHD."

SHD armband for grade 3 as denoted by the stripe of aluminum Tresse running the entire length of the top of the armband.

Bilheimer

Howard

Grade 7 with wide aluminum Tresse top and bottom (inscription machine-embroidered).

177

b. Trade Insignia (Tätigkeitsabzeichen): The trade insignia were worn on the left lower sleeve. The oval measured approximately 6cm high and 4cm wide. Each had a 2mm wide (inclusive in overall measurements) green border, and a different base color in each case. The insignia were machine-woven or machine-embroidered. Trades were as follows:

- Fire Brigade and Decontamination Service (Feuerlösch- u. Entgiftungsdienst): White Gothic letter F on a red base encircled by green.
- Maintenance Service (Instandsetzungsdienst): White Gothic letter I on a brown base encircled by green.
- Veterinary Service (Veterinärdienst): White Gothic letter V on a violet base encircled by green.
- Training in Gas Detection (für im Gasspüren und Entgiften Ausgebildete): Black letter G on a yellow base encircled by green.

Veterinary
Service

Instandsetzungsdienst—white "I" on a brown field encircled by a green oval.

Training in gas detection.

The following insignia, presumed to have taken the form of an armband, were abolished with the introduction of the above trade insignia:

- Gas: G
- Water (Wasser): W
- Canalization (Kanalisation): K
- Electricity (Elektrizität): E

c. Positional Armbands: The armbands for telephone operators and messengers were green 10cm wide, and with the woven or printed inscription Fernsprecher (telephone operator) or Melder (messenger) in white Gothic lettering. They were worn on the upper left sleeve.

Other armbands authorized by regulations for wear were:

- Stretcher Bearer (Hilfskrankenträger): Black title Hilfskrankenträger (on a single line) on a white field.
- Medical Service: Red cross on a white field.

Feuerlösch- und Entgiftungsdienst (Fire Brigade and Decontamination)—white "F" on red field encircled by a green oval. Note the fire fighter with the specialty insigne worn on the upper left sleeve.

SHD enlisted man wears the Instandsetzungsdienst specialty insigne on the upper left sleeve rather than the lower sleeve as prescribed by regulations. He wears a RLB buckle and a Luftwaffe overseas cap.

179

"Fernsprecher"—telephone operator.

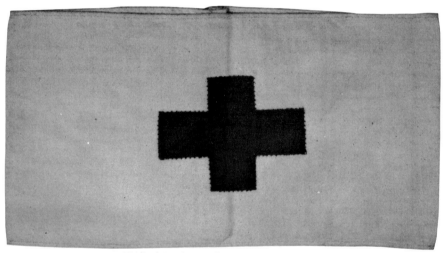

Medical Service—red cross on white field.

2. SHD Insignia of 1940: By order (BLB 40, No.454) dated 27 March 1940 a new system of ranks and rank insignia was introduced. It was basically identical to those of the LWD. The shoulder cords (Schulterschnüre) were worn on both shoulders. They were made of a flat cord, which formed a sling for buttoning. The backing was darkgreen cloth, but frequently the straps were without backing. The length was approximately 11.5cm. The shoulder cords replaced the 1939 pattern armbands as an identification of rank.

SHD shoulder strap for grade 4 Innendienstleiter as introduced in March 1940. However, the following year, the rank structure underwent a change, and this strap without the silver pip(s) was eliminated, and one and two silver pips were added for grades 4 and 5 respectively. Dark green 2cm wide cords doubled, and with an outer aluminum cord.

Grade 5 Zugführer.

SHD grade 6 Bereitschaftsführer with two gold pips.

SHD grade 8 Abteilungsführer with one gold pip. This specimen varies in that it has a dark-green wool base whereas it normally is without such an underlay.

a. Rank Insignia:

Rank	Military Equivalent	Description
1. SHD.-Mann	Private	2 dark green 1.5cm wide cords of artificial silk
2. SHD.-Truppführer	Gefreiter	Same, with 1 silver pip
3. SHD.-Gruppen-führer	Unteroffizier	Same, with 2 silver pips
4. SHD.-Innendienst-leiter	Hauptfeld-webel	As Grade 1, but with a .5cm wide aluminum border
5. SHD.-Zugführer	Leutnant	2 aluminum cords with dark green center cord with an over-all width of 2cm
6. SHD.-Bereit-schaftführer*	Hauptmann	As Grade 5, but with 2 gold pips
7. SHD.-Abtei-lungsführer**	Major	7mm wide aluminum cord braiding with dark green

181

| | | center cord, with an overall width of 2.5cm |
| 8. SHD-Abteilungs-führer | Oberst-leutnant | Same, with 1 gold pip (for commanders of three or more Bereitschaft (company-size units)) |

(NOTE: * = same for specialist rank of Fachführer; ** = same for specialist rank of Sachbearbeiter)

The rank insignia on the left upper sleeve of the work jacket were made of black cloth, and demonstrated ranks as follows:

Grade 1 None

Grade 2 One 7mm wide and 8cm long stripe

Grade 3 One 7mm wide stripe running about the sleeve seam to seam

Grade 4 As Grade 3, but with a stripe as Grade 1 centered below

Grade 5 Two stripes as Grade 3, but spaced 1cm apart

Higher grades were not addressed—probably because there was no need to wear work clothing.

    b. Trade Insignia: The oval insignia was worn on the upper left sleeve with the armband worn below it. Trade insignia for Fire Brigade Service, Gas Detection and De-contamination Service, Maintenance Service and Veterinary Service as worn by the LSW remained the same. Other trade insignia authorized for wear were:

- Medical Service (to include ambulance drivers): A 3.8cm high white caduceus on a blue-grey base encircled by green.
- Wreckage Service (Havariedienst): A white fouled anchor on a blue base with green border. The insigne was originally introduced for the Waterways Air Protection organization, but with a light blue border.
- Unknown: A white St on darkgreen base with lighter green border

Medical Service.

Unidentified.

Wreckage Service.

Medical leaders were identified by the usual insignia of their branch in the form of a gold metal device centered on the shoulder straps:

- Doctor: Caduceus
- Dentist: Caduceus with the letter Z
- Apothecary: Letter A
- Veterinarian: Snake

   c. Armband: Rank armbands were no longer worn. However, the basic SHD armband was worn on the left sleeve. This armband may have given way to a cuffband (usually the standard armband, but folded to measure 5cm wide by 44cm long bearing the same designation, and worn 14cm above the edge of the left cuff. Wear of the positional armbands for telephone operators and messenger was continued. A 10.5cm wide red armband with black 5.2cm high imprinted SHD was also worn.

3. SHD Insignia of 1941: Ranks and rank insignia were slightly altered per manual L.Dv.788 dated 1 August 1941. The basic system of shoulder straps and the other insignia were retained. Grades 1 - 3 remained unchanged. Alterations were as follows:

Rank	Description
4. SHD-Hauptgruppenführer (Feldwebel)	2 dark green artificial silk cords with aluminum cord border and one silver pip; overall width of 2cm
5. SHD-Stabsgruppenführer (Oberfeldwebel)	As Grade 4, but with two pips
6. SHD-Zugführer (Leutnant)	2 aluminum cords with dark green cord between, with an overall width of 2cm
7. SHD-Oberzugführer (Oberleutnant)	As Grade 6, with 1 gold pip
8. SHD-Bereitschaftsführer (Hauptmann/Fachführer)	As Grade 6, with 2 gold pips
9. SHD-Abteilungsführer (Major/Sachbearbeiter)	Braided aluminum cord with dark green cord in the center, with an overall width of 2.5cm
10. SHD-Abteilungsführer (Oberstleutnant)	As Grade 9, but with 1 gold pip (by special order)

4. SHD Insignia of 1942: Effective 1 May 1942 the SHD-Abteilungen (mot.) became mot. (Motorized) Luftschutzabteilungen of the Luftwaffe, while all others became Luftschutzpolizei (as a volunteer organization of the Ordnungspolizei). The lowest rank was now designated Flieger.

Future ranks changes will be addressed in a series dealing with police organizations.

D. Transfer to the Luftwaffe:

The motorized SHD-Battalions (SHD-Abteilung [mot.]—SHD-Abt.[mot.]) were established by order (Ob.d.L. Führungsstab Ia/Arbeitsstab 2L 2L/Ia No.5655/39 geh.) dated 25 November 1939. Leaders and NCOs were transferred from the police and fire police.

By order (Der Reichsminister der Luftfahrt und Oberbefehlshaber der Luftwaffe GenSt.Arbeitsstab LS/Gen. QU.2.Abt. No.6773/42 Gkdos. [IIIE]) dated 10 March 1942 the motorized SHD-Battalions were transferred to the Luftwaffe, and renamed motorized Air Protection Battalions (Luftschutz-Abteilung). They were a special branch within the Luftwaffe Construction Branch (Lw.Baueinheiten). Details were regulated by several orders released shortly afterwards.

Its members now had the status of soldiers with the standard uniform and insignia, etc., of the Luftwaffe. There was a brief period when wear of the SHD uniform continued, since issue of the Luftwaffe uniform was not immediate.

SHD leaders in a training course. All are now wearing the breast insigne of the Luftwaffe.

The branch color was black. The Latin letters LS (of the typical ornamented Luftwaffe style) were embroidered in black with a narrow white border on each letter for enlisted soldiers and junior NCOs, in white metal for senior NCOs, and in gold metal for officers.

The ranks were renamed as follows:

An order (LV 42, No.1509) dated 2 June 1942 established the lowest rank as Flieger, which may indicate the branch piping was yellow.

The ranks were now corresponded as follows:

Private	Flieger
Truppführer	Gefreiter
Obertruppführer	Obergefreiter
Gruppenführer	Unteroffizier
Hauptgruppenführer	Feldwebel
Stabsgruppenführer	Oberfeldwebel
Innendienstleiter	Hauptfeldwebel
Zugführer	Leutnant
Oberzugführer	Oberleutnant
Bereitschaftsführer	Hauptmann
Abteilungsführer	Major or Oberstleutnant

E.   Air Protection Police:

By an order dated 19 March 1942 (Ob.d.L. #Gen. St. Gen. Qu. 2. Abt./Arbeitsstab LS Nr. 3425/41 g. (1 1a)) the stationary (not transferable to another location) SHD Ist Grade was transferred to the Police Reserve and renamed Air Protection Police (Luftschutz-Polizei—LS-Polizei), and came under control of the Reich Police as part of the Order Police (Ordnungspolizei).

At first, the uniform of the SHD was retained, but with insignia of the police worn on the cap, sleeve, collar, rank, etc. Later in 1942 the green police uniforms were issued. For a transition period, a mixture of uniforms of both organizations were worn.

SHD personnel after having been placed under the control of the police. Note the wear of the police eagle on the upper left sleeve by what appears to be an instructor.

The new ranks were named as above, with Wachtmeister for NCO ranks instead of Unteroffizier, Feldwebel. The ranks Meister and Obermeister of the police were added between senior NCOs and officers.

Motor vehicles of the Luftwaffe in the service of the LS-Police were equipped with license plates of both the Luftwaffe and the police. When on service with the LS-Police, the license plates of the police were to be affixed to the vehicles.

In the periodical *Uniformen-Markt,* No.21 dated 1 November 1942, p. 166, there was a strange note that members of the LS-Police were not permitted to wear the rank insignia of the police, and that police insignia already in wear were to be taken off. However, it was not noted which insignia would replace those of the police—possibly the previously worn SHD insignia. By an order dated 19 May 1943 (Runderlass des RFSSuCHd Dt Pol O-Kdo g4 (Pla) Nr. 115/42 (1)) ranks and rank insignia of the police were introduced.

The first page from *Uniformen-Markt,* dated 1 July 1940, illustrates uniforms and insignia which had been ▶ introduced for the SHD in the spring of 1940.

Uniformen-Markt

7. Jahrgang   Folge **13**

Berlin, 1. Juli 1940

Fachzeitung der gesamten Uniformen-, Ausrüstungs-, Effekten-, Fahnen-, Paramenten-, Orden- und Abzeichenbranche ✦ Mitteilungsblatt der Fachuntergruppen Uniform-Industrie, Uniform-Ausstattungs-Industrie, Mützen-Industrie, Fahnenhersteller und der Fachabteilung Mützen-Zutaten-Industrie

Der „UM" veröffentlicht die Bekanntmachungen der Wirtschaftsgruppe Einzelhandel, Fachgruppe Bekleidung, Textil und Leder, in Verbindung mit seinem eigenen Einzelhandels-Nachrichtendienst für die Fachabteilung Uniformen und Gleichtrachten

Verlag: (Bezugs- u. Anzeigenbestellungen, Bezugsquellen, Bücherverkauf usw.) Verlag Otto Dietrich, Berlin SW 68, Zimmerstr. 72—74. Fernruf: 17 17 51. Postscheckk.: Berlin 201 01   Schriftleitung: (Inhalt betr. ausschl. Anzeigen) A. F. Dittberner, Berlin-Grunewald, Trabener Str. 29 a. Fernruf: 96 16 03 (10—4 Uhr). Besuche nur nach telephon. Anmeldung.

Bezugspreis: Monatlich RM 1,— einschl. Bestellgeld.   Einzel-Nummer 0,50.   Anzeigenpreis: Die 1 mm hohe und 22 mm breite Zeile RM 0,18.   Erscheint halbmonatlich.

SHD.-Dienstbekleidung und Abzeichen

Zur Zeit werden Schulterschnüre eingeführt

UM. Wir sind autorisiert, die Dienstbekleidung und die Rang- und Tätigkeitsabzeichen des Sicherheits- und Hilfsdienstes (SHD) bekanntzugeben. Eine Bekleidungsvorschrift befindet sich noch in Ausarbeitung.

Unsere Abbildungen zeigen: Tuchbluse mit Hose und Mantel, Farbton wie Luftwaffe, Breechluse mit Hose (rohgrau) mit Armbinden der Rangstufen, dunkelgrün mit Schrift „Sicherheits- u. Hilfsdienst": Die unterste Rangstufe trägt eine Armbinde ohne Streifen (zwischen Rock und Mantel dargestellt), die

dienst, auf lila Grund) und (unten links) G (für im Gasspüren und Entgiften ausgebildete, auf gelbem Grund). Sämtliche Tätigkeitsabzeichen haben einen dunkelgrünen Rand. Die grünen Tätigkeitsabzeichen G (Gas), W (Wasser), K (Kanalisation) und E (Elektrizität) kommen jetzt in Fortfall. Ferner zeigen wir das Hoheitsabzeichen für Luftschutzhelm, Mützen und Koppelschloß und die Armbinden für Melder und Fernsprecher.

Die Beschaffung erfolgt über das Luftwaffen-Beschaffungsamt; in Ausnahmefällen kommt es vor, daß sich Führer die Dienstkleidung persön-

angriffen nötig werden kann, oder das Luftschutzrevier vermittelt im Bedarfsfall die konzentrierten und kasernierten Hilfskräfte des SHD, wenn der Luftschutzwart Hilfe anfordert, weil es mit dem Schadenfall nicht fertig wird. Der SHD ist dem Polizeipräsidenten als örtlicher Luftschutzleiter unterstellt; mit dem SHD stehen in Verbindung: Feuerschutzpolizei (für Brandschutz), TRK und die öffentlichen Gesundheitseinrichtungen (für Luftschutz-Sanitätsdienst) und die öffentlichen Einrichtungen für den Luftschutz-Veterinärdienst. Vorgesehen sind besondere Gasspürertrupps, Entgiftungstrupps und Spezialtrupps von Facharbeitern. — Alle Geräte sind genormt, Ausstattung mit vorzüglichen Hilfsmitteln. Der SHD ist im ganzen Reich vollkommen durchgearbeitet und kann auch evtl. schnell Hilfe aus einem Nachbarort herbeiziehen. Der Dienst ist ebenso Pflicht, wie der Dienst bei der Wehrmacht.

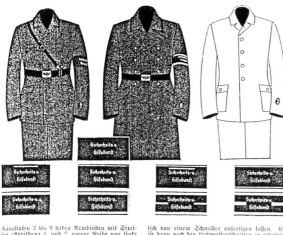

Rangstufen 2 bis 9 haben Armbinden mit Streifen (Abbildung 1. und 2. untere Reihe von links nach rechts). Diese Rangabzeichen werden nur noch für den Übergang beibehalten, denn es gelangen jetzt Schulterschnüre ähnlich denen der Sonderführer der Luftwaffe zur Einführung, die wir wegen Platzmangels erst in der nächsten Folge abbilden können. — Die zweite Bildtafel zeigt Schiffchenmütze (es gibt Tuchmütze und Drillichmütze), Tuchbluse mit aluminiumfarbigem Beschlag, die Tätigkeitsabzeichen F (Feuerlöschund Entgiftungsdienst, roter Grund), J (Instandsetzungsdienst, brauner Grund), V (Veterinär-

lich von einem Schneider anfertigen lassen. Es ist dann nach den Luftwaffenschnitten zu arbeiten. Kragenspiegel und hier nicht erwähnte Abzeichen werden nicht getragen.

*

UM. Grundlage des Luftschutzes ist der Selbstschutz (Luftschutzgemeinschaft). Aufgabe des erweiterten Selbstschutzes ist auch die Betreuung von Stätten mit größeren Menschenansammlungen (Schulen, Kirchen, Bauten, Kaufhäusern usw.). In Fabriken usw. wirkt der Werkschutz. Wo diese Kräfte des Selbstschutzes einer Erweiterung bedürfen, sorgt der SHD gewissermaßen als Dachorganisation für die Kräfte, deren Einsatz bei oder nach gegnerischen Luft-

Zeichnungen: SHD / „UM"-Bildstöcke

187

CHAPTER 25

HERMANN GÖRING & HIS UNIFORMS

ermann Göring was the most flamboyant personality among the leaders of the Third Reich. At the end of World War I he was a famous fighter pilot, and commander of the famed Richthofen Fighter Squadron. His feats of heroism in the air earned him the highest Prussian decoraton for bravery, the Pour le Mérite. He joined the Nazi Party in the early 1920's, and subsequently became one of Hitler's most ardent followers.

Göring was a respected personality and an able organizer. Eventually he rose to be the heir-apparent to Hitler in 1939. As a power behind the power, he exerted considerable influence on virtually every aspect of German political and economical life until he fell from Hitler's favor during the closing months of World War II.

His various governmental and political positions during the period of 1933 - 1945 made him the second most powerful man in Germany. A summary of the more significant positions follow:

General of Infantry: The rank of General of Infantry was bestowed upon Göring by President Hindenburg in August 1933. He was promoted to the rank of Generaloberst (of the Luftwaffe) on 20 April 1936.*

General der Infanterie Hermann Göring.

Minister of Interior of Prussia: Following the elections in 1933, which established the Nazi Party as a dominant party** in the Reichstag,*** Göring was named to the cabinet as Minister Without Portfolio. He was further given the post of Minister of Interior for the Prussian State, a post that gave him total control of the Prussian Police.

The vehicle that carries Göring bears the fender flag denoting his position as Minister of the Interior of Prussia. Note the very small Luftwaffe national emblem on the rear door.

Head of the Prussian Police: As Head of the Prussian Police, he held the rank of General der Polizei, and wore the uniform when it suited his purposes. He created a personal State Secret Police (Geheime Staatspolizei—Gestapo), which later came under the control of Himmler's SS.

President of the Reichstag: Although the Nazi Party held a minority in the Reichstag in 1932, they were able to form a successful coalition with the Center Party to elect Göring as President of the Reichstag.

Reichsminister of Aviation: This position allowed him to extend his control over every aspect of the development of German aviation. It was this post that allowed him to secretly build the fledgling Luftwaffe, which had been outlawed by the Versailles Treaty.

Administer of the Four Year Plan: Appointed to this post in September 1936, it gave him virtual total control over Germany's economic system.

Reichs Forestry and Hunting Master: (Reichsforst- u. Jägermeister)—8 July 1933 to end of the war.

Chief of the SA: Göring was named as temporary head of the SA in May 1925.

---

*See Vol. 1, p. 154, Annotation 1.

** The NSDAP had won seats in the Reichstag in increasing numbers since about 1928.

***The Reichstag was the German parliament.

R. Valdez

Göring as President of the Reichstag.

190

Charita

Göring photographed sometime after 1934. Note the unique pattern of the chained SA dagger being worn. His position as temporary head of the SA ended sometime before Röhm was appointed by Hitler. His high SA rank was without true function.

Göring as Reich's Forestry and Hunting Master.

Honorary President of the DLV, Hermann Göring, wears collar patches that were not covered in regulations. These were hand-embroidered 1929 pattern national emblems surrounded by a full circular oakleaf wreath on a white collar patch with outer twist cord piping.

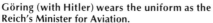

Göring (with Hitler) wears the uniform as the Reich's Minister for Aviation.

Göring wears a cape with his Fliegerschaft uniform. The pattern is identical to that of the later Luftwaffe, but was not mentioned in regulations.

His various ranks and duty positions within the Luftwaffe will be addressed with its corresponding uniform.

One side of Göring's personality was his well-known predilection for medals and splended uniforms. Where the Luftwaffe uniforms were concerned, he rarely strictly abided by the regulations, even though he fully expected his subordinates to do so.

1. General der Flieger—1 March 1935: It would appear that Göring held closely to the uniform regulations while holding this rank. One diviation from the norm was the grip of his 1934 pattern Flyer's Sword, which had a horizontal rather than a diagonal wrap, and with a tighter wrap pattern as was his 1934 pattern Flyer's Dagger. He was presented a distinctive sword by the officers of the Luftwaffe on his wedding day, 10 April 1935.

General der Flieger Göring wears the 1934 pattern Luftwaffe "Fliegerschwert" but unique to him in that it has 14 horizontal cords on a grip rather than the normal nine diagonal.

General der Flieger Göring wears the standard pattern undress uniform except for the unique slash breast pocket.

2. Generaloberst—20 April 1936: A distinctive uniform worn by Göring while holding this rank, in addition to the standard pattern uniforms, was a light blue uniform, to include the standard pattern general's visor cap, tunic, pants, and standard length double-breasted greatcoat (also with light blue lapels) with gold buttons. The greatcoat was of a uniform light blue color with collar patches and shoulder boards. He also wore a standard pattern white general's visor cap, but with a white cap band, with the white uniform during the 1935/36 time period.

Hermann Göring as Generaloberst.

3. Generalfeldmarschall—4 February 1938: It was while holding this
    rank as General Field Marschal that Göring began wearing distinc-
    tively designed uniforms in addition to the standard patterns. Some
    of the peculiarities were:
    a. Standard pattern Dress Uniform: This consisted of the blue-
        grey general's visor cap, four-pocket tunic, breeches with
        white side stripes and boots. There was nothing unusual about
        the uniform except the brocade dress belt was of the pattern he
        wore with the Deutsche Fliegerschaft and with the distinctive
        wedding sword. This same uniform was also worn with the
        gold shoulder cord and general officer's cape with collar pip-
        ing and gold cape closure.

Generalfeldmarschall Göring wears
the standard pattern dress uniform of
the Luftwaffe. At his side is the
unique pattern wedding sword.

b. Flyer's Blouse (blue-grey): Buttoned up to the collar, and with hidden button-holes; with slightly wider collar than normal; commemorative sleeveband on the lower right sleeve; regulation collar patches and shoulder boards; gold twist cord piping about the collar. Worn with the blouse was a wide belt with double open-claw buckle and shoulder strap. It is interesting that he continued to wear the shoulder strap well after it was abolished for wear after all other Luftwaffe officers in November 1939.

GFM Göring wears the flyer's blouse buttoned to the neck. Note wear of the belt with cross strap, which had already been discontinued.

c. Flyer's Blouse (white): As the blue-grey above only in white, and worn without the commemorative sleeveband. It appears to have had turned-back french cuffs.

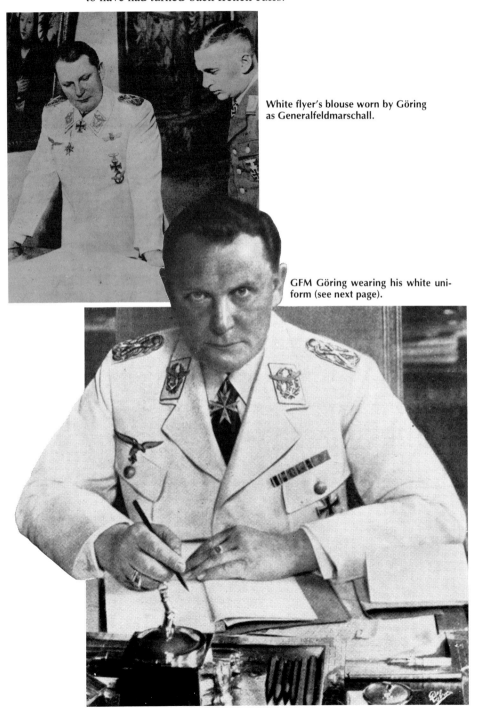

White flyer's blouse worn by Göring as Generalfeldmarschall.

GFM Göring wearing his white uniform (see next page).

d. White Uniform: Four pocket single-breasted tunic with turned-back cuffs; standard pattern collar patches and shoulder boards; worn with standard pattern white breeches (without adornments) with black riding boots, and with the standard pattern white-topped general officer's visor cap. He also wore the blue-grey straight pants without side stripes.

GFM Göring wearing the white uniform. With him is Italian General Balbo.

e. Undress Tunic of General Officers: Worn with and without white lapels and white piping on the cuffs; with and without collar patches. The GFM collar insignia were of the standard pattern on a white collar patch. However, he wore the standard pattern collar insignia, but with a blue-grey collar patch on the tunic without the white lapels. The national emblem for this latter tunic was on a white backing. A short opening for an inserted pocket (probably for his monocle) was positioned approximately parallel to the edge of the left lapel, and centered between the second and third button.

GFM Göring in the undress uni-form. Note the distinct pattern of the GFM collar patches almost giving the impression that the eagle and batons are metal rather than hand-embroidered.

Below: Göring wears the standard pattern blue-grey mess uniform, but with unique GFM insignia on the collar. To the right is the French Ambassador, Coulondre.

f. Blue-grey Mess Jacket: The uniform was of the standard blue-grey pattern, but with specially designed GFM insignia embroidered directly into the collars. The insigne consisted of an eagle in flight surmounting crossed batons.

199

g. Greatcoat: In addition to the regulations pattern blue-grey and leather greatcoats, he also wore a blue-grey greatcoat that reached only to the knees, without white lapels, patch side pockets with horizontal straight-edged flaps, and with two rows of three buttons each—a marked departure from the standard pattern. His standard pattern blue-grey greatcoat was worn with and without GFM collar patches.

h. Civilian Dress: A metal lapel badge distinctive of his GFM rank, and of identical pattern as that embroidered into the collars of the mess jacket, was worn on the left lapel.

Göring wears the metal stick pin of identical design to that pattern GFM insignia worn on his mess uniform.

4. Reichsmarschall—19 July 1940: After the victorious French campaign, Hitler promoted Göring to the new singular rank of Reich Marshal of the Great German Reich (Reichsmarschall des Grossdeutschen Reiches) on 19 July 1940, and awarded him the only Grand Cross of the Iron Cross to be awarded during the period 1939 - 1945.

From the time of his promotion he wore the newly designed RM insignia on his blue-grey uniform. It wasn't long after that he had specially designed and tailored uniforms to emphasize his unique rank. It is necessary to describe the rank insignia before discussing the various uniforms and his accouterments.

a. 1st Pattern Reichsmarschall Collar Patches: Introduced on 19 July 1940 on the occasion of his promotion, the newly designed collar patches were first worn in August, 1940. They took the form of a paralellogram (rhomboid) measuring 45mm high and 65mm long inclusive of a 3mm gold twist cord piping. The hand-embroidery was on a silver-brocade fabric, and consisted of an border of branches with laurel leaves and berries. On the patch worn on the right collar was a Wehrmacht eagle (with down-turned wings) with eagle head facing towards the neck, while on the patch for the left collar were two over-lapping marschal batons crossed at an acute angle. These were worn on all uniforms requiring collar patches until the introduction of the 2nd Pattern.

Göring wears the 1st pattern collar patches on the light blue flying blouse.

Right side

Left side

1st pattern Reichsmarschall collar patches worn with the white tunic.

1st pattern Reichsmarschall collar patches worn on the undress tunic of general officers.

b. 2nd Pattern Reichsmarschall Collar Patches: Identical to the above, but with the right collar patch taking the design of the left in a mirror image, the 2nd pattern was introduced March, 1941. It appears that several specimens were requested, with those produced by the Firm of Tröltsch und Hanselmann, Berlin, being accepted.

2nd pattern Reichsmarschall collar patches. Note the distinctive backing.

Above as worn on the white tunic.

Göring wearing the 2nd pattern Reichsmarschall insignia.

203

The Reichsmarschall shoulder board remained unchanged during the period. It was introduced for wear in August 1940. The basic design was that of field marschals-a braid of three equal gold cords with five bends on a stiff white backing. Centered on the boards was a pressed gilt metal insigne depicting the Wehrmacht eagle (with swastika in the static position) with two marschal batons (bearing the same design as the real baton) crossed below the wreath. The head of the respective eagle faced to the front, causing the head of the eagle worn on the left side to face its right wing, and that of the right to face the left wing.

The shoulder board itself was three gold entwined cords on a white field. Surmounting the board was a massive national emblem with two crossed Reichsmarschall batons in heavy gold metal.

Shoulder boards as above worn on the shirt.

There exist shoulder boards with eagle and batons of identical pattern and size, but gold embroidered on a base of golden-yellow cloth. These, however, are strongly believed to be post-war copies.

For a brief period Göring wore his standard pattern blue-grey service uniform with his new rank. However, to emphasize his exalted position he had soon designed an entirely new uniform, which deviated from the regulation blue-grey—especially by its light-grey color, which sometimes was also termed dove grey (taubengrau). Because Göring now held the highest rank in the Armed Forces, the light grey uniform was frequently (albeit incorrectly) been termed as an Armed Forces Uniform (Wehrmachtuniform).

The national emblems on the caps and breast were slightly larger, and with longer wings as compared with the normal pattern. He continued to wear the cross-strap with his leather belt, but discontinued wear of the Richthofen cuff title.

The distinctive features of the light grey uniform were as follows:

    a. Flyer's Blouse: Cut and style of the standard pattern blue-grey flyer's blouse, but worn with the distinctive RM insignia. Backing of the gold hand-embroidered national breast emblem was white. This was worn with or without the brown leather belt with cross-strap. In lieu of the inserted hip pockets with

Göring and his daughter, Edda, on her fourth birthday.

Reichsmarschall insignia worn on the light-grey flyer's blouse distinctive to Göring.

curved opening, a variant had pockets with a straight slanted opening and a buttoned flap. A modification of this blouse consisted of a blue-grey body with light grey collar piped in twist gold cord and the standard 2nd pattern RM collar patches and shoulder boards.

b. Undress Tunic: The double-breasted tunic had the cut of the blue-grey undress tunic, but was with longer lapels as it was buttoned by only two of the three double rows of gold buttons each. Standard pattern RM insignia were worn. A variant had white lapels and white piping on the front edge and around the upper edges of the cuffs.

Göring wears the light-grey undress uniform as Reichsmarschall.

c. Distinctive Tunic: This was a totally new design consisting of a double-breasted design with the left side buttoning over the right, and secured to the upper chest (also worn with the lapels turned back with the top two buttons unbuttoned) by six gold buttons. The leading edge of the front closure, the lapel and collar edges and upper edge of the turned-back cuffs were piped in white. The backing of the gold hand-embroidered national emblem was white.

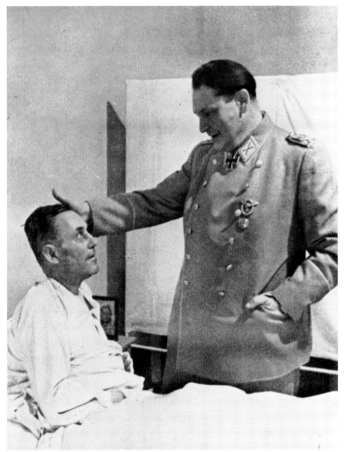

Göring, wearing the above-described uniform, visits General Bodenschatz who was wounded in the 20 July 1944 bomb attempt on Hitler.

d. The light grey breeches were with or without the side stripes of generals. Trousers had a white piping down the outer seams, and sometimes were with the wide white outer stripes of generals.

e. Visor Cap: Introduced in 1940 the style was virtually the same as the standard pattern blue-grey, but without the front center seam of the top. The national emblem was either embroidered directly onto the cloth or separately embroidered on a white backing and sewn on. There was a gold mesh-wire piping about the top. The cap band was made of grey velvet, and piped top and bottom with gold mesh-wire. The tri-color Reich rosette had a narrow rope-like surround. The wreath consisted of six laurel leaves with two fruits at either side, and was bound together at the base. The lateral wings consisted of four horizontal feathers each. The wings continued in a laurel leaf embroidery which formed Vs open toward the rear where they met at the rear seam of the cap band. He owned several visor caps, to include the same pattern, but without the laurel leaf embroidery about the crown. It would appear that the pattern without the laurel leaves became the preferred visor cap as the war progressed.

On this example, the national emblem and wreath are hand-embroidered directly onto the cap material.

This version has a separately embroidered national emblem, and a directly hand-embroidered wreath and laurel leaf decoration.

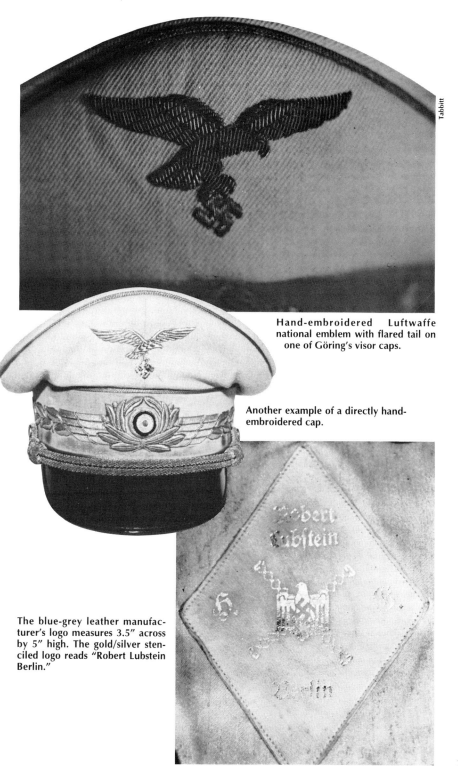

Tabbitt

Hand-embroidered Luftwaffe national emblem with flared tail on one of Göring's visor caps.

Another example of a directly hand-embroidered cap.

The blue-grey leather manufacturer's logo measures 3.5" across by 5" high. The gold/silver stenciled logo reads "Robert Lubstein Berlin."

209

As above, but note laurel leaves on a black cap band, circa 1940.

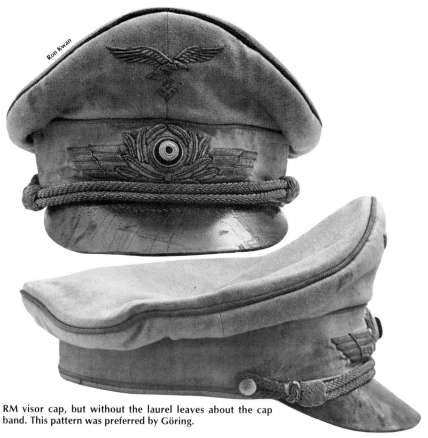

RM visor cap, but without the laurel leaves about the cap band. This pattern was preferred by Göring.

Göring, wearing a cap as above, with Krupp von Bohlen and Halbach.

f. Visored Flyer's Cap: The light grey cap was identical in cut and style as the blue-grey visored flyer's cap. Yet another pattern existed, and was with hand-embroidered laurel leaf design running about the turn-up. Piping around the top was gold mesh-wire. This latter cap has never been observed in wear, but a specimen does exist. However, period of manufacture is not known.

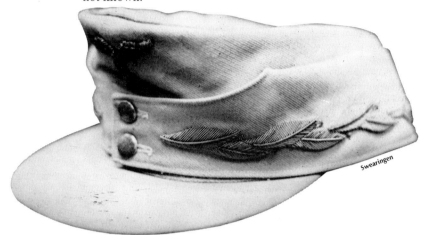

Visored field cap for RM. The interior is marked "Extra Ausführung, Marke Berlin," and with Göring's initials.

An unadorned version worn at the time of Göring's surrender.

g. Greatcoat: There were four different types:
1) Light grey in the cut and style of the blue-grey greatcoat with or without the white lapels, white underside of the collar and white piping on the front edges of the cuffs. The RM shoulder boards were of the sew-in variety. Worn with or without the brown leather belt with gold double-claw buckle and cross-strap.
2) Knee-length greatcoat as described for the blue-grey uniform, and with white piping around the collar and cuffs. A winter variant had additional muff pockets. Worn with the RM collar patches and shoulder boards. This pattern greatcoat was only worn for a short period after August 1940.

A variant of the above-described knee-length greatcoat with white lapels and flapped side pockets. Also note the dark colored cap band.

3) Light grey in the style of the blue-grey greatcoat except the front closure was with concealed buttons. The lapel facings were without adornment. The top of the turn-back cuffs were piped in white. The RM collar patches and shoulder boards were worn.
4) Grey leather of the standard cut and style; worn without collar patches, but with slip-on shoulder boards.

Göring wears the light grey greatcoat with concealed front buttons.

Göring wears a similar greatcoat as above, but with a large fur collar.

Göring chats with a female while wearing the leather greatcoat with slip-on shoulder boards only.

   h. Cape: the cape was of the cut and style of the blue-grey cape. The collar was piped in gold cord, and the chain fasteners were gilt. A large national emblem unique to his rank in gold hand-embroidery on white was worn on the left side. The eagle had

A special cape eagle was introduced in 1940 for wear on the left side of the blue cape. It was done in hand-embroidered gold bullion on a white field, consisting of the national emblem with two crossed RM batons. Note also the special cap insignia worn by the Reichsmarschall.

its head turned to its right wing. The horizontal wings were composed of five feathers each, and the rump had a pattern of diagonal lines. The eagle clutched a swastika standing on its point, the center bars of which were superimposed on two stylized marshal's batons crossed at a right angle.

i. Boots: Reddish-brown leather calf-high riding boots with spurs.

Other known examples of the RM uniforms worn by Göring are as follows:

a. Shirt: During the summer Göring wore a long sleeve pale blue shirt with fall down collar. Slip-on RM shoulder boards and a gold hand-embroidered breast eagle on a white backing were worn. There were two pleated patch pockets on the breast with pocket flaps secured by white button. Buttons down the front were also white.

b. White Summer Tunic: Of the standard cut and style, and worn with the RM collar patches and shoulder boards. There was a reinforced hole at the right breast to accommodate a screw-on gold metal national emblem. Trousers were of the light grey variety. The visor cap was with fixed white top and light grey velvet body.

c. The Grey Uniform: This uniform was probably tailored either late 1944 or early 1945. Only known illustrations of this uniform was when he surrendered. It consisted of the following:

1) Tunic: The front was buttoned up to the collar by five

Göring's white uniform with 2nd pattern RM insignia.

As above in wear.

exposed buttons. The collar was slightly wider than the standard blue-grey cloth tunic, and had a gold twist cord piping about the collar. The breast and hip pockets were of the patch variety, and were with a center pleat and scalloped buttoned flaps. The sleeves were with turned-back cuffs. The gold national emblem was hand-embroidered , and positioned over the right breast pocket. The RM collar patches were not worn. A unique pair of shoulder boards were worn with this tunic—a stiffened board with basic cloth with rounded end, and piped in gold cord. The RM insignia on the shoulder boards were embroidered rather than of the metal variety. The boards were of the slip-on variety. The leather belt, to include the cross-strap, continued to be worn.

2) Breeches: Without white seam piping or side stripes, and worn with black high boots.

Reichsmarschall Göring soon after his capture by U.S. Forces.

3) Greatcoat: The greatcoat had the basic cut of the double-breasted blue-grey greatcoat, but overlapped at the front for only approximately 10cm, and buttoned by a center row of four buttons. It was without the white lapels and piping.

Göring wears the above greatcoat while visiting his division in East Prussia, late 1944.

Jack Ingram

RM Göring wears another version of a blue-grey greatcoat with hidden front buttons.

Other Uniforms Items Distinctive to Göring:

    a. Batons as a badge of positions:

        1) Field Marshal's Baton and Interim Staff: Apparently, Göring's Field Marshal baton and interim staff were very similar, if not identical, to the 1940 batons and staffs presented to the newly promoted field marshals of the Luftwaffe.

Göring in his capacity as Generalfeldmarschall.

    • Baton: Hitler presented Göring with his baton in early April 1938. The baton had an overall length of 49.5cm, with the center shaft measuring 38.5cm, and weighing approximately 950 grams. The center shaft was a

3.4cm diameter aluminum tube covered by a very fine light blue velvet. On the shaft were four vertical rows of five eagles, three/two Iron Crosses and two/three Balken Crosses (also referred to as Flyer's Cross) each with the cross pattern alternating vertically (a total of 20 insignia on the tube), in a pattern alternating vertically and horizontally. The gold eagles were of the Wehrmacht eagle pattern. The silver Iron Crosses and Balken Crosses (1.6 x 1.6cm) showed a black interior surface. Construction of the gold capitals, from base to end, was as follows—an inscription ring of silver measuring 1.2cm wide and 3.3 cm in diameter bordered on both sides by a 1cm wide band of five rolls each, with the fourth roll (counted from the inscription band) being larger than the others. Next came an eight-edged part of .9cm high, with each side being rounded. The eight-edged end discs, measuring 1.3cm in width and 5.6cm in diameter, screwed to the center brass axis inside the shaft. The rim of the discs was decorated by crossed ribbons at the eight edges, and bordered on both sides by a 2mm wide rim. The upper end of the baton was decorated by a gold Luftwaffe eagle, while the lower end was decorated by a silver and black Balken Cross measuring 3.7 x 3.7cm. Both the eagle and cross were positioned in a circle on the surface of the end discs, with the circles measuring 4.7cm in diameter. The inscriptions were made of gothic letters separately affixed to the silver band, and in two lines each. It showed the rank, name and date of promotion to that rank as follows: Top capital—Der Führer dem Generalfeldmarschall Hermann Göring; Bottom capital—Zum Freiheitskampf des—4. Februar/ Grossdeutschen Volkes.—1938.

Upper right: Detailed photo of the upper portion of the baton showing a diamond-studded gold Luftwaffe eagle.

NOTE: A Luftwaffe marshal's baton was jointly designed by the firms of Godet and Wilm, both of Berlin, but was rejected. An alternative to the end capital with the Balken Cross was a sun-wheel swastika, and the national emblems on the tube were of the Luftwaffe pattern.

- Interim staff: This was a black staff with a silver knob and a 55cm long black/white/red tassel. The overall length was 78.5cm, with the wooden portion measuring 62cm. The diameter at the base of the knob was 1.9cm and at it end 1.1cm. The 16.5cm long knob enlarged conically, and curved concavely to its largest diameter of 3.8cm. On the neck of the knob was a 1.5cm high crown with a pineapple fruit measuring 2.2cm in height and diameter. Near the bottom end was a 1cm wide inscription band bordered by a 3mm wide ring on each side, made of two rolls each. On the band was the name of the recipient affixed in separate silver Gothic letters. The conical part of the knob was decorated by two gold National emblems and two Balken Crosses in an alternating pattern.

Design of the Luftwaffe
Marshall's baton. Original
drawing in scale 1:1.

Hitler greets Göring in France, 1940. Note that the
Field Marshal holds his black interim staff.

BERLIN
und
GEBR. GODET u. C

2) Reichmarschall Baton and Interim Staff: The interim staff (about 85cm long) was the same pattern as that he carried as a field marshal, but with a white staff and gold knob and point. However, there was a marked departure in the baton! The Reichsmarschall baton was taken as a token of surrender from Göring by Lieutenant General Alexander M. Patch, and currently resides in the West Point Museum. It is described as being an ivory baton with gold Wehrmacht eagles, ten Iron Crosses and ten Balken Crosses, 360 matched diamonds distributed in the top and bottom capitals, with most in the end plates and the surround of the knobs. The inscription rings and the eagle and swastika on the end plates were made of platinum.

Göring holds the Reichsmarschall baton and wearing the RM Degen receives French Marshall Petain.

L.M. Olney, of the Savings Bond Division of the U.S. Treasury, hands the Reichsmarschall baton to Colonel Ralph P. Swofford of the U.S. Military Academy.

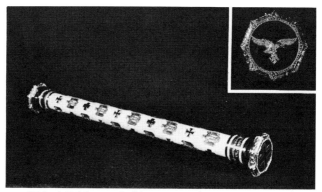

Göring's Reichsmarschall baton. Note the very ornate capitals.

Clearly shown is the white staff of the RM Interim Staff vice the black of GFM.

225

b. Sidearms:
1) 1934 Pattern Luftwaffe Sword: Standard pattern sword, but with variation grip wrap.
2) General's Degen: Before the introduction of the general's special sword Göring frequently wore the so-called memorial sword (Erinnerungsdegen), which was presented to him by the Duke of Saxonia-Coburg in 1934. This sword set the design pattern for the general's sword that was to follow the next year.

Göring wears the Prussian Honor Degen. This was identical to the "Fliegergeneralsdegen" that was introduced at a later date, but with the Prussian State insigne on the grip rather than the Luftwaffe national emblem. Note the silver portepee with light blue stripes.

Göring wears the 2nd Pattern "Fliegergeneralsdegen" during the presentation of awards of the Spanish Cross to former members of the "Legion Condor," 5 June 1939.

226

The newly designed General's Degen was in two patterns:

    1st Pattern: Identical to the above, but with the Luftwaffe national emblem on the grip instead of the Prussian insigne.

    2nd Pattern: A sword of similar design, but significant modifications. The clamshell guard bore a large silver Luftwaffe national emblem, and the grip was yellow-orange with diagonal wire wrap.

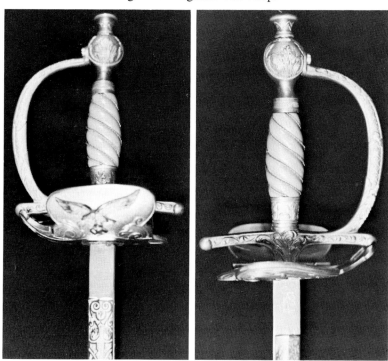

The 2nd pattern General's Degen.

3) 1934 Luftwaffe Dagger: Standard pattern dagger, but with variation grip wrap.

4) Göring Wedding Sword: The officers of the Luftwaffe presented a sword designed by Paul Casberg to Göring on the occasion of his wedding on 10 April 1935. It was a totally unique sword that reflected many aspects of Göring's career. Two almost identical swords of this design were produced as follows:

    1st Pattern Wedding Sword: The massive sword weighed 5 lbs, 11 ozs. It depicted the Luftwaffe national emblem as a crossguard, and a round pommel bearing a facsimilie of the Pour le Mérite (Prussia's highest award for valor) on the obverse, and Göring's coat-of-arms on the reverse. The grip was concave. The ornate damascus blade was hand-forged by Paul Dingler, and bore the

227

R. Valdez

Göring shown here with his wife, wears the newly introduced Fliegerdolch at a function on 9 May 1935. The closely wrapped grip wire appears to run parallel. The upper chain has nine rings rather than the normal seven, and the lower chain also has an additional six rings. The original negative shows this piece to be a presentation piece as the upper scabbard band is heavily engraved.

Obverse and reverse of the 1st pattern Wedding Sword.

sentiments of the Luftwaffe—the raised gold dedication 10 April 1935 - Die Reichsluftwaffe Ihrem Oberbefehlshaber (10 April 1935 - The National Air Force to its Commander-in-Chief) on the obverse, and Getreu dem Führer für Volk und Reich (Loyal to the Führer for People and Nation) on the reverse. The scabbard was sharkskin dyed a royal blue to match the Luftwaffe uniform, and with ornate gold fittings.

2nd pattern Wedding Sword: In an effort to reduce the weight, it was returned to the designer for modification. The major changes were the grip was now convex, the blade was not damascus, and the pommel now bore a swastika in the form of a sunwheel on the obverse.

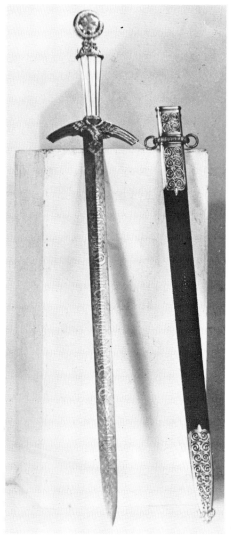

Damascus blade showing the "PD" (Paul Dingler) monogram, creator of the blade, and the Eickhorn Firm trademark. The raised areas of the blade were finished in gold.

Underside of the crossguard bearing the name and location of the jeweler, Prof. K. Dluzewski, that created the hilt and scabbard fittings.

The 1st pattern Wedding Sword.

Charles Lindberg, private emissary from the United States, inspects the wedding sword, 23 July 1936. Note the hanger, which is rarely seen.

Hermann Göring wearing the 2nd pattern Luftwaffe Wedding Sword during a ceremony of the RLB.

RM pattern degen in wear. It is virtually identical to the standard 2nd pattern degen except that the scabbard is brown leather rather than black. The knot is aluminum, and the leather hanger is brown.

5) Reichsmarschall's Degen: Basically identical design as the general's sword, but with reddish-brown leather scabbard rather than the black.

6) Reichsmarschall's Dagger: Yet another totally unique dagger design produced exclusively for RM Göring, to include

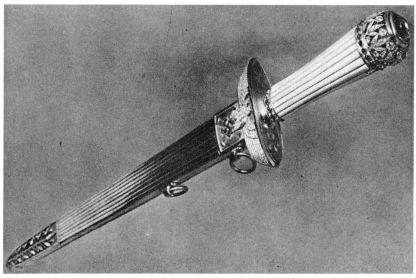

Reichsmarschall's dagger.

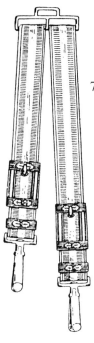

the dagger hangers used to suspend this dagger. The cross-guard featured the RM emblem. It was first referenced in 1940, was found among the treasures found in 1945, and has not been heard of since.

7) .38 caliber revolver carried in a brown leather holster with large covering flap.

c. Other Miscellaneous Items:
   1) Reichsmarschall Insigne: This gold hand-embroidered insigne on a red field and with black accents is possibly for a funeral sash considering the background color. It measures 18cm high x 17cm wide (outer edges).

Hand-embroidered RM insigne in gold on a red backing.

2) Gold cuff links in the form of the Luftwaffe national emblem with dark blue gem stones in the arms of the swastika.

Gold cuff links with blue gem stones.

3) Silver cuff links in the form of a swastika.

Silver swastika cuff links.

4) Gold signet ring bearing Göring's coat of arms. Companion cuff links of the same design.

Gold signet ring bearing Göring's title and coat of arms.

d. Distinctive Flags, etc.: For details, see the chapter dealing specifically with this subject.

Other uniforms and items belonging to Hermann Göring:

Göring was an avid hunting enthusiast, and wore many costumes related to that activity. He wears the uniform of the German Hunting Association with he characteristic hunting cutlass.

Göring wears a hunting vest, but with another hunting dagger.

Another costume of the German Hunting Association. Note the membership badge on the upper left breast. He wears a distinctive dagger given to him by the brother of his wife.

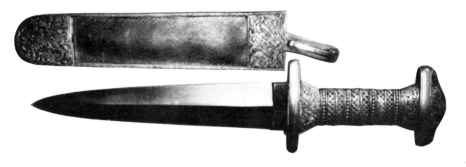

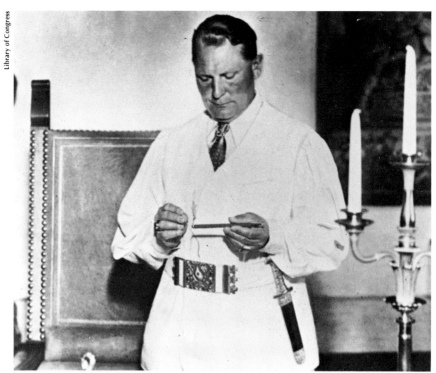

Still another hunting costume as worn by Göring at Carinhall on 7 June 1939. Note the massive Hunting Association buckle probably unique to him.

This special Hunting Association belt and buckle is similar to the one worn above. The green leather belt has a gilt clasp and decorations, on which are mounted precious stones, and obviously for wear with one of Göring's more extravagant hunting suits.

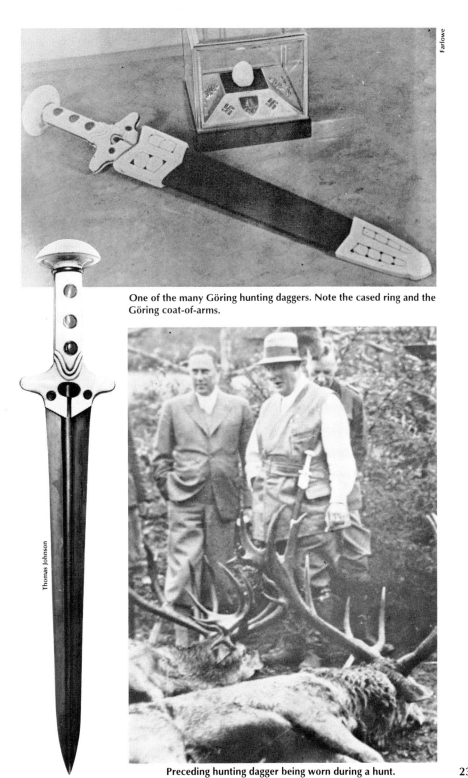

Farlowe

Thomas Johnson

One of the many Göring hunting daggers. Note the cased ring and the Göring coat-of-arms.

Preceding hunting dagger being worn during a hunt.

237

Unique Honor Cutlass of the German Hunting Association presented to Göring as Reichsjägermeister. The blade is original damascus, and bears the mark "Gebrüd. Mauer, Wien."

Library of Congress

Hanseatische Auktionhaus

And yet another Hunting Association dagger in wear.

Boar spear head engraved with presentation to Göring commemorating a successful hunt.

Göring wears one of the more famous and distinctive Hunting Association daggers given to him as a gift. The grip fittings are jewel-encrusted. The obverse at the scabbard throat bears the emblem of the German Hunting Association, while the reverse bears his coat-of-arms. Above: Note he is wearing the green leather belt illustrated previously.

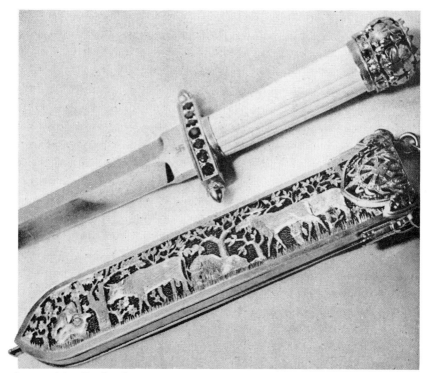

The materials utilized in the construction of the hunting dagger include silver-gilt, tourmalines and green leather.

Obverse.

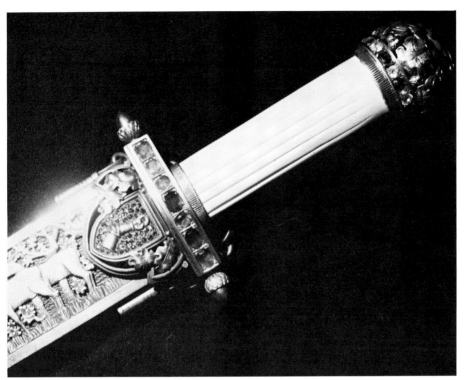

Reverse.

Another example of an exquisite
Göring hunting dagger.

The edge of the silver scabbard is engraved, "Meinem Freunde Hermann Göring Gabe in Treue 20.V.1938 Günther" (My Friend Hermann Göring Gift in Loyalty 20 May 1938 Günther).

Scabbard obverse and reverse.

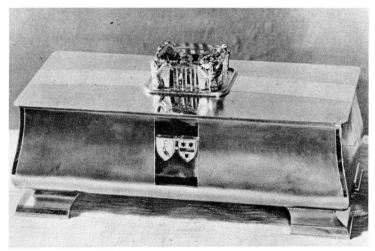

"Herm.-Göring-Strasse" (Hermann Göring Street) street sign in white on dark blue. It measures 6" wide x 23.5" long, and is in enamel.

Miscellaneous

This box, nearly 14 inches long, made by students of Berlin Technical Academy, has an ornate knob of silver-gilt and aquamarines.

An interesting desk stand used by Göring. The "inkwell" on the left houses a secret dictaphone.

243

Top: This desk organizer can be seen utilized by Göring on page 197. This piece was apparently presented by the city of Berlin (coat-of-arms of Berlin on the front).

Left: An ornate cigar box.

Below: Possibly a stationery holder.

Göring Presentation Pieces and Sports Awards produced by H.J. Wilm of Berlin.

Challenge trophy for the signals troops.

Challenge prize for the flying troops.

Challenge prize for the Göring Regiment.

CHAPTER • 26
GENERAL GÖRING / HERMANN GÖRING UNITS

The parent unit of all General Göring/Hermann Göring units was a police detachment of the newly formed Prussian State Police (Landespolizei), which was constituted on 23 February 1933 as Police Detachment at Special Purposes (Polizeiabteilung z.b.V.). However, details of this police element will not be discussed here, but rather in a detailed coverage of police formations in a future work. Instead, we will jump to 24 September 1935 when Regiment General Göring was officially transferred to the Luftwaffe. It was composed of two rifle (Jäger) battalions, a Flak battalion, two guard companies, one motorcycle company, one engineer company and a mounted platoon. After several reorganizations, the bulk of the regiment consisted of two Flak battalions and a guard battalion at the end of 1938.

During pre-war years, and possibly during the early years of the wars, replacement personnel were carefully selected volunteers only. The recruits had to meet high physical standards, and were rigorously trained. The extension to division size made necessary the transfer of army specialists, e.g. staff officers, offices and NCOs of armored units or of artillery, all to serve in training and leadership functions.

The General Göring (GG)/Hermann Göring (HG) units were elite units with a superior quality of personnel and material, and were usually deployed at main points of combat at the various theaters of war. The designation as a parachute armor division and later parachute armor corps would indicate a role as parachute troops. Actually it was only an elite term, and there was never any parachute training.

A brief organizational history stemming from this 1935 date indicates the following:

- Führer Flak Battalion (Führer-Flakabteilung): Constituted in 1940 from parts of the Flak battalions for the protection of the Führer Headquarters.
- Guard Battalion (Wachtbataillon) GG/HG: Initially, part of the regiment, but at the end of 1941 it was expanded to an independent guard regiment. Besides this unit, a separate guard

battalion of the Luftwaffe continued to exist at Berlin for other guard duties.

- Reinforced Regiment (motorized) (Verstärktes Regiment (mot.)): Established 1 March 1942 and renamed Hermann Göring.
- Führer Escort Regiment (Führer-Begleitregiment): Formed by units of the guard regiment HG at the end of 1942.
- Brigade HG: Expansion to brigade strength since 15 July 1942, it was composed of a rifle (Schützen) battalion, an armored company, a Flak regiment and separate smaller units.
- Division HG: Expansion to division strength since 21 May 1943. When deployed to the African Theater of War in May/June 1943 it was designated Division (mot. Trop—motorized, tropical) HG.
- Panzer Division HG: Reorganized and designated 1 July 1943.
- Parachute Armor Division (Fallschirm-Panzerdivision HG): Redesignated February 1944, it was under the tactical command of the 1st Parachute army until transfer to the new Corps HG. All units of the division were renamed with the prefix Fallschirm- to their standard designation.
- Parachute Armor Corps (Fallschirm-Panzerkorps HG): Formed since 1 October 1944 it composed of the Fallschirm-Panzerdivision 1 HG and the Fallschirm-Panzerdivision 2 HG. However, the corps never came to full strength.
- Replacement and Training Units: An Ersatzabteilung GG/HG was formed after the beginning of the war, which eventually expanded to regiment size and a brigade in 1944.

1. **Uniforms and Insignia of the GG/HG Units:** By an order (LV 36, No.348) dated 12 March 1936 the Regiment GG was issued with the standard blue-grey uniform of the Luftwaffe, replacing the previous police uniforms. The same order introduced the white branch color, which appeared in the color of the collar patches, for NCOs and privates as piping of the visor caps, and for officer as the backing of shoulder boards. The flyers cap of NCOs sometimes had a white piping around the flap, but this was against regulations.

   a. Branch colors: A subsequent order (LV 36, No.453) dated 3 April 1936 prescribed the standard aluminum cord piping about the collar patches of officers, but the following pipings about the collar patches of NCOs and privates:

   • Flak units: bright red
   • all other units: rifle-green (jägergrün)

It is possible that the IVth (Parachute) Battalion, which was the redesignated former Ist (Rifle) Battalion, had a golden-yellow piping of the collar patches, but this has not been confirmed.

General Staff Corps officers, medical officers and NCOs and privates of the medical service and of other special branches e.g. ordnance personnel) retained their basic branch color, and were identified by their cuff title only.   **249**

As the division HG comprised units of various branches, which were otherwise not found in the Luftwaffe, a differentiation of the branches by colors became necessary. Therefore, branch colors were introduced in association with the system of the army. By order (LV 43, No.127) dated 4 January 1943 the branch colors were introduced as follows:

- NCOs and Privates: Shoulder straps were piped in white

"HG" shoulder strap for Private ranks—blue-grey with white piping.

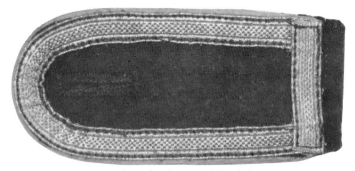

As above, but for Unterfeldwebel.

As above, but for Feldwebel.

Branch	Piping of collar patches
Grenadier Regiments, Guard Regiment	white—with narrow black line next to white patch
Panzer Regiment, Reconnaissance Battalion, Tank Destroyer Battalion	pink
Artillery Regiment, Flak Regiment, Führer Flak Battalion	bright red

Engineer Battalion	black
Signal Battalion	golden-brown
Supply Units	light blue

- Officers: white collar patches with a twist aluminum cord piping, and white backing on shoulder boards, without any differentiation of branches.

The order also prescribed that the Guard Regiment and the Führer Flak Battalion retain their collar patches on greatcoats and surcoats, the separation of which on those garments was generally prescribed by an order (LV 42, No.1453) dated 29 May 1942.

Collar patch worn by a Feldwebel assigned to a flak unit of the "HG" as denoted by the white patch and red piping—as per the 4 January 1943 order.

Collar patch of the Panzerjägerabteilungen as denoted by the green patch and pink piping—as per the 4 January 1943 order.

Right: White collar patch for Oberleutnant. Far right: Major.

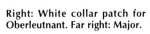

Panzertruppenschule, Münster

251

Hauptmann.

Major.

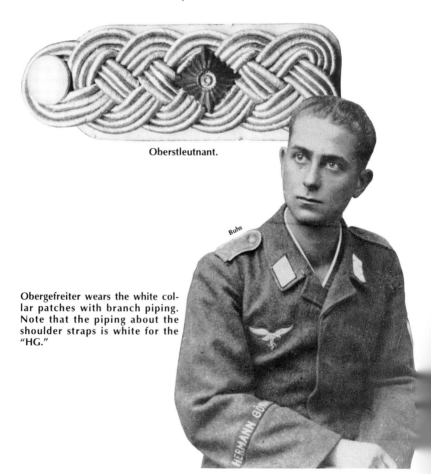

Oberstleutnant.

Buhs

Obergefreiter wears the white collar patches with branch piping.
Note that the piping about the
shoulder straps is white for the
"HG."

Rupert

NCO service tunic of the "General Göring" Regiment. The collar, in addition to the NCO Tresse, is piped with white twist cord. Note also the white collar patch piped in red and white piping on the shoulder strap. The interior markings above the pocket slit represents the wearer's size and the tailor, while those below represent date and assignment to the "General Göring"—in this case, Staff Battery, 1st Battalion, GG.

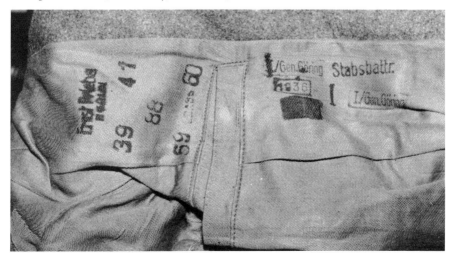

A subsequent order (LV 43, No.709) dated 2 April 1943 considerably modified the system as follows:

- The piping of the white collar patches of NCOs and privates was abolished, and the shoulder straps were now piped in the branch color.
- The backing of the shoulder straps of officers was of the branch color (in lieu of the former white backing).
- The new branch colors were as follows:

Division Headquarters	pink
Grenadier Regiments, Guard Regiments	white
Rifle Regiment (Jägerregiment)	rifle-green
Panzer Regiment	pink
Armored Reconnaissance Battalion, Flight Detachment	golden-yellow
Artillery Regiment, Flak Regiment, Führer Flak Battalion	bright red
Engineer Battalion	black
Signal Battalion	golden-brown
Supply Units, Administrative Service, Military Police	light blue
Replacement and Training Regiment HG	branch color of the respective branch

NOTE: The light blue branch color of the military police was altered to orange by an order (LV 43, No.1115) dated 3 June 1943.

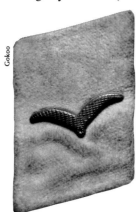

Gokoo

An order dated 2 April 1943 abolished the branch piping about the white collar patches.

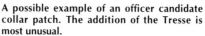

A possible example of an officer candidate collar patch. The addition of the Tresse is most unusual.

Wood

Oberfeldwebel of the "HG" as an officer candidate as indicated by the aluminum twist cord piping.

Kontrolliert durch

The HG officer above wears white collar patches and white underlay on his shoulder board while in the field. The artillery Gefreiter at right wears white collar patches and red piped shoulder straps on his flying blouse.

255

Wear of the white collar patches, which were quite popular and striking, was prohibited with the field uniforms by a divisional order of January 1944. Additionally, the metal wings of the collar patches of NCOs and privates were frequently affixed directly to the collar of blouses, etc. By the same order the wear of the subdued matte grey NCO Tresse was required.

Note this Unterroffi-zieranwärter (here an Obergefreiter) wears the metal rank wings affixed directly to the blouse collar. This photo was taken at Limmen, Holland, on July 20, 1944.

b. Cuff Titles: The introduction order of the Luftwaffe uniform dated 12 March 1936 (LV 36, No.348) introduced a cuff title to be worn by all soldiers of the Regiment GG. The 3.3cm wide band of blue cloth was with the Gothic inscription "General Göring" with the following variances:
- Officers: silver hand-embroidery with 3mm wide silver (aluminum) Tresse borders of the Soutache type top and bottom
- NCOs: machine-embroidery of matte grey cotton yarn, and with 3mm wide matte grey border Tresse
- Privates: as NCOs, but without the border Tresse

General Göring

NCO pattern.

General Göring

Enlisted ranks pattern.

Oberfeldwebel of the "G.G." Regiment. Note the pattern of each capitol "G" on the sleeveband.

Enlisted personnel of the "General Göring" wearing the standard blue-grey Luftwaffe uniform. Note the enlisted sleeveband.

Knight's Cross holder Rudolf Graf wears the officer's version of the "General Göring" sleeveband.

The cuff title was worn on the lower right sleeve of the tunic immediately above the upper edge of the cuff or immediately above the dual Tresse rings of the Hauptfeldwebel. Officers wore the title also with the flyers blouse, and the white tunic at the corresponding position.

As a result of the name change to Hermann Göring, a new cuff title with the inscription "Hermann Göring" was introduced by an order (LV 42, No.1381) dated 22 May 1942, with the expected delivery of the new title not earlier than late August 1942. At first the inscription was "Hermann Göring" in Gothic lettering, but this was soon altered to "HERMANN GÖRING" in Latin capitals. The cuff title was worn by all soldiers of the HG units. However, it was not always worn with the field uniforms. There is also photographic evidence that it was also worn by officials of the HG units, albeit against regulations.

The first pattern "Hermann Göring" sleeveband in Gothic lettering.

The enlisted ranks' version of the "HERMANN GÖRING" sleeveband in Latin.

Generalmajor Josef Schmid, commander of portions of the division in North Africa, wears the officer's version of the "HERMANN GÖRING" sleeveband.

Soldiers of the GG/HG units attached to the Führer Headquarters in any function, to include the Führer Flak or Escort Battalions, were distinguished by a special cuff title worn on the lower left sleeve. The first pattern title was a black cloth band with the Gothic inscription "Führer-Hauptquartier" machine-embroidered in golden-yellow yarn or, for officer, gold hand-embroidered with 3mm wide gold Tresse borders top and bottom. An order (HM 41, No.40) dated 15 January 1941 introduced a new cuff title—a black band with the aluminum or matte grey Gothic inscription "Führerhaupt-quartier," and with aluminum or grey borders.

2. **Peculiarities of the Regiment GG:** When the Regiment GG was transferred to the Luftwaffe the national emblem of the Luftwaffe was adopted. It was worn above the right breast pocket of the police style tunic and on the police visor cap above the Luftwaffe winged rosette with oakleaves.

The rank designation Jäger were used with Rifle (Jäger) and Parachute Battalions.

In 1935/36 and until the issue of the Luftwaffe uniform, the army pattern field blouse and long trousers were additionally issued to be utilized for the service uniform. The rank insignia of the police were retained, and the NCOs were distinguished by the aluminum Tresse along the front and lower edges of the dark green collar of the field blouse. The cuff title was worn on the sleeve. The long trousers were tucked into army pattern buckled boots or marching boots. The black leather belt was worn with the rectangular Luftwaffe buckle.

Between 1 April and 30 September the Guard Battalion of the Regiment GG wore the white-topped visor cap when on guard duties.

The Mounted Platoon (Reiterzug), which was expanded to a Mounted Troop in 1938, wore garments and equipment of Mounted personnel, consisting of riding breeches, riding boots, saddle bags, etc.

The army pattern uniform was initially worn in 1935/36.

Enlisted visor cap with removable white top for the Regiment "G.G."

The interior is reddish-brown with gold stenciling indicating the size, unit and year of issue.

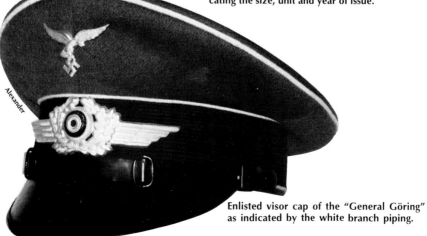

Enlisted visor cap of the "General Göring" as indicated by the white branch piping.

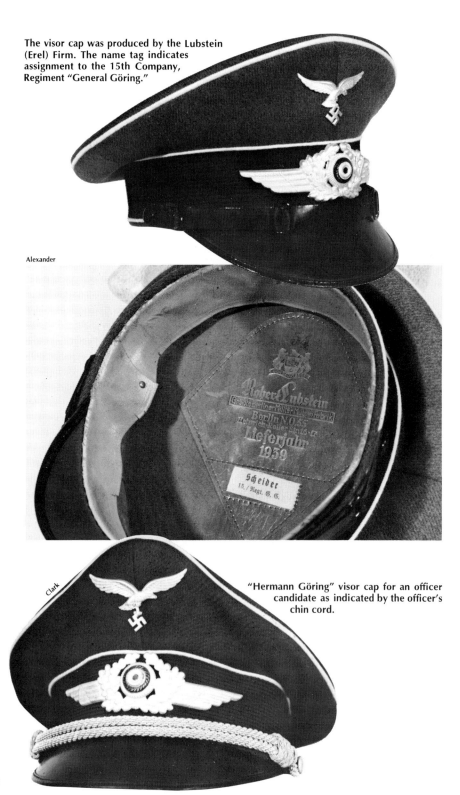

The visor cap was produced by the Lubstein (Erel) Firm. The name tag indicates assignment to the 15th Company, Regiment "General Göring."

Alexander

Clark

"Hermann Göring" visor cap for an officer candidate as indicated by the officer's chin cord.

262

Unteroffizier of Regiment "G.G."
Note the stag grip dress bayonet.

Visorless field cap with white piping,
which was against regulations, but
still done.

263

Blue-grey M43 visored field cap with white piping of the "HG."

Recruit Hans Schmitz, photographed in Berlin-Reinickendorf, wearing the standard pattern M43 visored field cap.

Luftwaffe M40 single decal combat helmet of the "Hermann Göring Panzer Division" as indicated by the white disc with green "clock hand." The green "2" represents the 2nd Pz. Gren. Rgt.

By an order (BLB 38, No.161) dated 23 April 1938, the crews of armored reconnaissance vehicles of the reconnaissance company were issued with the black protective cap of the army-pattern Panzer uniform. The cap had the form of a large beret with a padded interior, and was probably adorned by the Luftwaffe national emblem and the tri-color rosette at the front. Apparently, the black field jacket and trousers were not issued.

3. **The Black and Field-Grey Panzer-type Uniforms:** The HG Division and Corps included armed units, which were issued with the army pattern Panzer-style black or field-grey field uniforms. The specific HG insignia were worn with these uniforms, and the jackets were adorned with the Luftwaffe national emblem on the right breast.

    a. Black Uniform: The black uniform was worn by Panzer, Armored Reconnaissance and Heavy Tank Destroyer units. It was also sometimes worn by members of Panzergrenadier units with armored personnel carriers.

       • Field Jacket: The wrap-around jacket was with a wide collar and wide lapels. The front was buttoned by four black plastic buttons (right) and a hidden buttonhole tape at the slightly slanted left front edge. The row of buttons continued upwards with three smaller buttons to button the left lapel. The sleeves had a buttoned slash. Since about 1942 the collar was made smaller, and its piping was omitted. Since 1943 the lapels were reduced in width, and the front was buttoned by three buttons and one button for the lapel. The collar was piped in pink with jackets of army stocks.

This was soon replaced by a white piping. Since about the end of 1943 the piping of the collar was omitted. Officers sometimes wore an aluminum twist cord piping.

The following collar patches were worn (without distinction of rank):

- Black rectangular army-pattern patches measuring 7 - 7.5 x 3.5cm with pink piping and an aluminum-colored metal death's head affixed to the center. The patches were usually worn on collars with pink piping. It may be assumed that these jackets were worn by personnel transferred from army units to serve the HG units.

- Black patches of the same size and make, but with white piping (green piping for members of the Panzergrenadier or Rifle units). These patches were worn for a transition period only until issue of the white patches.

Hauptmann Karl Rossmann, a Knight's Cross holder and battery commander of 16./Flak-Rgt. (mot.) "General Göring."

Black Panzer jacket for a Hauptmann of the "HG" Division. Note the black Panzer collar patches with white piping.

Ishihara

Bowermann

Hermann Göring collar patches—black with white piping. Note the non-regulation angle of the skulls.

Bowermann

As above, but with the 2nd pattern SS skull.

Hermann Göring collar patch—white with red piping. The cloth behind the eyes and nose is also red. Specimen is cut directly from the collar.

As above, but green patch with red piping.

"Hermann Göring" Panzer jacket made of tropical tan material. The NCO shoulder straps have the subdued Luftwaffe pattern Tresse. The national emblem is embroidered on the same backing as the jacket. The specimen jacket is complete with the Panzer Überfallhose of the same fabric. Note the offset position of the skulls on the collar patches.

Note a member of this flamethrower crew wears white piped, army-style collar patches.

- White rhomboid patches of the Luftwaffe pattern, but with a centered aluminum death's head in lieu of rank insignia. Patches of officers had an aluminum twist cord piping.

White collar patch with metal skull was introduced for wear by Panzer personnel of the "HG" in April 1943.

Panzer NCO of the "HG" wears the white collar patches introduced in 1943.

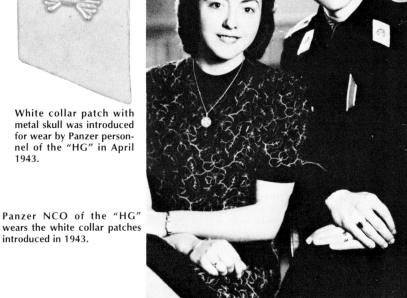

Alexander

Anderson

Black Panzer jacket of a Feldwebel of the "HG" Division. Note the white unpiped collar patches and the pink branch piping.

Oberleutnant assigned to the "Hermann Göring" Division. Note the plain white collar insignia with metal skulls.

271

NCO Candidate wears the unpiped collar patches with metal
skulls. The patches appear to be
pink.

- Without patches when the wear of the white patches was
  prohibited with the field dress, but with the death's head
  usually affixed directly onto the collar.

Young Private of the "HG" wears
the large metal skulls without
patch backing.

- Trousers: The waist of the trousers was cut straight, and was with six or eight narrow belt loops of basic cloth. Two front pockets and two hip pockets had slightly scalloped buttoned flaps. The ends of the legs were tapered for a length of 12 -15cm, and with a slash at the outside seam so they could be worn bound with ribbons in a bloused fashion over the boots or shoes.

    - Shirts: A variety of shirts was issued—made of dark grey tricot, dark grey or grey-green fabric, with or without patch breast pockets with buttoned flaps. All shirts had a permanent collar, and were worn with a black neck tie.

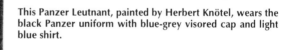

This Panzer Leutnant, painted by Herbert Knötel, wears the black Panzer uniform with blue-grey visored cap and light blue shirt.

- Field Caps: The usual field cap was the standard flyer's cap (visored field cap) made of black cloth. Officers were sometimes distinguished by an aluminum piping or cord around the top.

Gefreiter Horst Flemming of the 14./Sturmgesch. Art. Rgt. "Hermann Göring" in Italy, 1943. Note he is wearing the white collar patches with metal rank wings.

Horst Flemming

As below, but for officers with aluminum piping.

274 Black visorless field cap of the "HG"—white embroidered national emblem on black field at top, and the national tri-colors below. The pattern is the standard Luftwaffe boat form.

Former armor officers of the army frequently retained their black field cap of the boat form, with the army pattern national emblem above, and an aluminum piping around the top and the front cut-out of the flap. A pink or white Soutache in an inverted V sometimes surrounded the national rosette.

It was not unusual for officers to wear their Luftwaffe visor cap with the black uniform.

National emblems worn on the black uniform were identical in pattern to those worn on the various blue-grey garments, but were embroidered in white on a black backing. One pattern, worn on the M43 visored field cap, was trapezoidal in shape, and had the national tri-colors embroidered below the national emblem. The individual national emblems were in three sizes (measured from wing tip to wing tip):

- Breast insigne: 87mm
- Visored and visorless field caps: 70mm
- Visorless field cap: 55mm

Black visored field cap with trapezoidal insignia. The lining is black.

Trapezoidal insignia as worn on the above cap. The fabric backing is black.

Black visored field cap with two-piece insignia. The national emblem is the characteristic white on black.

"HG" pattern national emblems—top is for the breast, while the lower two are for the M43 visored field cap and the visorless field cap.

National emblems could be encountered in the earlier droop-tail pattern as well.

b. Field-grey Uniform: The field-grey uniform was issued to Assault Gun units and also, but not generally, to Panzer-grenadier units. Cut and design were identical to the black uniform. Apparently, a uniform of identical cut, but made of blue-grey cloth was also issued.

Field-grey assault gun uniform of the "HG."

This Panzerschütze wears the blue-grey version of the special black Panzer uniform. His jacket has no collar patches, but has pink piped shoulder straps. Painting by Herbert Knötel.

277

The piping of the collar of the jacket was white or bright red with uniforms of army stocks. The piping was later omitted. The collar patches encountered were as follows:

- Rectangular field-grey patches of the army pattern with white or bright red piping, and with a metal death's head centered.
- White rhomboid patches with a death's head; an aluminum twist cord piping for officers.

Hermann Göring collar patch as worn on the assault gun uniform—grey with white piping.

Adolf Forster

18-year-old Uffz. Albert Plapper wears the field-grey jacket with white rhomboid collar patches and white collar piping. He was a Knight's Cross holder who was killed in East Prussia on January 28, 1945.

- Without patches, but with the death's head affixed directly onto the collar.

Unteroffizier assault gun uniform of the "HG." Note that metal skulls have been affixed directly into the collar. The piping on the shoulder straps is red.

Liban

Field-grey M43 visored field cap worn by assault gun personnel of the "HG." The insignia is trapezoidal.

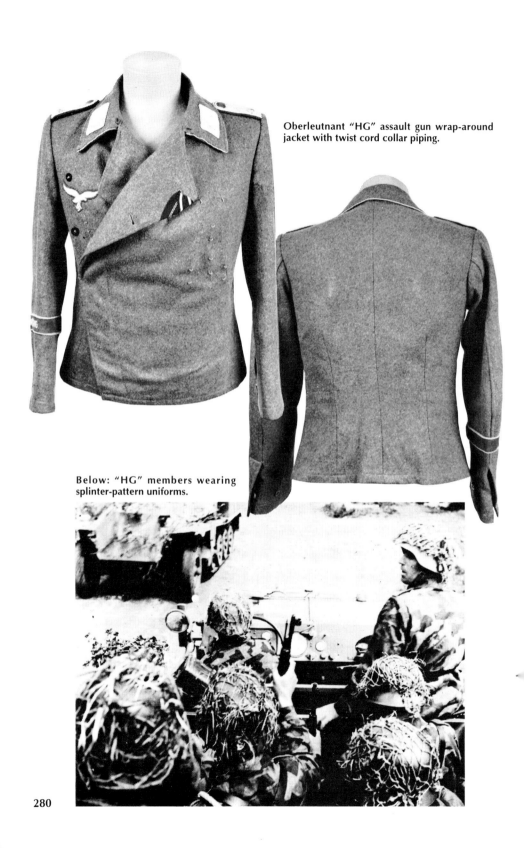

Oberleutnant "HG" assault gun wrap-around jacket with twist cord collar piping.

Below: "HG" members wearing splinter-pattern uniforms.

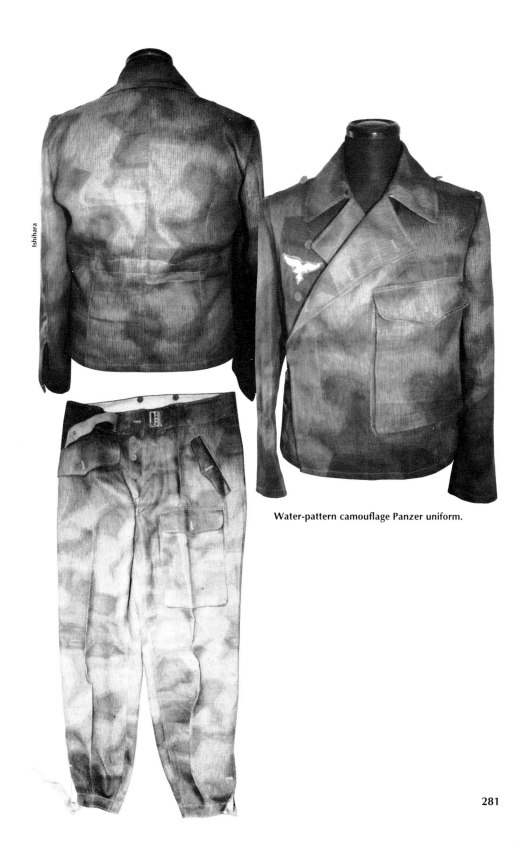

Ishihara

Water-pattern camouflage Panzer uniform.

281

"HG" members wear the three-quarter length, splinter-pattern camouflage jacket.

This "HG" mortar crew wears the SS camouflage helmet cover and smock, Italy 1944.

Late war brownish ersatz material Hermann Göring NCO service tunic with six-button front closure (when closed to the neck). The pockets are of the unpleated patch variety. There are metal belt ramps at the front and back. The interior is without markings. Shown below are the pants for the above. It has the "female" four-button side closures, and pockets with buttoned flaps. The fabric is identical to that of the tunic. The cuff has a drawstring for tightening.

Sevier

A "Hermann Göring" enlisted man wearing the tan tropical uniform.

Stabszahlmeister Alfred Otte just before his movement to Sicily in 1943. He wears the tropical uniform with the officer's cuff title.

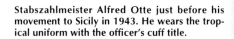

Insignia of the Sports Dress: A woven insigne was sewn on the center of the breast of the sport shirt and prabably also on sport suit. The insigne took the shape of a shield measuring 7.6 x 8.5cm. The light green center shield (6.4 x 6.9cm) was surrounded by a 5mm wide white border and an about 3 mm wide light green border. Centered of the shield was a white swastika standing on the point and measuing 3.9 x 3.9cm; its arms were 8mm wide. A black Gothic "G" was at the center of the swastika.

CHAPTER • 27

THE TROPICAL DRESS

I n late 1940 the Italian troops were fighting a losing battle in Italy's North African territories against the British forces. In spite of superior Italian strength, the British Army forced the Italians to withdraw from the Cyrenaica into Libya. Hitler, after deciding that the Italians might lose North Africa altogether, opted to send a German Expeditionary Force, the German Africa Corps (Deutsches Afrikakorps—DAK) under the command of General Erwin Rommel, to assist the Italian forces. The first German units disembarked in Tripoli in February 1941. To assist the German ground forces, the Luftwaffe sent air units, especially fighters, signals and flak units to North Africa.

To meet the needs for a tropical uniform better suited to the hot climate, a special light "tropical" uniform was quickly designed in late 1940. The army, airforce and navy independently designed their own models of tropical dress. Introductory orders of these uniforms have not been encountered.

The tropical uniforms were initially issued only to units in the North African theater of war. Additionally, units stationed or fighting in Italy, in the southern part of France, in the southern countries of the Balkan peninsula, on the islands of the Aegean Sea, and units in the southern part of Russia were also issued tropical dress for wear during the summer months.

Even though strictly prohibited, the wear of a combination of blue-grey and tropical uniform parts was nevertheless done. Frequently, especially in North Africa and during the early period, personnel wore garments of army or Italian issue, probably due to shortages of normal supplies.

The design of the tropical dress was a very similar to the blue-grey uniform garments. All garments were made of a light but durable cotton fabric, with a variety of color hues of the original khaki brown (khakibraun) color. It was common for the original color to bleach in the sun or as a result of washing, causing an off-white color.

By order (BLB 41, No.497) dated 25 April 1941 the following garments were to be issued:
- flyer's cap (Fliegermütze)
- tropical helmet (Tropenhelm)

Luftwaffe unit tailor does final alterations on a tropical tunic. Note that he wears a standard pattern wool sweater.

- tunic (Rock)
- long trousers (lange Hose), bloused trousers (Überfallhose), short trousers (kurze Hose)
- greatcoat (Mantel), weather coat (Wettermantel), motorcycle coat (Schutzmantel für Kraftfahrer)
- shirts with short and long sleeves (Hemden mit kurzen und langen Ärmeln)
- tie (Kravatte)
- under shirt (Unterziehhemd)
- under pants—short and long (Unterhosen kurz, lang)
- stocking, sport stockings (knee-length stockings) (Strümpfe, Sportstrümpfe [Kniestrümpfe])
- drill tunic, drill trousers (Drilchbluse, Drilchhose—of the blue-grey uniform)
- lace-up shoes (Schnürschuhe)
- knee-high, front-laced boots (knee—discontinued by order (LV 42, No.99) dated 1 January 1942
- knitted gloves (gestrickte Fingerhandschuhe—of the blue-grey uniform)
- sports shirts, sports trousers, sports shoes (Sporthemd, Sporthose, Laufschuhe—as with the blue-grey uniform)
- handkerchief (Taschentuch)

287

- suspender (Hosenträger)
- belt with buckle and bayonet frog (Leibriemen mit Schloß und Seitengewehrtasche)
- canteen, messkit (Feldflasche, Kochgeschirr mit Essbesteck, Fettbüchse—of normal design)
- tent equipment (Zeltausrüstung)

Personnel responsible for their own uniforms, i.e. officers, etc., were issued garments and equipment as a loan and without cost.

A subsequent order (LV 42, No.1025) dated 13 April 1942 ordered the issue of the following garments, etc. Note the prefix "Tropen" (tropical):

- tropical visored cap with neck protection pad (Tropenschirmmütze mit Nackenschutz)
- tropical tunic (Tropenrock)
- tropical bloused trousers, tropical short trousers (long trousers ommitted)
- tropical shirts with short and long sleeves
- tropical underwear
- tropical suspenders
- tropical motorcycle coat
- tropical clothing bag (Tropenkleidersack) with small bag (Tasche zum Tropenkleidersack)
- tropical goggles (Tropenbrille)
- mosquito net equipment (Moskitonetzausrüstung)

Garments and equipment with the prefix "tropical" were of special design. All other garments and equipment was standard issue. The special clothing (Sonderbekleidung) for flight duties, paratroops and motor driving duties was retained.

Description of tropical garments, etc., was announced for a later date as a "special addition" of the L.Dv.422, section A, but was never edited, however.

An order (LV 42, No.492) dated 14 February 1942 restricted wear of tropical uniforms to units on duty south of the line Naples-Foggia, at the isles of Sicily and Sardinia, at Greece and at the isle of Crete. During the warm season, the soldiers were issued with the following garments besides their normal blue-grey uniforms—flyer's cap, tunic, long trousers or bloused trousers, short trousers, shirts with long and short sleeves, and tie.

Wear of short trousers with shirt was permitted only at airfields, at flak firing positions, within barracks or by closed formations. Otherwise wear of tunic, long or bloused trousers, and shirt with tie was prescribed. A mix of blue-grey and tropical garments was strictly prohibited. On leave or at duty in the home area, wear of the blue-grey uniforms was required.

An order (LV 42, No.1113) dated 4 June 1942 prescribed issue of tropical visor caps instead of the flyer's cap and of tropical underwear, waistband (Leibbinde), and lace-up shoes.

Army style tropical uniforms were issued to the first units under command of the Afrikakorps, probably because the Luftwaffe-style tropical uniforms were not yet developed and issued. The rank insignia, usually including collar patches, were those of the Luftwaffe.

The Luftwaffe officer at right wears the army style tropical uniform early in the North African campaign.

A mix of tropical and blue-grey garments was quite frequently encountered, and frequently worn by officers. Some examples—tropical pants with flyer's blouse, blue-grey shirt with tie, blue-grey visored cap; blue-grey or white visor cap with the tropical uniform; leather belts in lieu of web belts.

Rank Insignia: The above order of 13 April 1942 prescribed wear of rank insignia as follows:

- Officers and officials of officer rank: detachable shoulder boards made of matte grey artificial silk (the normal boards were frequently worn).

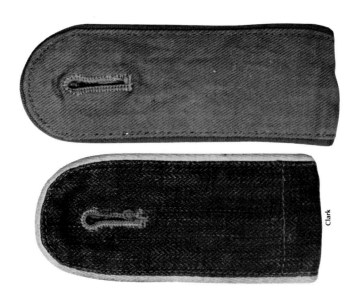

Two variations of the enlisted tropical shoulder straps.

- Enlisted personnel: detachable shoulder straps of khaki brown basic fabric with piping in branch color. The blue-grey straps were frequently worn. Greatcoat with blue-grey straps and with sleeve chevrons on a blue-grey base.
- NCO's: shoulder straps with brown Tresse of the pattern of the standard aluminum Tresse, and with aluminum pips. Sometimes the collar of tunics were bordered in NCO style with the same Tresse, but this was against regulations. Strangely, the order required a Tresse bordering the collar of the tropical shirt, but this was certainly an error.
- Ranks of Gefreiter, etc.: chevrons of brown Tresse on a triangular base of tropical fabric on the center o the left upper sleeve.
- Collar patches: these were not worn. However, numerous photos show wear of the collar patches by all ranks on the tunics.

Other Insignia:

- National Emblems: Those of tunics, shirts and caps were of white-grey machine embroidery on a tropical fabric or woven in white-grey on khaki brown . Frequently the standard national emblem of the flyer's blouse, i.e. on the blue-grey base, was worn. Infrequently, officers wore the metal national emblem (of the white tunic) affixed to the tunic. National emblems of general officers were gold colored.
- Cockade: woven on the square khaki brown base or machine embroidered (without base).
- Trade and specialist insignia: Wear of the standard white-grey insigne on a blue-grey base.

Note the wear of the metal pin-on national emblem being worn on the tropical tunic.

Steve Wilson

- Cuff Title "AFRIKA": By orders (LV 42, No.622) dated 25 February and 6 March 1942 a cuff title (Ärmelstreifen) "AFRIKA" was introduced as a general insigne of all members of Luftwaffe units in Africa. Wear of the title was permitted while on duty with those units, by wounded personnel in European hospitals, and by personnel on home leave also with the blue-grey uniform.

The order described the cuff title as a 3.3cm wide band of dark blue cloth with the title "AFRIKA" in Latin capital letters (without palm trees)—for officers, of aluminum-colored embroidery; for NCO personnel and officials of NCO rank of matte grey machine embroidery. Strangely enough, enlisted personnel were not mentioned in the order. There are several known non-regulation variants:

- dark blue, 3cm wide, silver-colored hand-embroidery with a narrow silver border at top and bottom; title 7.8cm long and 1.8cm high
- blue, white-grey machine-embroidery, border stripes of white "soutache" band
- navy blue band, 3.7cm wide, light grey machine-embroidery; title 7.8cm long and 1.8cm high
- dark blue band, title in Gothic letters of white-grey machine-embroidery

Two variations of the "AFRIKA" dark blue sleeve band. The bottom pattern is the regulation variety.

Stone

NCO on his wedding day wears a tunic bearing the "AFRIKA" sleeve-band.

- Cuff Title "AFRIKA" with palm trees: By order (LV 43, No.283) dated 28 January 1943 a new cuff title (Ärmel-

Regulation pattern "AFRIKA sleeveband with palms on the brown camel hair cloth.

band) was introduced as a "battle insigne" (Kampfabzeichen). It was awarded on individual merits, e.g. after six months of fighting in Africa. The title was a 3cm wide band of brown camel hair cloth and with the Latin capital letters "AFRIKA" with palm tree at either side—all of white grey machine embroidery, and bordered by a 3-4mm wide white grey "soutache" stripe top and bottom. The order described the borders as "silver", which was an error. Non-regulation cuff titles were produced and worn:

- aluminum hand-embroidered title and border stripes on brown or blue bands
- silver-grey machine embroidery on dark blue band, and without border stripes
- silver-grey machine embroidery on a blue band, and with aluminum border stripes

As above, but on a Luftwaffe blue-grey backing.

As above, but without soutache stripes to and bottom. The sleeveband is dark blue.

All cuff titles were worn on the left lower sleeve of tropical and blue tunics, flyer's blouses and greatcoats 1cm above the open cuffs or at a corresponding height.

The man in the Luftwaffe tropical uniform at right is wearing the army pattern "AFRIKA-KORPS" cuff title. Also of interest is that he is wearing the national emblem from a tropical pith helmet sewn onto his visored field cap.

- Insigne of the Special Unit (Sonderverband) 287: This unit was constituted in mid-1942 as an army unit for possible employment in the Near East. Its members were distinguished by a special insigne, which was worn centered on the right upper sleeve. There were a few Luftwaffe personnel attached for liaison duties, who wore the insigne on their Luftwaffe tropical uniforms. An introduction order has not yet been located.

The sleeve insigne measured 5.5 - 6.2cm high and 4.8 - 5.3cm wide. It was machine-woven, and took the form of an oval depicting a wreath of palm fronds with a swastika at the base. Within the wreath was a desert landscape with a rising sun with sunbeams, and an inclined palm tree at the left. The sun was light yellow with other depictions in white or off-white on a bluish-dark green field.

Arab members of Special Unit 287 wear the unit insigne on the upper right sleeve.

Detail discussion of the tropical uniform follows:

1. Headgear:
    a. Pith Helmet (Tropenhelm): Due to the intensity of the sun, a tropical headgear was necessary for wear with the tropical dress. Pith helmets were issued to the first German troops, both army and air force, but apparently was found to be unsuitable to the harsh service conditions. Distribution was phased out in late 1941 or early 1942. The above order of 13 April 1942 no longer listed a pith helmet.

The tropical pith helmet was made of pressed rigid construction cork covered with six segments of khaki brown, olive-green or blue cloth sewn together. A 2.2cm wide band of the same cloth was around the crown, and **295**

Standard pattern Luftwaffe pith helmet in tan with tan leather trim and strap. The national emblem is silver.

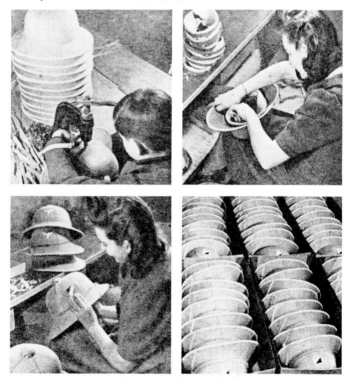

Assembly of the Luftwaffe pith helmet.

joined at the rear, and with the vertical seam covered by a vertical cloth band. There was a 4cm diameter circular opening at the top for ventilation, crowned by a screw-on cloth-covered hemisphere (1.5 - 2cm high and 4.5cm in diameter) with two or four semicircular ventilation holes.

A sun-shade was attached all around the helmet at a slight angle, and cloth covered on both sides, with panels connected by lateral seams. The sun-shade was 5cm wide at the sides, 7cm wide in the front, and 8cm wide at the rear. The rim was covered with a blue-grey or tan (army pattern in brown-olive) colored leather "tape"—7mm wide on the upper side, and 9mm wide on the lower.

The issuance of tropical clothing.

Olive-green pith helmet with tan leather trim, and gold national emblem (general officer).

    The interior normally consisted of a stiff 2.3cm wide felt ring, a 5cm wide brown leather sweatband, and at the top a grommeted 4cm diameter circular ventilation hole. The lining was of red or olive-green thin fabric. Variant specimens exist without lining.

Blue pith helmet with blue leather trim, and standard silver national emblem.

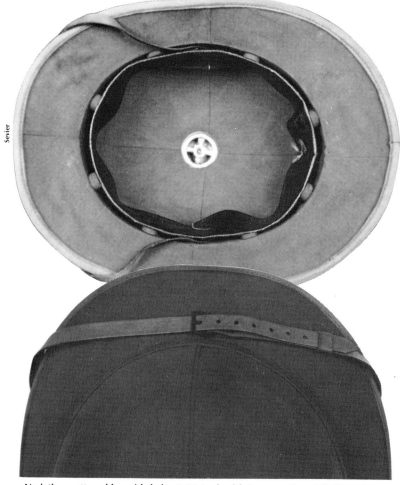

Variation pattern blue pith helmet. Note the fabric covered cork buffers about the sweatband and the buckle on the brown leather chin strap.

Gold-embossed manufacturer's logo in the sweat band of a standard pith helmet.

Blue-grey pith helmet with wind goggles being worn.

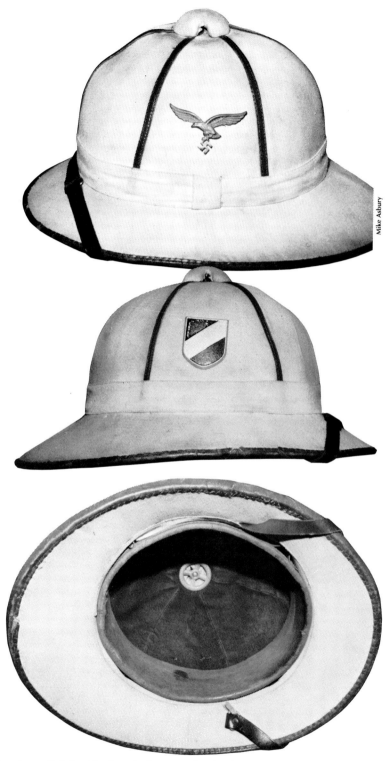

This unique pith helmet is of standard construction, but is covered in white cotton material and trimmed with tan leather. The lining is red and the metal insignia are standard issue.

A 1.9cm wide two-part leather chin strap in the same color as the rim reinforcement was affixed to the interior felt ring at the right , while the left side had a metal hook secured to the left side. The strap was normally worn across the front of the sun-shade.

The insignia worn on the pith helmets consisted of stamped metal national black/white (aluminum-colored)/red shield (4.2cm high and 3.5cm wide) with pebbled base and a narrow aluminum-colored raised rim affixed to the right side .8cm above the crown band, and a stamped metal Luftwaffe pattern national emblem flying to the front affixed to the left side.

An infrequently worn model, procured from army stocks, was made of pressed felt-like material of brownish-dark green color. The top was seamless, and the leather trim and chin strap was dark olive-green.

    b. Field Caps:
        (1) Visorless Field Cap: It is presumed that the visorless field cap was distributed in limited numbers, and only saw wear during the early months of the North African campaign. The above order of 13 April 1942 no longer mentioned the visorless field cap.

It was of the same pattern as the blue-grey field cap as worn by NCO's and privates, but made of tropical tan fabric. The lining was of red or brown fabric, and without sweatband.

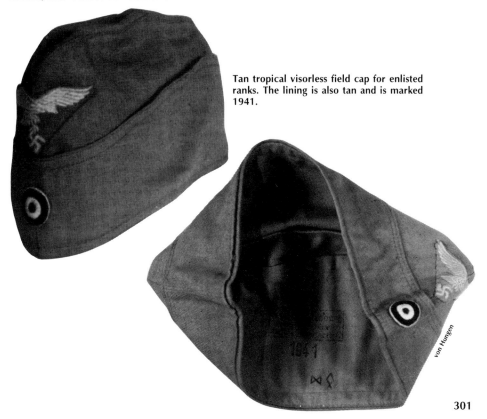

Tan tropical visorless field cap for enlisted ranks. The lining is also tan and is marked 1941.

von Hungen

Tan tropical enlisted visorless field cap. The interior lining is tan, and marked with the manufacturer's logo dated 1941.

Gefreiter Franz Georg Haider, born 1921 in Krems, Austria, served with the Luftwaffe in North Africa. He wears the tropical pattern breast eagle and overseas cap emblem. The tropical overseas cap is tan cotton. Note the continental shoulder straps in wear.

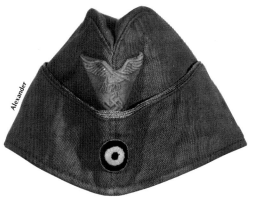

Officer's tropical visorless field cap as denoted by the aluminum wire piping.

Knight's Cross recipient Albert Scheidig wears the officer's tropical visorless field cap (as denoted by the aluminum wire piping) as he prepares for a tactical mission. Note the wear of the flare shell holder at the waist.

The insignia consisted of the machine-embroidered national emblem (white grey or blue-grey) and national rosette, each on a tan backing. The caps of officers had an aluminum web piping about the top of the turned-up flap.

(2) Standard Issue Field Cap: The visored standard issue field cap was most often worn, and became the characteristic mark of the tropical dress. The lightweight field cap was without reinforcements, and was made of the same basic design as the army pattern visored field cap, but of tan tropical fabric. It had a long cloth visor to provide protection from the sun. There was a one layer cloth, non-fold-down flap sewn along the upper edge, and with a semicircular dip at the front. The flap ended about 2cm below the edge of the crown. The lining was of red or brown fabric. At either side were two (sometimes one or none) metal grommets for ventilation.

Standard pattern issue field-—enlisted version. Note lack of air vents. The national emblem flies from left to right.

304   A Luftwaffe mortar crew in North Africa, January 1943.

Sevier

Visored tropical field cap with leather national emblem and rosette with leather backing.

Enlisted man wears the standard pattern tropical visored field cap.

305

The national emblem and cockade were of the same pattern and make as the visorless field cap. The national emblem was centered on the front above the flap, while the cockade was centered on the flap.

Caps of officers usually had an aluminum (gold for general officers) web piping around the crown and the front cutout of the flap. Field-made or modified enlisted pieces were sometimes with twist cord piping.

Luftwaffe tropical visored field cap for officer as indicated by the aluminum piping and hand-embroidered national emblem. The interior is red with a size mark.

General Ritter von Pohl wearing the above pattern cap.

Visorless field cap at left, and two officer pattern standard issue field caps.

Officer's tropical visored field cap with hand-embroidered national emblem and tri-color rosette.

Hodgin

GFM Albert Kesselring, in Italy in 1944, wears a tropical visored field cap with single button closure.

(3) Tropical Visored Cap with Neck Protector (Tropen-schirmmütze mit Nackenschutz): The cap was included in the above order of 13 April 1942, but was probably introduced earlier. It was worn predominantly by officers, and not generally issued.

The cap was made of tropical fabric and of a soft construction resembling the navy-style visor cap.

The nearly circular crown had a diameter of about 28cm. The four parts of the crown (that portion above the cap band) were sewn at the front, the sides and at the rear. There was a piping of basic cloth around crown, and at the top and bottom of the 5 - 5.5cm wide lightly stiffened cap band. The interior was lined with red, green or light brown fabric, and had a light brown leather sweatband. A rather large round ventilation hole, covered by mesh wire, was positioned at either side of the lateral seams on each side of the crown. The visor was covered top and bottom by cloth, with a seam around the front edge 3mm distance from the edge.

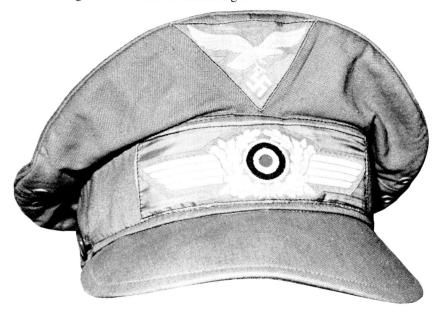

Note this version has two standard ventilation grommets on each side of the cap.

A 1.5cm wide adjustable brown leather chin strap was buttoned to a brown button affixed at either side of the cap band. However, it was not unusual for officers to wear the aluminum (or gold) twist cord as found on the blue-grey visor cap.

Insignia consisted of the blue-grey or white-grey machine-embroidered national emblem on a base of tropical cloth, and machine-embroidered national tri-color cockade. However, the characteristic insignia was the machine-woven national emblem and wreath and cockade on a tropical backing.

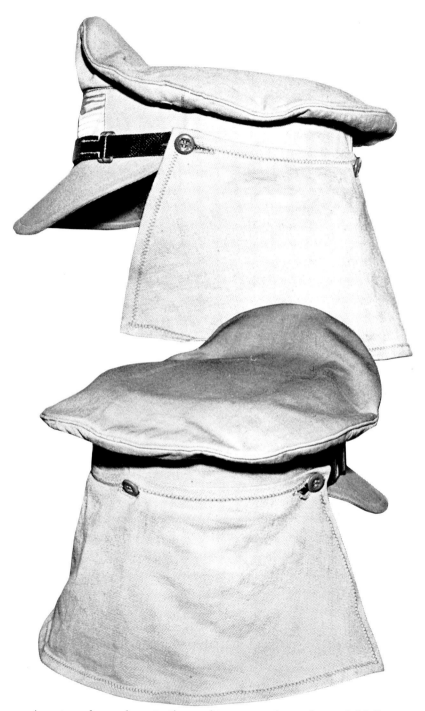

A rectangular neck protection pad to protect the neck was initially sewn on, but with later patterns affixed at three points (the two side buttons and a button at the rear of the cap band). Most frequently the cap was worn without the button-on pad, and the three buttons were later omitted.

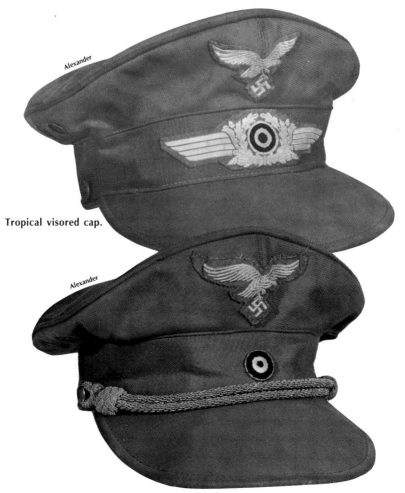

Tropical visored cap.

Tropical visored cap with non-regulation insignia and officer's chin cord held in position by two aluminum metal side buttons.

General Ramcke wears the tropical visored cap with a non-regulation chin strap.

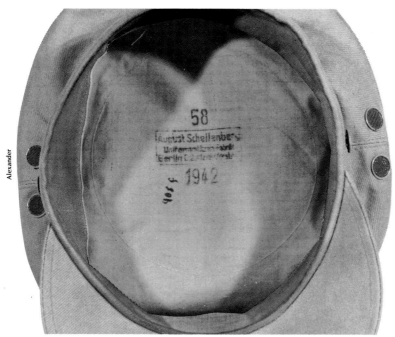

Alexander

Red interior with manufacturer's logo and 1942 date. Clearly shown are the wire-mesh air vents.

Note insigne of Sonder-verband 287.

2. Tunic: The tunic was made of tropical cloth and was similar in cut and style as the blue-grey four-pocket pattern tunic, with open collar and lay-down lapels. There were four buttons at the front. If worn closed up to the collar, it was hooked by a small hook and eye, with the lapel buttoned by a button positioned underneath the right lapel. Tunics of later production were without hook and eye and lapel button and buttonhole. The center back seam ended in a slit. The two breast pockets had a center pleat, while the large hip pockets were without the pleat. The sleeves had a 7 - 8cm high false cuff, which apparently was omitted with later production patterns.

Breast and shoulders were lined on the inside. At either side was an inside breast pocket. There was a pocket for the first-aid pouch on the right inside panel.

Standard pattern tropical tunic with four button closure and patch lower pockets.

Jim Plante

Farnes

Mason

The tropical four-button front tunic in wear. Note the tan shirt and tie.

Standard pattern four-button front closure. Note the collar button and hook that would allow it to be closed to the neck.

Oberleutnant Hans-Joachim Marseille wears the tropical four-button front tunic.

Standard pattern Luftwaffe tropical tunic, but with five button front closure.

Biasutti

Officer's pattern tropical tunic with concealed lower pockets and pin-on breast national emblem. Note the rarely encountered tropical fabric waist belt. It is speculated that the tunic is a privately tailored piece as there are a number of variations from the standard pattern.

Long/Halcomb Smith

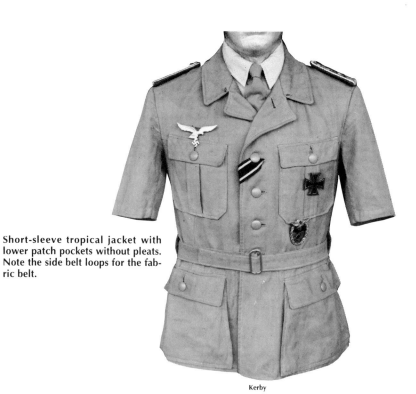

Short-sleeve tropical jacket with lower patch pockets without pleats. Note the side belt loops for the fabric belt.

Kerby

As above, but Sahariana pattern with long sleeves and pleated lower patch pockets.

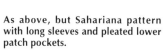

Liban

315

An interesting mixture shown in this tropical tunic, which is of the army pattern (to include the breast emblem), but with other Luftwaffe insignia added.

Humsaker

Luftwaffe personnel also wore a reed-green tropical uniform. This officer's example is adorned with continental insignia.

Jim Plante

As at left but with NCO shoulder straps, and a tropical belt and buckle.

Gibbons

Unspecified pattern tropical tunic.

The machine-embroidered national emblem was sewn on above the right breast pocket, and was with a tropical or blue-grey backing. Collar patches were not authorized by regulations, but often worn. Also against regulations was the wear of a brown Tresse ("Borte") by NCO's about the collar.

Shoulder straps and boards were affixed by a loop near the shoulder head seam and retained by a button. Shoulder straps were made of tropical cloth, but the continental blue-grey straps were also worn. The rank chevrons of privates were of brown Tresse on a triangular tropical cloth base. The standard pattern chevrons were also worn.

Buttons were pebbled tan or blue-grey for enlisted personnel and officers, and gold for general officers.

Charita

Private wearing tropical tunic with tropical pattern shoulder straps.

Rarely encountered tropical Fliegerbluse (dated 1941) with standard pattern hand-embroidered breast eagle.

Tannahill

A Sahariana pattern tunic, which apparently was in short production, was also in wear by the Luftwaffe.

Kerby

Oberleutnant Sahariana-pattern tropical tunic.

Oberleutnant Heinrich Eppen wears a variant Sahariana pattern jacket.

Oberst Eduard Neumann wears a similar version of the above pattern jacket.

3. Trousers: The trousers were made of the same material as the tunic. The basic design of the body portion was the same as the blue-grey long trousers. They were cut with a horizontal waist edge and a 4 - 5cm wide waistband with a built-in belt made of light webbing or double-laid uniform cloth. The right end of the belt was triangular, and on the left front had a sewn-on three-pronged metal buckle or a friction buckle—a rectangular frame with a moveable center bar. Around the waistband were five or six vertical cloth loops, each about 6cm long and 2cm wide, to hold the belt when worn without the tunic. The fly was buttoned with 5 - 6 buttons.

   a. Long Trousers (lange Hose): Long trousers were only listed in the order of 25 April 1941 (BLB 41, No.497), but omitted in the order of 13 April 1942 (LV 42, No.1025). This indicates a short-term production only. These were hardly ever worn.

Two side pockets with slanted openings, one (right) or two rear pockets with or without buttoned flap, and a watch pocket (with or without flap) were the same as with the standard blue-grey trousers.

   b. Shorts ("Tropenhose kurz"): The shorts were of the same design and cut as the long trousers, but reached down nearly to the knees, and with slightly widening legs.

Knee-length stockings and ankle-high lace-up boots were the prescribed wear with the shorts. However, the high tropical boots were also worn. Socks were commonly rolled down to the top of the lace-up boots, but this was against regulations.

K. Peters

Shorts worn with ankle-high lace-up boots and rolled down socks.

As below.

K. Peters

Enlisted man wears the regulations tropical shorts. Note the socks rolled down over the top of the ankle high boots in contradiction to regulations.

321

c. Bloused Trousers ("Überfallhose," "Tropenüberfallhose"): The bloused trousers were the most commonly worn. The body portion was identical to that of the long trousers and shorts. The pockets had buttoned flaps with a short center point and an inside buttonhole. The button was placed a the center of the edge of the pockets. There was a large sewn-on rectangular pocket on the upper part of the left thigh, and the bottom edge positioned in the height of the knee. The buttoned flap was identical with the other pocket flaps.

The cut of the legs was very wide and slightly narrowing towards the ankles. The ends of the legs narrowed to a sewn-on rim, and wear with an ankle-high outside slit that was bound with bands sewn to either edge of the rim. In this manner the ends of the legs were bound around the ankles, and with the pant leg bloused over the rim of the lace-up shoes.

Biasutti

Tropical bloused trousers.

This officer wears the above described bloused trousers.

322

NCOs wearing the tropical bloused trousers.

Luftwaffe officer in the fore ground wears a visored field cap with aluminum piping, to include the scalloped front. Note that the eagle flies from left to right.

4. Shirts: The shirts with long (most commonly encountered) or short sleeves and with collar were of identical cut and style, and made of lightweight light-brown tropical fabric in various shades due to bleaching by washing. The usual design was with a 35 - 40cm long slit at the chest, buttoned by three small buttons and one button on the collar. A tape with buttonholes was sewn to the left edge of the slit. Shirts produced later were open totally at the front.

There were two breast pockets measuring about 17x21cm and with 3.5cm wide pleats. The scalloped flaps measured abut 6cm at the point, and were usually buttoned by pebbled buttons as on the tropical tunic (but this varied).

Sleeves of the long-sleeve shirt were with a 13 - 14cm long slash at the outer side; its front edge was usually reinforced by a 2.5-3cm wide tape. The 7cm wide cuffs were buttoned by one or two small buttons. The length of the short sleeves covered about two-thirds down to the elbow.

Clark

Above: Long sleeve pullover shirt. The cuffs have the double button closure.

As above, but with single button closure at cuff.

Hackney

Charita

At left Major Maltzahn wears the long sleeve shirt with the sleeve rolled up, a practice characteristic of the tropical areas. A Generaloberst presents the Iron Cross 1st Class.

Clark

Tropical short sleeve shirt with full front button closure.

325

Enlisted personnel, having been awarded the Iron Cross IInd Class, wear the short sleeve tropical shirts. Note the white visorless field cap being worn at the right.

Short sleeve shirt worn with the tropical uniform.

The small buttons were made of brown plastic. Slip-on shoulder straps/boards were (normally) affixed by a pebbled button and a loop near the sleeve head seam. Rank chevrons of privates or collar patches were not worn.

The national insigne as worn on the tunic was frequently sewn above the right breast pocket.

If necessary, shirts were worn with a brown neck tie of wool or cotton.

Standard pattern machine-embroidered tropical national emblem as worn on the shirt.

Machine-woven national emblem on a blue-grey backing worn on the tropical shirt—although done, it was rare.

Rarely encountered tropical shirt of the sahariana style.

The above shirt in wear.

Clark

5. Greatcoat: The order of 25 April 1941 (BLB 41, No.497) included: greatcoat, weather coat, and motorcycle coat. The subsequent order of 13 April 1942 (LV 42, No.1025) omitted greatcoat and weather coat, which actually were never issued in a tropical version. For tropical wear, the standard blue-grey greatcoat was issued.

Charita

Standard pattern Luftwaffe blue-grey greatcoat being worn in North Africa.

6. Motorcyclist's Protective Coat: The "(tropical) protective coat of motor drivers" (Tropen-Schutzmantel für Kraftfahrer) was generally known as "motorcycle coat." It was made of heavy-duty brown cotton fabric, and in cut and style of the standard blue-grey rubberized motorcycle coat. The collar was made of the same cloth, and the pebbled buttons were brown. Shoulder straps/boards were of the button-on variety, but generally not worn.

7. Footwear:
    a. Knee-high, front-laced tropical boots (Schnürstiefel) were listed in the above order of 25 April 1941, but omitted in the order of 13 April 1942. The army provided the standard pattern army tropical boots for wear. The listing of the boots in the 1941 order must therefore be regarded as an error.
    b. Another pattern knee-high tropical boot, largely attributed to the Luftwaffe, had a virtually identical foot portion, but with a wrap-around legging secured by a long leather strap passing through a hole at the base, and again through a hole at the top, and secured by a friction buckle at the outer side. Like the army pattern, the fabric was normally olive-green, but it is believed that a blue-grey canvas-topped tropical boot also was produced.

Officer at extreme right wears the knee-high tropical boots.

Halcomb Smith

Luftwaffe tropical wrap-around boots being worn during a briefing. Note the sandals being worn by the officer in the center.

Luftwaffe officials inspect the army pattern knee-high tropical boots prior to issue.

Ankle-high tropical lace-up boots being worn with the tropical uniform during an inspection.

c. Lace-up Shoes: The ankle-high, lace-up tropical shoes were officially termed "lace-up shoes with khaki-brown canvas upper part" (Schnürschuhe mit Segeltuchschaft khakibraun). These were similar to the black leather lace-up shoes, but made of brown canvas, and reinforced with brown leather around the sole, at either side of the front slash, and over the rear seam. The number of eyelets depended on the shoe size.

Low-quarter tropical lace-up shoes being worn. No mention of these has been found in regulations.

An order of 2 April 1942 (LV 42, No.99) prescribed issue of the standard black leather lace-up shoes after stocks of tropical shoes were used up.

331

8. Belts: Enlisted personnel wore a tan, greenish or even rarely a blue webbed belt, since the webbed belt was more durable in tropical conditions than the leather belt. The standard issue leather belts, however, were also issued and worn, especially by troops in Italy and Greece.

Luftwaffe foreign volunteers wear the webbed tropical belt with the tropical uniform.

The enlisted webbed belt measured 4.2 - 4.5cm wide. The buckle was attached by two prongs to a back strap (either web or leather) with double eyelets. The buckle was of the standard Luftwaffe pattern with smooth rectangular surface, and finished in olive or blue paint.

Standard pattern tan webbed tropical belt with tan paint finish to the enlisted buckle.

Luftwaffe enlisted buckle, painted blue-grey with a webbed tab of the same color.

Regulations for a special web belt for officers has not been observed, but production probably existed. Officers usually wore their standard brown leather belt. Officers of front-line fighting suits (paratroops, etc.) usually wore the enlisted version belt with the battle dress.

9. Miscellaneous Garments and Equipment: The color of garments was olive-brown, while that of equipment was more of an olive green.

As assortment of Luftwaffe tropical gear in wear.

- Bayonet Frog (Seitengewehrtasche): This was made of stiff webbing of a similar design as that of the black leather, but straight-edged rather than with a taper. It came with and

333

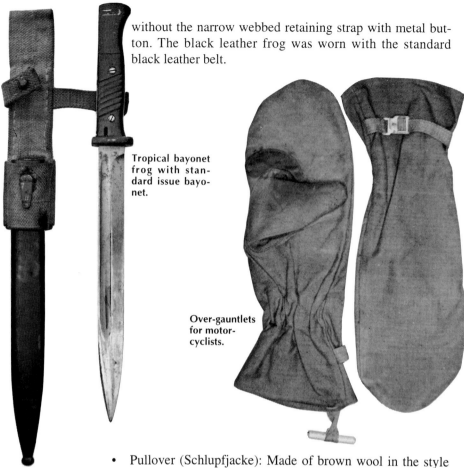

without the narrow webbed retaining strap with metal button. The black leather frog was worn with the standard black leather belt.

Tropical bayonet frog with standard issue bayonet.

Over-gauntlets for motor-cyclists.

- Pullover (Schlupfjacke): Made of brown wool in the style of the standard issue pullovers.
- Stockings and Socks (Strümpfe): Knee-length stockings (Sportstrümpfe or [Tropen-] Kniestrümpfe) of light wool with an inside rubber band at the end. Brown woolen socks (Strümpfe or [Tropen-] Strümpfe) or standard issue grey socks.
- Scarf (Halstuch): The quadratic scarf was made of light cotton fabric.
- Gloves (Fingerhandschuhe): Knitted wollen gloves of the standard issue model.
- Over-gauntlets (Überhandschuhe): The over-gauntlets of motor-cyclists were made of durable canvas-like olive-brown cloth without lining, and reached up to the mid-fore-arms. There was a buckled narrowing-strap at the wrist.
- Rucksack: This was the standard pattern issue blue-grey rucksack.
- Straps, etc.: All equipment straps were made of strong webbing, and with light-metal friction buckles. The other end was usually with a triangular light metal mounting.

- Canteen, mess kit, etc.: Of standard issue. The cover of canteens and the paint of mess kits, etc., was brown, and the straps were of webbing.
- Bread Bag (Brotbeutel): The bread bag was of standard issue pattern. Blue-grey bread bags were also issued.
- Clothing bags (Tropenkleidersack—Tasche): The sack and bag were standard issue. Blue-grey standard issue sacks and bags were also issued.

Double decal Luftwaffe helmet with tropical tan finish.

Tropical painted gas mask cannister.

Göring inspects troops of his division who are outfitted with tropical uniforms and equipment.

Steel helmet with tropical paint.

- Tent equipment (Zeltausrüstung): The standard issue shelter quarter was olive-brown.
- Steel helmets and gas masks: Painted olive-brown.

- Goggles (Sonnen- und Staubschutzbrillen): There were several goggles of various design. The surround was usually of grey rubber for protection against dust.

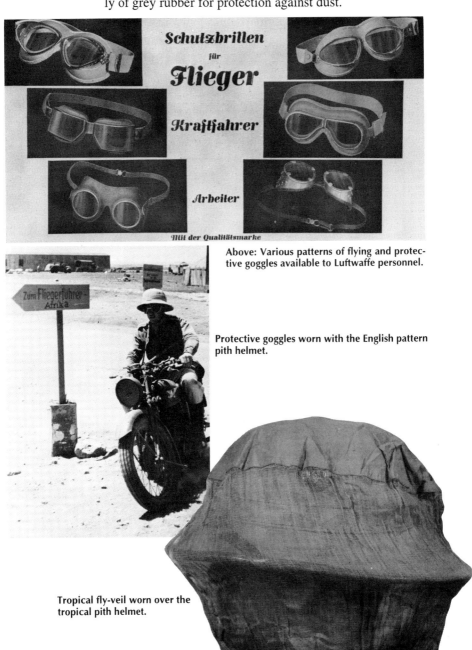

Above: Various patterns of flying and protective goggles available to Luftwaffe personnel.

Protective goggles worn with the English pattern pith helmet.

Tropical fly-veil worn over the tropical pith helmet.

- Fly-veil (Mückenschleier): Also served as a mosquito net, it was in the pattern of a green or olive-brown mesh hood worn over the head.

CHAPTER • 28

MOUNTAIN, WINTER, CAMOUFLAGE CLOTHING

A **• Mountain Clothing:** Following a testing, the following garments were introduced by an order (BLB 39, No.31) dated 19 December 1938 and issued for personnel assigned to mountain duties: mountain cap, wind jacket, mountain trousers, mountain boots, ankle puttees, and over-gauntlets. Additional garments were introduced in 1943, but the information has not yet been located. These garments were: over-jacket, over-trousers and three-finger over-gauntlets.

The garments were identical in cut and style as those of the army. Even during the war years, issue was still restricted to personnel of units designed for mountain duties.

Descriptions are based on army regulations, inspection of original garments and period photographs.

    1. Mountain Cap: The distinctive mountain cap (Bergmütze) was similar in design to the cap used by mountain troops of WWI. It was replaced by the standard visored field cap (Einheitsfeldmütze) by order (LV 43, No.1824) dated 27 September 1943, but was continued to be worn out. The edelweiss badge of the mountain troops of the army was not worn.

The mountain cap was made of blue-grey basic cloth. The top was slightly tampered backwards. The two lateral parts of the body were 9.5cm high in the front, 9cm high on the sides, and 8cm high at the back. A 2.5cm wide and 8.5cm high stiffening pad of blue-grey twill with horsehair filling was sewn inside the front lining to prevent the cap from folding at the front. The pad was abolished sometime during the war.

The folding flaps were sewn to the lower edge of the cap body. Unfolded they were 16cm wide and diminished, beginning in the middle of the side parts, in a circular front scallop to 3cm on the upper and on the lower part. The lightly rounded ends of the folded flap were buttoned by one blue-grey plastic (and also probably metal) 13mm button on the right end, and one buttonhole on the left end. At both sides of the cap body was a reinforced ventilation hole 1cm below the top seam.

Unteroffizier wear the distinctive mountain cap. Note the single button front closure.

This wounded NCO wears a short-billed ski cap.

The visor of the standard pattern was made of basic cloth covering a flexible pad of plastic material or leather. The visor was 27 cm wide at the base, and at an angle of about 20 degrees.

The lining was grey, and the sweatband was of blue-grey or brown leather or artificial leather.

The national emblem of off-white or light grey machine embroidery on a blue-grey base and the machine-embroidered cockade were placed at the front of the cap body.

An order (LV 43, No.234) dated 22 January 1943 introduced the following for officers, etc.: 3mm twist aluminum cord or Litze piping around the top; national emblem of aluminum colored metal with an approximate 4cm wing span; 1.2cm diameter metal button at the front. Officer piping, insignia and button were aluminum, while general officers were gold colored.

2. Ski Cap: An order (L.D. No.40296/36 D IV 3 a III.Ang.) dated 23 March 1936 permitted the wear of a privately purchased ski cap (Skimütze) for wear at skiing with a privately owned ski dress. The cap was made of blue-grey basic cloth, and was with the national emblem. While details were not published, the style and cut was similar to that of the mountain cap.

As a result or an order (BLB 39, No.205) dated 10 March 1939 the ski cap was substituted by the mountain cap. Ski caps were to be altered in the following way: width of the upper and lower part of the front scallop reduced from 5cm to 3cm; ends of the folded flap buttoned by one 13mm plastic or metal button (in lieu of the previous two); a 2.2cm machine-embroidered cockade was positioned below the national emblem.

These members of Parachute Regiment 1 wear army issue, mountain clothing over their blue-grey uniforms for transport to Narvik in June 1940.

3. Windjacket: The double-breasted wind jacket (Windjacke) was made of waterproof cotton cloth of a blue-grey color (olive-green, almost grey color of the army pattern jackets). Since it was designed to be worn over the uniform with equipment, the cut was loose fitting.

There were two front and two back panels connected by lateral, shoulder and back seams. The front panels reached 8.5cm beyond the center line, with five button holes on each side 2cm back from the edges. Correspondingly, each front panel had five grey or blue-grey buttons.

The back had a 7-8cm wide open pleat from the collar to the bottom edge. A half-belt in two parts, each 6cm wide and 23-30cm in length with rounded ends, was sewn into the lateral seams at the waistline. The left part was with two buttonholes, while the right part had two buttons.

The lay-down collar was made of the same cloth, an was made with a stiffening pad between its two panels, and measured 9cm in the front and 7cm at the back. It was closed by a hook (right) and eye. There was a 10cm long and 3.5cm wide cloth bridle sewn to the left underside of the collar to hold the collar in a turned-up position. The bridle had two buttonholes and a rounded, free end. It was secured by a single button, and buttoned to a button on the opposite collar when in use.

There were two patch pockets, one on each side, measuring 17cm wide and 20cm high with a 3cm wide center pleat. The pocket flaps were scalloped with a center buttonhole and a center button on the pockets. Above the side pockets were muff pockets with inside pockets-bags measuring 20cm wide and high and with 15-17cm wide openings at a slant. The openings were reinforced with a 4cm wide tape of basic cloth. The pointed pocket flaps had a center buttonhole, with the button on the jacket.

The sleeves were made of two parts with a front and back seam. A flap (or bridle) was inserted into the front seam 4cm above the sleeve's edge. This allowed the sleeves to be narrowed at the wrist. The flap was 11.5cm long, 4cm wide at the seam, and 3.5cm wide at the pointed end, and had a buttonhole. Two buttons were sewn to the sleeve to secure the flap, thus narrowing the sleeve opening.

Buttons were grey or blue-grey horn or plastic. The buttons of the collar and the flaps were smaller.

Slip-on shoulder straps/boards were normally worn, but not always. Sleeve chevrons of private ranks were not worn.

4. Mountain Trousers: The mountain trousers (Skihose) were in the style of civilian ski trousers then in fashion with tapered legs (so-called Keilhose design) The trousers were made of waterproof, blue-grey cloth. The trousers were cut in two front and two back panels joined with a lateral seam and a center seam. The upper body section was the same as with the long trousers. The legs were tapered from the upper part of the thighs down so they could be tucked into the mountain boots without folding below the ankels. The outer lateral seams of the legs ended with a 12cm long slash with its front having a 2cm overlap, and bound by two blue-grey ribbons measuring 40cm long and 1cm wide each, with one ribbon sewn to the front edge of the slash, the other one 7cm from the rear edge and 1cm above the end of the legs.

There were two front pockets with slanted openings of 16cm in length, and a rear pocket at the right hip, with a 15-16cm long opening 14cm below the upper edge of the trousers and 4 cm from the lateral seam. All pockets were with scalloped flaps secured by a button. There was also a watch pocket on the right front, secured by a button.

There were two narrow straps made of basic cloth with lining positioned on the left and right hip. Each forward strap was sewn on 4cm from the lateral seams, and mesured 5cm in length and 4cm wide at the front and 2cm wide at the end with a friction or two-pronged metal buckle. The rear straps measured 13cm long each, 3cm wide at the sewn on pointed rear ends, and tapering to 2cm wide at the front.

The seat, crotch, and inside of the legs were reinforced with basic cloth. The lining and buttons were as those of the long trousers.

5. Mountain Boots: The mountain boots (Bergschuhe) were worn with the mountain trousers. They were designed for use in difficult mountainous terrain, and could also be used as ski boots.

The boots were made of strong leather of natural fawn, brown or black color, and usually lined with fine brown leather. The height in the front was 14-16cm, and at the rear 13-15cm. A 1.5cmwide grey cloth or felt band was sewn to the upper edge. There was a 2.5cm wide leather band above the sole

Mountain boots.

around the sides and the front. The rear seam was covered by leather. A semicircular or rectangular leather cap was sewn on at the heel extending 4.5-5.5cm in height. A double-laid web strap was inserted at the rear between the leather and the lining, and measured 2cm wide and 9cm long, reaching 5cm above the edge. In wear the strap was put inside. It was omitted in 1940.

The leather boot laces measured 1m long and 3mm in diameter, and secured the boot through five pairs of eyelets below, and four pairs of hooks above. The leather tongue was sewn up to the upper edge.

6. Ankle Puttees: The mountain trousers were designed to be worn with ankle puttees (Gelenkbinden or Knöchelwetzstreifen—ankle protecting tapes) to give a snow-tight connection between trousers and boots. The puttees were elastic woven, grey (army pattern) or blue-grey woolen tapes measuring 73cm long and 8cm wide. One end was folded in a triangular shape with a woven fastening strap 20cm long and 2.5cm wide with a movable buckle sewn on. The other slanted end had a small metal hook positioned 8cm away from the end, which was hooked to the edge of the front slash of the boots. The puttees were wrapped around the ankle from the inside outwards, first with two layers, and then with each of the following layers half covering the lower one. The fastening strap was

Ankle puttees in their rolled configuration.

wrapped and secured by the buckle over the last layer. The puttee wrap was to reach arout a hand's width above the boots.

7. Over-gauntlets: The canvas over-gauntlets were made of the same fabric as the windjacket. They measured 40cm long with an 18cm wide opening. On the inside of the wrist was an elastic band. The sewn on thumb was 12cm long and 9cm wide. The cuffs were worn over the sleeves of the windjacket, etc., and tied by two ribbons sewn to the cuffs on the upper and lower sides 5.5cm from the opening. The 1.9cm wide band was 5cm long (with a friction buckle) and with a 12cm long corresponding band. The palm and thumb were reinforced by blue-grey leather patches. Sewn to the opening on the left hand glove was a 5cm long strap with a wooden crossbar at the end, and a 6cm long cloth loop on the right glove to serve as fastening device when carried between bayonet grip and frog.

B. Winter Clothing: The peacetime winter clothing was also intended for wartime wear. It consisted of several additional garments—toque, woolen pullover, overcoat, over-stockings, knitted gloves, over-gauntlets, and felt boots. Some garments were issued only to soldiers in the performance of certain duties. All those garments were issued for use during the winter months only, and taken back again in the spring for storage at the unit's clothing depots. The basic winter issue was apparently sufficient in any normal central European winter, but not in the severe winters of eastern Europe. The Russian winters were far worse than anything the German troops had ever experienced or had expected.

The Wehrmacht was not prepared for the severe Russian winters, neither in clothing nor in equipment, weapons and material. The German troops improvised in winter clothing to endure the bitter cold, from using captured stocks of Russian-type quilt jackets and trousers, to makeshift improvisations of all kind, using everything they could get, from civilian garments to captured clothing. In the winter of 1941/42, a nation-wide but hastily improvised collection of warm clothing for use by the troops was organized with great propaganda effort; however, it came too late for the first Russian winter, and brought an insufficient quantity of material fit for use by the troops.

In early 1942, development of a suitable winter clothing began. Since autumn of 1942 it reached the front troops in large numbers. On 19 April 1942, the newly developed winter clothing was presented to Hitler at his headquarters. It consisted of jacket, trousers, cap, mittens and snow boots, and was worn over the standard uniform. The loose-fitting design allowed its wear over the basic uniform without hindering the movements of soldiers. Up to three layers of clothing retained the body heat, while the external layers were waterproof and windproof.

By an order (LV 42, No.5) dated 2 December 1942 personnel who were responsible for procurement of their uniforms by themselves (i.e., officers and officials, etc.) were required to provide for their personal winter clothing by themselves and at their costs when stationed in Norway, Finland, and in the 343

Eastern countries. Only by exception, i.e. when on service in areas with high grades of cold they could be issued with winter garments of stocks and without paying for them. However, an additional order dated 17 December 1942 prescribed that officer personnel were also issued winter garments as their troops.

An official price list of garments and equipment of 1942 lists the following winter garments:

- fur cap (Pelzkappe, Pelzmütze)
- woolen cap (Wollmütze)
- hood (Kopfhaube, Kappe)
- toque (Kopfschützer)

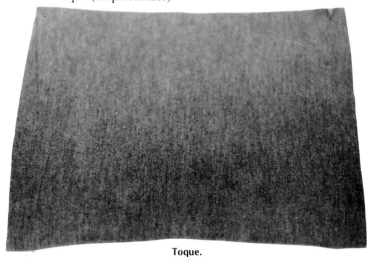

Toque.

Klaus Peters

The toque in wear by paratroopers.

- face mask (Gesichtsmaske, Nasen- und Wangenschutz)
- over-jacket, over-trousers, with or without white side (winter dress) (Überziehjacke, Überziehhose mit und ohne weisse Tarnseite - Winteranzug)
- snow shirt (Schneehemd), snow suit (Schneeanzug, Jacke, Hose)
- fur coat for guards (Postenpelz)
- fur jacket (Pelzjacke), fur vest (Pelzweste), fur trousers (Pelzhose) made of lamb's skin, rabbit's skin or other fur
- plush jacket (Plüschjacke)
- undertrousers, lined (undervest not mention although they were worn together)
- breast warmers, back warmers (Brust- und Rückenwärmer)
- mittens with long cuff (Fausthandschuhe mit Stulpe)
- knee protector (Knieschützer)
- long felt boots (Filzstiefel)
- straw boots (Strohschuhe)
- felt socks (Füsslinge aus Haarfilz)
- warming bag (Wärmebeutel)
- identification signal: a dual-colored armband of red and black (Armbinde rot-schwarz)

Dates of introduction and information about design and make have not been found. The following descriptions are based on the winter clothing of the army and on existing garments:

1. Winter Suit: The winter suit was a jacket and trousers, and was worn over the standard uniform. It came in three models:
    a. Light Winter Suit (leichter Winteranzug): made of doubled cloth (Doppeltuch—reversible) with a blue-grey side and a white side.
    b. Medium Winter Suit (mittlerer Winteranzug): doubled cloth with an inside woolen lining.
    c. Heavy Winter Suit (Schwerer Winteranzug): grey reversible to white cotton twill with a quilted internal layer of wadding or similar material.

It is presumed that production of the three models did not last throughout the remainder of the war due to the worsening supply of raw materials.

One side of the reversible winter suit was white for use as snow camouflage. The other side was blue-grey or grey with suits that came from the army stocks, but since 1943 it was colored in a splinter or water camouflage pattern. Because the white became easily dirty, it was to be worn outwards only when absolutely necessary.

Both sides of the winter suit were identical in size and position of pockets, openings, flaps, etc. The front of the jacket and the trousers slit were buttoned by additional inner and outer flaps to provide the best possible protection against wind and snow.

    1). Winter Jacket: The double-breasted jacket (Winterjacke) was with a sewn on hood, and reached down to the mid-

Heavy winter suit reversible from blue-grey to white. Note the different shade of blue on the button seal strip and hood.

thigh. The right front panel was with six buttons 12-13cm distant from the front edge. A flap with six buttonholes was sewn on a 17-18cm distance from the edge, which was buttoned over the the buttoned left front edge to serve as protection agains wind and snow. The inside of the jacket was a mirror image of the outer side.

The reversible heavy winter suit worn with the white side out. Note the button on the upper sleeve for attaching the dual-colored identification armband.

A 4cm wide passage with two seams for an inside drawstring for narrowing was at the waistline. It came out for fastening by two slits, which were positioned 7cm from the right front edge and 21cm from the left ledge. A similar drawstring was at the bottom end of the jacket.

There were two slanted hip pockets with a 17cm long opening, and a buttoned 8cm wide flap slightly pointed with rounded corners. Hidden by the flap was a slit for easy access to the pockets of the uniform.

A 6cm long and 2.5cm wide flap with a buttonhole was sewn into the rear sleeve seam. It was buttoned forward, with a second button to narrow the sleeves. A variant had a passage with an inside band coming out through two slits.

The hood of a double layer of cloth was cut large enough to fit over the steel helmet. It was sewn on around the collar line. A drawstring allowed it to be drawn tightly around the face. A vertical 3.5cm long buttoned loop was 347 sewn on just below the seam of the hood, centered on the back, for the purpose of holding the connecting cord of the mittens (per order HV 44B, No.278, dated 7 June 1944).

The buttons were of the style of the cloth tunic—blue-grey (black after 1943) on the outer side, and painted white on the white side.

Although sleeve rank insignia were prescribed for wear on the winter jacket, they were rarely worn.

One or two small buttons were sewn to the upper sleeve of the white side for fastening the identifying dual-colored armband used for recognition of friendly troops when both sides were wearing the white snow suit. The bands were worn or the colors were altered by the order of the day.

Winter heavy suit coat with water pattern camouflage introduced in 1943. The interior lining is blue-grey satin. It could also be reversible to white.

A medium winter suit of a splinter pattern camouflage. It is lined in silver-grey material and is not reversible.

Robert Olney

349

2). Winter Trousers: The winter trousers (Winterhose) extended over the waist, with the back cut slightly higher than the front. White webbed suspenders measuring 3.5-4cm wide were sewn to the back edge, sewn together crosswise at the back, and with two buttonholes on each running end to be fastened to small horn buttons in the front. Suspenders accompanying the 1943 pattern camouflage trousers were reversible camouflage and white, and with buttonholes on each running end.

The 31-32cm long trouser slit was prolonged on both edges by triangular flaps, which were put one upon another and buttoned by a buttonhole in the upper corner, and a button on the corresponding position on the other side of the slit. A 28cm long tape was sewn in on the right front, and with three buttonholes to be secured to one or more of three buttons on the left part. A variation model had slanted edges at the trouser with four buttonholes along the left edge to be secured to four buttons on the right front part.

Note the suspenders for the reversible trousers.

Feltrin

There were two slanted pockets with 18cm long openings and with buttoned flaps. There was often a slit below the flap for access to the uniform pockets.

There was a 12cm long open slit at the outer seams of each leg end, which was fastened by drawstring bands on the ends. A reinforcing pad was often sewn over the knees, finished with the same fabric and color.

The buttons were as those of the jacket, or black or white horn buttons. The trousers were sometimes quilted, probably depending on the material used for the internal layer.

2. Undersuit: An undersuit, consisting of a vest (Zwischenweste) and trousers (Zwischenhose) was developed at the same time as the winter suit, and was intended for wear under the standard field dress. For comfortable wear, however, the uniform garments should have been two sizes larger than normally worn by the wearer—albeit a somewhat unrealistic requirement.

The undersuit was made of a fabric of a brown shade, which was frequently slightly glossy, and was quilted with an inside lining of wadding material.

The vest was without collar, and was made with or without sleeves, buttoned or tape-fastened, and with a drawstring waist. The trousers had a drawstring waist, and were tapered and of calf-length.

Fur vests of many variations were also used, and were with or without sleeves. These fur vests were often of non-military origin. Individual improvisations included fur jerkins and quilted or pile jackets of many styles.

Quilted chest and back warmer being worn as an outer garment.

A sheep-skin vest in wear.

3. Hood: The reversible hood (Kappe or Kopfhaube) was usually made without an internal layer, and cut in form of the head with a wide collar protecting the shoulders. When closed, it formed an open oval around the face, and had elongated neck neck flaps reaching to the opposite side of the neck. The flaps were put one above the other, and fastened by a tape running as a drawstring half around the neck, and put with the ends through slits of the flaps. The hood was manufactured in three sizes.

4. Face Mask: The face mask (Gesichtsmaske) measured 15x30cm and was made without internal lining or wadding. It had a straight lower edge and rounded lateral edges, and was with two circular or semi-circular eye openings. Two bands were sewn on at either side to be fastened around the head.

There was a face mask made of dark brown leather with inside lining which covered the entire face. It had openings for eyes and mouth, and a sewn on triangular nose (for illustration, see chapter dealing with operational flight gear).

There are indications, however, that neither the hoods nor the face masks were produced or issued in large numbers, probably because the winter suits were usually worn without them.

5. Mittens: The padded reversible mittens (Fausthandschuhe) were of the color and material of the winter suits. They had an index finger to allow for firing the rifle. The cuffs were without internal lining and were secured around the wrist by a running band. Mittens without cuffs had a running band at the end. Each pair was connected by a long tape, which was secured by a loop at the back of the jacket to prevent loss. Fur mittens and fur gloves of all kinds were also used.

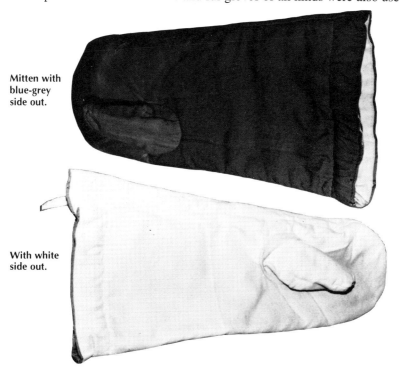

Mitten with blue-grey side out.

With white side out.

6. Footwear: Snow boots (Schneestiefel) were developed and introduced for wear with the winter suits. After enjoying only limited use, further production was probably discontinued.

The boots were made of waterproof, stiff, white webbing. Between the two layers of the legs, which were open at the upper rim, paper or straw for insulation was to be put in. The front of the legs was reinforced from the sole upwards by a narrow leather tape, ending in a 10cm long slash, which was laced up by a white leather tape or crod running through 6 to 8 pairs of grommeted eyelets. There was a wide leather reinforcing patch around the front above the sole.

Fur or felt boots of every kind and origin were often worn, to include over-boots of fur or plaited straw.

Over-socks (Füsslinge) were made of soft felt. They reached up to below the ankles. Normally they had a seam at the heel and a slightly reinforced sole. If over-socks were worn boots and overboots had to be of a slightly larger size than normally worn.

GFM Milch wears yet another pattern of snow boots.

Snow boots.

7. Fur Overcoats: A wide range of pattern variations of fur overcoats (Pelzmäntel) were worn for sentry or driver duty. The most frequently used fur was sheepskin, but any other fur was also worn. They were usually worn with the fur to the inside.

The coats came single or double-breasted. They were normally fastened in the front by loops and short pieces of wood rather than the large buttons and loops. The lay-down collar was with fur on the inside when turned up. The side pockets were normally of the patch-on pattern with flap, less frequently of the slanted muff pattern. Generals and high staff officers often preferred knee-length coats.

Felt winter boots in wear at left. Note wear of the sheep-skin vest at the right.

354

There were no regulations concerning rank insignia. Officers sometimes wore shoulder boards or sleeve rank insignia.

Blue canvas-like sheep-skin lined coat with five button (exposed) front closure. There are slash pockets at both sides at the waist. The collar is closed with a tab and button under the collar. There are no markings.

One of many styles of fur overcoats.

An array of winter over-garments, to include the pants, in wear.

Characteristic style sheep-skin lined coat with rank insigne sewn on.

Various cold weather clothing worn during fighting in Italy, 1944.

Not found on list of winter clothing:

Surcoat worn over the greatcoat as additional winter protection.

Bqrt

Wool knit scarf in folded configuration.

8. Fur Caps: There appears to have been no standard issue pattern fur cap (Pelzmütze) as there were many variation models. Fur caps were usually made of white, dark brown, black sheepskin or various colored rabbit fur or artificial fur. The outside was the leather side of the fur, which was sometimes covered by blue-grey basic cloth.

The front forehead flap, the ear flaps and the neck flap could be turned up. The ear flaps were secured in this position by a button and tape loop or by strings.

A variety of insignia was worn (and frequently none) on the forehead flap or, less frequently, on the cap above the flap—national emblem as found on the visor cap, with or without metal cockades; the large metal national emblem as found on the officer's white summer tunic; machine-embroidered national emblem as found on the field cap, or the larger variety as found on the flyer's blouse, with or without embroidered cockade.

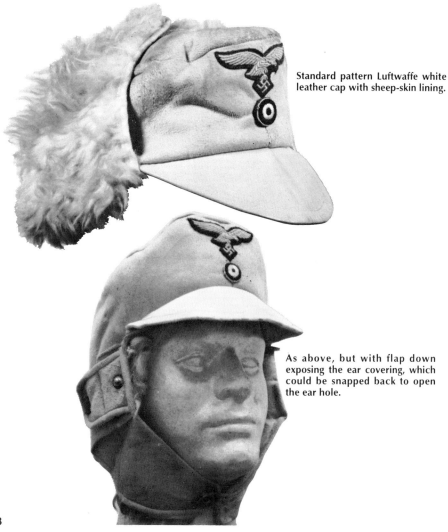

Standard pattern Luftwaffe white leather cap with sheep-skin lining.

As above, but with flap down exposing the ear covering, which could be snapped back to open the ear hole.

Charita

White leather cap in wear. Note the other pattern being worn in the center.

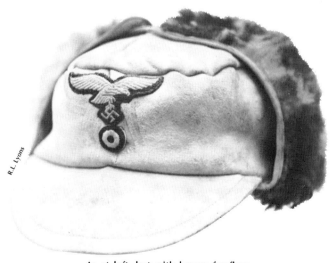

R.L. Lyons

As at left, but with brown fur flaps.

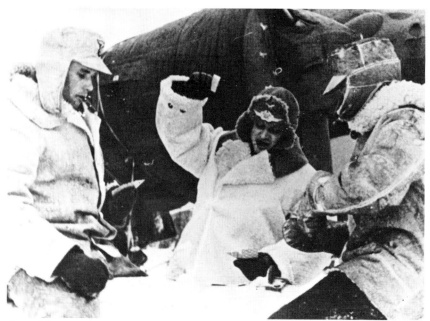

Three different patterns of fur caps being worn. Note the addition of the Luftwaffe wreath in the center.

Luftwaffe Hauptmann wears a variant pattern wool cap.

A frequently worn variant was of a similar design of the standard field cap with visor. The cap was rather high and was with visor, both covered with blue-grey cloth or felt. The fur was black, white or brown. The cap had an outside fur lining around the bottom edge of about one-third of its height.

Dark blue cap with fur lining.

White leather cap with wool lining.

Blue-grey fur cap with trapezoidal insignia sewn on.

Various winter caps in wear.

The ear flaps and the neck flap were fur-covered. The ear flaps were fastened by strings or buttoned over the head, or, when turned downwards, under the chin. Normally the national insigne of the visor cap or, less frequently, of the flyer's blouse was worn at the front, rarely with cockade.

White-painted M42 helmet with national emblem left exposed.

W.R. Maertz

This flak unit wears the reversible winter suit and white-painted helmet.

C. Camouflage Clothing: When the necessity of camouflage clothing for winter wear on a large scale and for all-year round wear arose it was developed in a short time in 1942—first by the Waffen-SS then by the army. However, white winter camouflage garments (snow smocks and anoraks) had been in wear by army mountain troops before the war.

A necessity for camouflage clothing, white or colored, arose only for the ground-combat elements of the Luftwaffe, i.e., the Hermann Göring units and the Luftwaffe Field Divisions. Introductory orders for camouflage clothing have not yet been located. Apparently, the army camouflage clothing was also produced for Luftwaffe units. For camouflage clothing of paratroops, see that respective chapter.

    1. Winter Camouflage Clothing:

        a. Steel Helmet: For winter camouflage, the steel helmet was normally painted white, usually with paint of a lime basis. As an expedient, the helmet was covered with white cloth fastened by a string or a rubber band around the helmet. For the doubled-colored helmet cover, see below.

        b. Snow Smocks: The snow smocks (Schneehemden) were made of light white fabrics, and came in various models, usually reaching down to any length between the knees and

Charita

Luftwaffe officer at the right wears the white snow smock.

Gen. Maj. Heidrich, commander of the 7th Flying Division, wears a snow smock.

ankles. Cut similiar to shirts, the smocks were loose-fitting to be worn over the equipment. The front slash opened down to the waist, and was buttoned by four to six buttons. While usually without collar, it sometimes did have a sewn-on hood or a wide collar. The sleeves were normally wide, often with drawstring closures at the ends. There were patterns with sleeves that reached down only to the elbows. Sometimes there were patch-on side pockets without flaps and with a pocket on the left breast. The back was often with a slit.

There were also capes buttoned down the front, and with or without a slit for the sleeves.

c. Anorak and Trousers: This suit was introduced at the end of 1942 or in early 1943. The suit was of a lightweight fabric— white on one side and reversible to a grey on the other, and worn over the standard field dress.

Buttons were normally grey/white cardboard, and sewn to the suit on both sides, usually with a reinforcing tape (dishpan or tunic buttons were infrequently used).

• Anorak: The anorak was cut in two panels with lateral and shoulder seams with a sewn-on hood with a drawstring rim around the face. The laced-up front usually had four pairs of grommeted eyelets. The laced front slit was covered by a sewn-on flap with three buttonholes on its left edge, and three buttons on the corresponding right side. A white drawstring cord allowed it to be tightened at the waist. Near the end of the sleeves was a 2cm wide fastening tape with a buckle on one end so that the sleeves were narrowed with the tape always on the outer side of the sleeve.

Three pockets were sewn on in a wide band across the front of the chest, both outer pockets with pleats, and the wider center pocket without. The pockets had buttoned flaps with a point in the center. Two rear pockets were positioned on both rear hips. The pocket bags were turned inside through horizontal openings with pointed, buttoned flaps.

A 5cm wide fastening tape was sewn on, centered on the back below the waistline, and was made of the same fabric as the anorak. Its purpose was to hold the anorak down by putting it between the legs and buttoning it to a button on the front. When not used, the tape was buttoned on the inside to a button positioned high on the back. One button on the front of the upper sleeves was used to fasten the armband worn to identify friendly troops.

Regulations prescribed the wear of sleeve rank insignia, but they were rarely worn. Privates were not authorized to wear sleeve rank insigna.

• Trousers: The trousers were held in place by drawstrings in the waistline. The ends of the legs were also secured by drawstrings. The trouser-slit was buttoned by a wide flap, usually with three buttons. Pockets with buttoned flaps were inserted into the lateral seams. The trousers did not enjoy the degree of issue as did the anorak.

2. Camouflage Clothing: It was not until 1942 that camouflage clothing was developed by the armed forces. Introductory orders for camouflage clothing have not yet been located.

Jackets tailored of camouflage fabrics of German or Italian origin were usually made of groundsheets, and in design and make of the blue-grey tunic, complete with shoulder boards/straps. They were sometimes worn by officers, especially general officers, of ground fighting forces.

a. Camouflage Patterns: There were two camouflage patterns, as those of the groundsheet and of the winter suit. The groundsheet pattern depicted the colors in an irregular geometrical

Three shades of splinter pattern camouflage.

splinter pattern, with the colors clearly divided from one another, and with short, narrow green or dark stripes all in the same direction across any color. The emphasis seemed to be on the green colors, with the light spring colors on one side, and the darker autumn colors on the other. The pattern developed for the winter suits had soft, dissolving colors blending into one another (water pattern) with emphasis on the brown colors.

Water pattern short pants—
probably made by a field tailor.

The Italian pattern, often used in makeshift uniforms for the camouflage and summer wear, especially in Italy, consisted of a sand-brown pattern with large color splotches of different colors.

Lt. Erich Hellmann wears a specially made jacket made of Italian camouflage material.

b. Camouflage Suits: The camouflage suit was introduced in 1942, but was generally issued to soldiers of ground fighting units. The suits were made of water-repellent artificial cotton fabric and came in both non-reversible and reversible to white models. Both splinter and water camouflage patterns were used on the non-reversible and reversible models, with minor variations in cut and manufacture, probably due to production conditions. The reversible suits were produced in limited numbers only. The suit was designed to fit over the standard dress, with the field equipment worn over the camouflage suit.

- Camouflage Smocks (Tarnjacke): The camouflage smock was a loose-fitting pullover without collar. It had a breast slit, reinforced on both edges, that was laced up by a cord passing through five pairs of grommeted eyelets. The wide bloused-fashion sleeves closed at the wrist by a narrow band buttoned at the rear by one of two buttons. There was a vertical or diagonal opening on each breast to allow easy access to the pockets of the blouse, with these openings often having buttoned flaps. Variations of the smock had slanted inside pockets with buttoned flaps on the hips. A drawstring fastening cord in the waistline allowed for a tighter fit. A variation model of the water pattern variety was with a sewn-on hood that eliminated the need of camouflage helmet covers. Although sleeve rank insignia were prescribed for wear, the smocks were most often worn without any grade insignia.

- Camouflage Trousers: The camouflage trousers (Tarnhose) for the smocks to which they belonged found even less distribution than the smock. They were held by a drawstring in the waistband. Drawstrings at the end of the slits allowed for a bloused effect with lace-up boots, or bloused over the top of the marching boots. The trouser slit was buttoned by a wide flap with tow or three buttons, similar to the trousers of the padded winter suit.

- Camouflage Coat: A camouflage coat with large fall-down collar, two concealed hip pockets with buttoned

Camouflage coat with metal "dish" buttons. The shoulder straps are the blue-grey with white ("HG") branch piping.

straight-edge flap, and buttoned cuffs was largely worn by the Luftwaffe Field Division units. It had a five button front closure to the neck, but was ususally worn with the top button open. Under each arm pit was a slit to allow for air circulation. A Luftwaffe national emblem, usually with the camouflage backing, was sewn to the right breast. Shoulder straps or boards were usually worn, denoting the rank of the wearer.

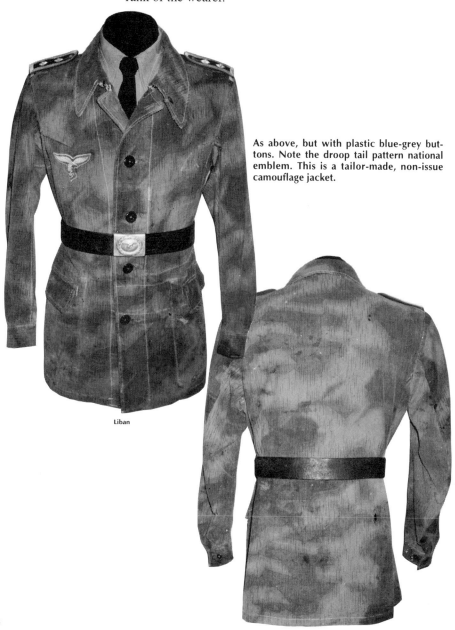

As above, but with plastic blue-grey buttons. Note the droop tail pattern national emblem. This is a tailor-made, non-issue camouflage jacket.

Liban

3. Helmet Camouflage: Until the end of 1942 there were neither prescribed regulations or standard issue material for helmet camouflage. Therefore, camouflage material—grass, foliage, etc.,— were retained on the helmet by makeshift inventions of the wearer. A common technique was the use of a wide rubber band, usually cut from old tire tubes, into which was placed the camoulflage material. Leather straps, carrying strap of the breadbag, wire, string, etc., were used as well. Crudely made helmet covers made of groundsheets or of sackcloth were sometimes used.

- Camouflage Helmet Cover: The helmet cover (Tarnüberzug) was introduced in 1942.It was made of groundsheet fabric in both splinter and water patterns. Some models were reversible with white on the other side. The cover was sewn together of five segments with a drawstring to hold the cover down below the rim of the helmet. **369**

Some models had five to seven fabric stripes evenly distributed around the cover for attching foliage, etc.

Splinter pattern camouflage helmet cover.

R.L. Lyons

Tan and green camouflaged, double-decal Luftwaffe helmet with wire frame for foliage.

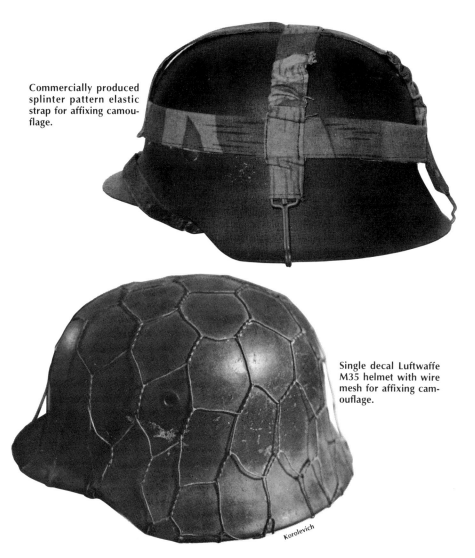

Commercially produced splinter pattern elastic strap for affixing camouflage.

Single decal Luftwaffe M35 helmet with wire mesh for affixing camouflage.

Korolevich

- Camouflage Net: The army pattern camouflage net (Stahlhelmtarnnetz) was introduced by order (LV 42, No.2326) dated 3 September 1942 for ground combat units. The rectangular net was knotted of thin string, with a drawstring drawn through the net. The net was put over the helmet and secured by pulling the drawstring below the rim of the helmet. To hooks, to be inserted fore and aft, between the helmet and its lining were linked with two small rings of the net. One longer end of the net was to fall down in front of the face for camouflage. Camouflage material was inserted between net and helmet. When not used for camouflage, the net was rolled up and put inside the helmet.

Gebrauchsanweisung

für das Stahlhelmtarnnetz.

1. Anbringung der Befestigungshaken am Stahlhelm.

a) Vorderer Haken: Der Haken (Abb. 1) wird zwischen Außenring der Innenausstattung und Stahlhelm durchgeschoben — wobei die Enden zweckmäßig etwas gedreht und flach nebeneinander gelegt werden — und in den Außenring eingehängt. Hierauf wird der Haken eng um den Stahlhelmrand gelegt und fest angedrückt (f. Abb. 2 und 3).

b) Rückwärtiger Haken: Der Haken wird zwischen Innenring und Außenring der Innenausstattung durchgeschoben und wiederum im Außenring eingehängt, sodann fest um den Stahlhelmrand gelegt und angedrückt (f. Abb. 2 und 3).

2. Anbringung des Netzes am Stahlhelm.

Das Netz wird mit der Spannschnur b) zwischen den beiden Knoten bei a) (Abb. 4) am Vorderhaken des Helms eingehängt. Dann wird es über den Stahlhelm gezogen, die Spannschnur gespannt und mit der Hand gedreht. Die dadurch unter dem rückwärtigen Haken gekreuzte Schnur wird in diesen eingehängt (Abb. 7 bis 9), der Ring er alsdann unter eine passende Masche geschoben, so daß er unter dem Netz liegt und zum Haken zeigt. Damit ist die Spannung gesichert.

Der Gesichtsteil wird bei Nichtgebrauch zurückgeschlagen und mit beiden Hälften im Netz eingehängt.

3. Gebrauch des Netzes.

Zum Tarnen wird der Verschluß geöffnet, wobei die verkreuzte Schnur aus dem Haken springt. Dann wird das Netz nach vorn über den Helm gelegt und auseinandergebreitet (Abb. 5). Nachdem Tarnmaterial daraufgelegt ist (Abb. 6), wird der Stahlhelm nachgestürzt und das Netz in gleicher Weise wie unter 2. beschrieben verspannt.

Zum Enttarnen wird das nach vorn gekippte Netz ausgeschüttelt.

4. Bei längerem Nichtgebrauch wird das Netz abgenommen und im oberen Innenraum des Helmes untergebracht.

5. Tarnmaterial.

Als Tarnmaterial eignet sich selbst empfindlichstes Material, wie trockenes Laub, trockenes Farnkraut, Steppenmoos, kurzes Gras, in gleicher Weise wie Rübenblätter, Heidekraut, Getreide, Schilf, Rindenstückchen, Laub und Stoffstücke.

Um die Tarnung besonders wirksam zu machen, empfiehlt es sich, das Tarnmaterial zwischen einzelnen Maschen des Netzes etwas herauszuziehen. Es ist ferner darauf zu achten, daß bei längeren Gras- oder Getreidehalmen diese die gleiche Richtung unter dem Netz haben wie das umgebende Getreide oder Gras usw.

Zur Tarnung der Schultern werden — wenn es das Gelände ergibt — einzelne Halme, Äsichen oder Gräser seitlich unter der Spannschnur herausgezogen. —

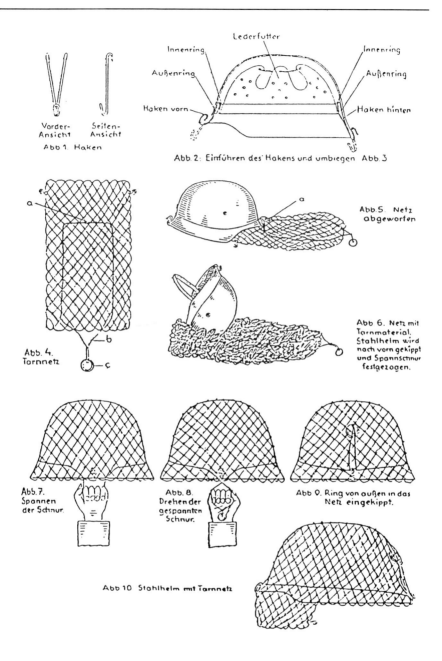

Vorder-Ansicht   Seiten-Ansicht

Abb 1. Haken

Lederfutter

Innenring   Innenring

Außenring   Außenring

Haken vorn   Haken hinten

Abb. 2: Einführen des Hakens und umbiegen Abb. 3

Abb. 5. Netz abgeworfen

Abb 6. Netz mit Tarnmaterial. Stahlhelm wird nach vorn gekippt und Spannschnur festgezogen.

Abb. 4. Tarnnetz

Abb. 7. Spannen der Schnur.

Abb. 8. Drehen der gespannten Schnur.

Abb 9. Ring von außen in das Netz eingekippt.

Abb 10. Stahlhelm mit Tarnnetz

CHAPTER • 30
THE PARACHUTE TROOPS

P aratroop units of the Luftwaffe and army were established respectively in early 1936 and early 1937, with the first units incorporated into the Infantry Demonstration Regiment of the army, and into the Regiment "General Göring" of the Luftwaffe. At the urging of Göring, who insisted that "everything that flies" was his sphere of authority, army components came under the auspices of the Luftwaffe on 1 January 1939, resulting in the amalgamation of both components to form the 1st Parachute Regiment of the Luftwaffe. Other parachute regiments were constituted after the outbreak of war. Since 1943, the parachute troops were considerably expanded to eventually comprise ten parachute divisions, two parachute corps and one parachute army. However, the divisions formed during the final phase of the war never reached their full Table of Organization and Equipment strength. It should be noted that the "Hermann Göring" units should not be regarded as part of the parachute troops despite their general prefix "Fallschirm-..." (parachute), which was awarded to these units in February 1944.

When the parachute forces were expanded in 1943, the number of volunteers apparently was insufficient to form the units as planned. Therefore, on 20 September 1943 (LV 43, No.1826) Göring proclaimed an appeal to volunteer because, "the Führer...had ordered a new considerable expansion of these units." Still, the number of volunteers did not meet the demands. So, on 29 November 1943, Göring issued another proclamation to move his soldiers to volunteer. Flying personnel and certain specialist listed in an annex of the second appeal were, however, exempted from volunteering.

The new parachute units gained their fame in the French Campaign (particularly operations bringing about the seizure of the fortress at Eben Emael), and in the airborne operation of Crete in 1941. Due to the heavy losses at Crete, however, major German airborne operations were inhibited in the future, with the consequence that the parachute units were employed at the focus of operations at all theaters of war. Parachute training did, however, continue, but on a limited scale.

The German paratroops developed their peculiar "esprit des corps," and were regarded as elite units. Their fighting spirit and the greenish color of their jump smocks earned them the epithet "green devils" by the Allied troops.

At the end of 1936, the army constituted its parachute unit as a Parachute Infantry Company (Fallchirm-Infanteriekompanie), which was incorporated as the 15th Company of the Infantry Demonstration Regiment (Infanterie-Lehrregiment) per order (HM 37, No.181) dated 31 March 1937. Their branch color was white, and they wore the insignia of the regiment, a Gothic "L" on shoulder boards/straps. The company was enlarged to an (independent) Parachute Infantry Battalion (Fallschirm-Infanteriebataillon) per order (HM 38, No.286) dated 15 March 1938, and to become effective on 1 June 1938. The shoulder straps/boards now displayed the intertwined Gothic letters "FJ." By an order (OKH No.4840/38 g.AHA/In 2 IX) dated 30 December 1938 the battalion was transferred to the Luftwaffe on 1 January 1939, and was absorbed with the designation of IInd Battalion, 1st Parachute Regiment. Recipients of the army pattern parachutist's badge were authorized to continue to wear the badge in lieu of the Luftwaffe pattern badge.* The army pattern badge took the basic form of the Luftwaffe pattern, but with a gold-colored oakleaf wreath with a national (Wehrmacht pattern) emblem above, and with the silver-colored diving eagle without a swastika. Development of the special paratroop clothing was executed by both the army and Luftwaffe. The special army pattern system of grade insignia of the jump smock (NCOs with Tresse and pips on the collar, and officers with Tresse rings on the lower sleeves) was worn in lieu of the Luftwaffe pattern. After the transfer of the army units to the Luftwaffe, the Luftwaffe uniform was issued as quickly as possible, but a mixture of army and Luftwaffe garments was worn during the transition period. The army pattern national emblem on the jump smocks and steel helmets continued to be worn, at least until mid-1940.

*Note: On December 18, 1943 all former members of the FIK/FIB were issued the Luftwaffe parachutist's badge, but none opted to wear it in place of their army issue.

This photo was taken at Stendal in August 1936. This early paratroop unit was entitled "Fliegergruppe (F)," but redesignated "Fallschirmschule 1" in late 1936.

These members of the Fall. Inf. Bn. wear the early, full double zipper smock and Luftwaffe paratroop helmet.

The Luftwaffe considered an eventual formation of parachute units since the end of 1935. By an order (Der R.d.L. u. Ob.d.L. No.262/36 g. III, 1A) dated 29 January 1936 15 volunteer officers and NCOs of the Regiment "General Göring" were committed to parachute training "in preparation of the Regiment 'General Göring' to jump training." These first "Parachute Rifles" (Fallschirmschützen) (as they were initially officially termed, but this was

Shoulder strap for NCO with "Fl" and strap slip tab with "Fz"—both with the army acceptance tags.

Army paratroops, some wearing the smock, prepare to depart via train. Note the wear of the "Fallschirmjäger Regiment 1" sleeveband.

White embroidered "FI" (the "J" is a German "I") on the Waffenrock of a Junior NCO of the Parachute Infantry Battalion.

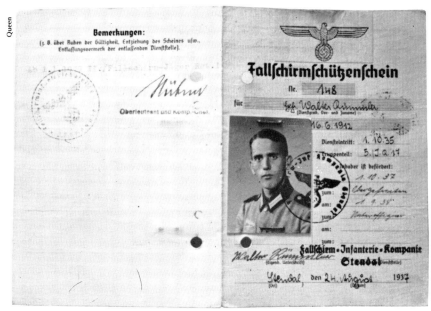

Army parachute license dated 24 August 1937.

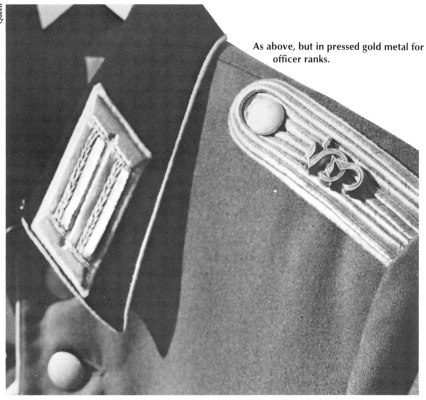

As above, but in pressed gold metal for officer ranks.

As above, but in pressed gold metal for officer ranks.

changed to "Fallschirmjäger" in March 1939) were to become the nucleus of the cadre and training personnel of all future volunteers.

Jump training was performed at the Parachute School at Stendal. After return to the regiment the parachutists were concentrated in the Ist (Rifle) Battalion [I.(Jäger-) Bataillon] and the Pioneer Company of the Regiment "General Göring." Since 1939, the organizational development of paratroop units was as follows:

- 1 October 1937: Renaming of the Ist (Rifle) Battalion and the Pioneer Company as IVth (Parachute) Battalion, Regiment "General Göring" [IV.(Fallschirmschützen-) Bataillon].
- March 1938: Transfer of the IVth Battalion to the newly formed Fallschirmjägerregiment 1 as its Ist Battalion. Until 1 January 1939, the regiment consisted of one battalion only.
- 1938: Constitution of the 7th Flying Division, which controlled parachute training, equipment, and air transport. It was reinforced by the 16th Infantry Regiment (of the 22nd Infantry Division), which was trained in airborne operations, and by an air landing battalion (Luftlandebataillon), which was temporarily formed by volunteers of the SA-Standarte "Feldherrnhalle" for the occupation of Sudentenland and Czechoslovakia, and for wartime mobilization. The division was disbanded in December 1940.
- 1 January 1939: Parachute Infantry Battalion of the army was transferred to the Luftwaffe with designation as IInd Battalion, Fallschirmjägerregiment 1.
- Early 1940: Constitution of the 2nd and 3rd Parachute Regiments (Fallschirmjägerregiment 2 and 3), Parachute Signal Battalion (Fallschirm-Nachrichtenabteilung), etc.
- December 1940: Concentration of all paratroops under the command of the XIth Airborne Corps (XI.Fliegerkorps).
- Early 1942: Constitution of the 1st Parachute Brigade (1.Fallschirmjäger-Brigade) for the North African Campaign. Under the command of Generalmajor Ramcke, thus also known as "Brigade Ramcke."
- 1943: Constitution of the 1st to 4th Parachute Divisions.
- 1944: Constitution of the 5th to 8th Parachute Divisions.
- 1944: Formation of the Ist and IInd Parachute Corps (I. and II.Fallschirm-Korps), and a Parachute Army (Fallschirm-Armee), including the necessary General Headquarters Troops.
- Early 1945: Constitution of the 9th and 10th Parachute Divisions.

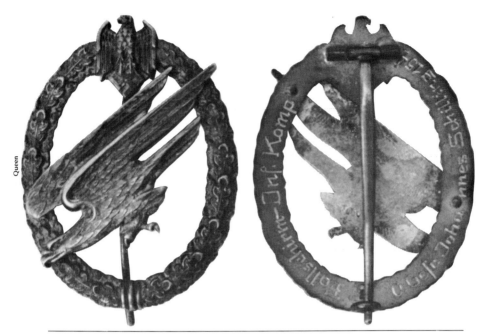

Army-pattern paratroop badge, made of "800" fine silver, and engraved on the reverse with O. Gefr. Schilling's name and unit (see his photo at lower right).

Below: As badge above, but with O. Gefr. Eger's name and unit engraved on the reverse. These badges in silver were not issued, but privately purchased from local jewelers. Note that the eagle is silver, and the wreath gold.

Award document for the army paratroop badge.

Queen

Queen

This aluminum version of the army paratroop badge has "Obj. Nikolas" scratched on the reverse. Heinz Nikolas was a member of "Sondergruppe Peters," and jumped on the bridge at Moerdijk. Note it has been repaired.

Queen

Queen

Another example of an aluminum badge which is totally unmarked.

O. Gefr. Johannes Schilling wears the metal version of the army paratroop badge.

Two assault gunners, both wearing the army pattern paratroop badge—left in metal, and right in cloth.

Machine-embroidered Luftwaffe paratroop badge.

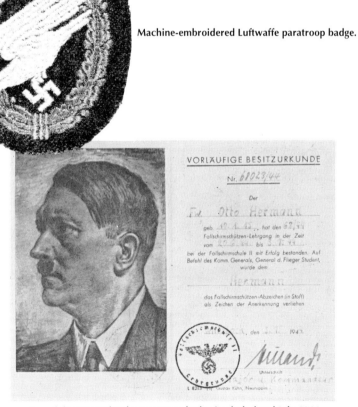

Award document for the paratroop badge in cloth dated July 1944.

Metal versions of the Luftwaffe Paratroop badge worn by enlisted paratroops.

Enlisted paratrooper at the right wears the embroidered
Luftwaffe pattern Parachutist's badge on his left breast pocket.

Paratroop NCO candidate wears the branch color of golden-yellow distinctive of the flying branch, of which the paratroop units were a part.

The paratroop units were not an independent branch, but rather a sub-branch of the Flying Branch, and therefore had as its branch color golden-yellow (without any further differentiation for artillery, engineer, etc.). Distinctive to the paratroop units were the lowest enlisted rank "Jäger" and lowest NCO rank "Oberjäger" (vice Unteroffizier). Graduates of the parachute school were awarded the Parachutist's Badge.

At ceremonial parades or, when so ordered, a distinctive parade dress was worn consisting of the paratrooper's unique articles—steel helmet, jump smock, trousers, lace-up boots, gauntlets, and parachute harness without parachute. Enlisted personnel with rifles wore the bayonet and ammunition pouches on the leather belt, while officers wore their brown leather belt with cross strap.

Paratroops on parade in Berlin, 20 April 1939 (Hitler's birthday). Note the wear of the parachute harness without the parachute, and the ammunition bandoleers.

The battalion colors of Fallschirmjägerregiment 1 differed considerably from the standard colors of the Flying Branch with the golden-yellow field. The Ist Battalion retained the colors of the Landespolizei design that it was awarded when it was designated as Ist Battalion/Regiment "General Göring," and was retained when it was renamed as IVth Battalion. The IInd Battalion, the former Parachute Infantry Battalion of the army, retained its white swallow-tailed standard. The award of colors to the IIIrd Battalion, which was formed in mid-1939, has not been confirmed, but if awarded, was probably the golden-yellow of the Flying Branch.

1. **Cuff Titles:** A cuff title (Ärmelstreifen) was introduced for the 1st Parachute Regiment, made of dark green cloth with the inscription "Fallschirm-Jäger Rgt.1" per order (Der R.d.L. u. Ob.d.L. No.7045/38 g.K.Iv, 1b) dated 2 February 1939. The order stated the inscription as "... Regt.1," but all cuff titles instead read "... Rgt. 1". Additionally, specimens exist with the inscription "Fallschirm-Jäger-Rgt.1". An order (BLB 39, No.567) dated 19 August 1939 introduced a cuff title "Fallschirm-Division" to be worn by all other paratroop units of the 7th Flying Division, including the Parachute School. The order stated that introduction of titles for the 2nd and **385**

3rd Parachute Regiments was to be "reserved." Actually, these were introduced at an unknown date in 1940. Specimens also exist without the dividing hyphen e.g. "Fallschirm Division."

The orders stated the color of the titles was to be dark green, but they were actually a medium (Jäger) green. The embroidered inscription was in Gothic lettering. The grade groups were distinguished as follows:

- officers: aluminum hand-embroidery with 3mm wide aluminum "soutache" border sewn on top and bottom.
- NCOs: matte grey or white-grey machine-embroidery with 3mm "soutache" border of the same color sewn on top and bottom.
- privates: same as NCOs, but without the borders.

The cuff title was worn on the right lower sleeve of the tunic immediately above the open cuff. Hauptfeldwebel ranks wore the title above the Tresse rings of the sleeve. Unlike enlisted personnel, officers were permitted its wear on the flyer's blouse and on the white summer tunic at a corresponding position. The right to wear the cuff titles was only granted to officers, NCOs and privates on TO&E positions of the respective units, and to officers of the body of reserves and retirees of these units. Wear, however, was denied to medical officers, medical personnel, officials and members of the Corps of Engineer and the Nautical Corps, but photographic evidence indictates this restriction was violated. Cuff titles were not generally worn during the war.

2. **Special Clothing and Equipment of Paratroops:** The basic special clothing and equipment (Sonderbekleidung and Sonderausrüstung) was originally developed in cooperation between the army and the Luftwaffe. All special articles were retained when the paratroop units were eventually employed exclusively in ground combat.

Unless otherwise stated, the following articles were introduced by an order (BLB 38, No.1450) dated 15 March 1938. Articles previously issued, which partially served for test and evaluation purposes, continued to be worn until replaced or worn out. Original German designations will be used, but remember that the prefix "Fallschirmschützen-..." was altered to "Fallschirmjäger-..." sometime in 1940.

  a. Jump Smock: The jump smock, officially termed "Fallschirm-schützen-Bluse" (paratroop blouse), was not-so-affectionately named "bones sack" (Knochensack) by the soldiers. The smock, which became the paratroops most distinctive article of clothing, was worn over the standard field dress, with the equipment worn over the smock (under at the time of the actual parachute jump).

Three different models existed—the first regarded as the test model for troop evaluation. The first two models were made of water-repellent strong cotton fabric mixed with artificial threads (Zellwolle), and had a greenish shade, which was officially termed "green mottled" (grünmeliert). These were of the step-in pattern with short legs reaching to about mid-thighs. The third model took the form of a jacket made of camouflage fabrics. Each model varied to some degree in details and color.

The Luftwaffe pattern national emblem was worn on the right breast. However, camouflage smocks frequently lacked the emblem. Smocks with the army pattern national emblem were still worn in mid-1940.

Privates wore their standard pattern grade chevrons (1cm wide blue-grey subdued Tresse on a backing of basic fabric) on the left upper sleeve. NCOs and officers wore their grade insignia as a system of white bars and wings on a backing of basic fabric, and of the patterns prescribed for the garments of the special clothing. It should be noted, however, that the grade insignia were sometimes lacking, especially on camouflage smocks.

Ernst Fromming (left) and Lt. Geiger (right) attend an awards ceremony in Berlin, October 1944. note the unauthorized wear of decorations on the smocks.

Period photos depicting wear of medals, badges and campaign titles on the smock are misleading as they were worn only on the day of award (if the

NCO tunic with the "Fallschirm-Jäger Rgt. 1" sleeveband without borders. Note the interior marking of the tunic also showing assignment to the same regiment.

See tunic
at left.

Senior NCO tunic with the sleeveband worn on the lower right
sleeve.

A NCO's version.

Private, preparing for a jump, wears his rank stripe on the upper left sleeve of his smock.

smock was prescribed for wear at the ceremony) and at special occasions when so ordered. Even then, they were only temporarily affixed.

- First (Test) Model Jump Smock: The step-in smock was with two metal zippers at the front, beginning at the collar with approximately 5cm between their ends, and running slightly diagonally down to the groin. The unzipped front flap allowed the wearer to rapidly disrobe by stepping out of the smock. When closed both zipper slides were secured by short cloth flaps, positioned below the collar seams, and sewn on by their right ends, while the left ends were fastened by a press snap. The soft stand-up collar measured about 3cm high, and was closed in the front from right to

Army paratroop wearing the first model jump smock as denoted by the two front zippers. Note the short cloth flaps securing the zipper pulls and the Luftwaffe decal on the helmet.

left by a flap with one press snap, and two lower parts of press snaps on the left side of the collar. The device was used to narrow the collar. The very short legs were with drawstring or elastic ends. There was an opening, closed by a zipper, at both sides in the side seam. This allowed the wearer to reach into the trouser pockets while wearing the smock. The sleeves had bloused ends, closed by a press snap, with two lower parts to narrow the sleeve.

Left and below: The first model jump smock in wear. Note the three snap closure on the leg flap of the man at far left. Normally the flap had two snaps. Note also the use of both the Army and early Luftwaffe breast eagle.

- Second Model Jump Smock: The standard model smock was made of greenish fabric, but grey smocks also existed—probably as a test and evaluation model. A splinter-pattern step-in pattern was produced in late 1940, and saw use during the invasion of Crete on 20 May 1941. Initial patterns were without pockets as the smock was intended as a "coverall" to prevent equipment from fouling the suspension lines. However, this was changed when the smock was adopted for standard wear. Transition smocks will have a varied number of pockets until such time the standardized version was fully introduced for distribution, at which time the earlier pocketless versions were used for ground training.

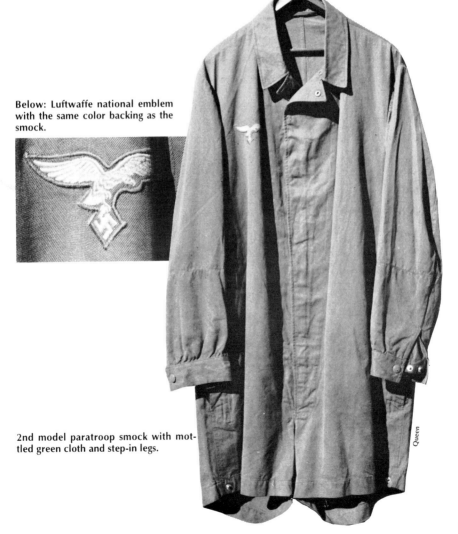

Below: Luftwaffe national emblem with the same color backing as the smock.

2nd model paratroop smock with mottled green cloth and step-in legs.

Queen

Charita

Heavy-weight Boxing Champion, Max Schmeling (left), wears the standard 2nd pattern jump smock.

Charles Hinz

This green, second model jump smock is a step-in version, and has breast and thigh zippered pockets with flaps.

Variant 2nd pattern smock with horizontal zipper thigh pockets as well as smocks without thigh pockets. Hitler has just decorated these heroes of the assault on Fort Eban Emal. Note that there are one and two breast pocket varieties, and all are with exposed zippers.

The cut was in two front panels, two back panels (with a center seam), two panels for each sleeve, and the collar. The legs were approximately 15cm long, and their ends were about 35cm wide and without drawstring or elastic seam. The bottom was rather widely cut so that the equipment could be worn underneath the smock. The weight was about 1.1kg.

The front was open from the collar to approximately 7cm above the crossing point of the seams at the crotch. Both edges reached over the vertical center line of the breast for approximately 4cm above and 1 - 2cm below. On the both inside edges a tape of basic fabric was sewn on with a width of 13cm above and 3cm below at the right edge and 7cm at the left edge. The left edge was additionally reinforced by a 6cm wide tape of nettle fabric between. The front was closed upwards by a zipper, with the zipper ending about 17cm below the collar. The upper portion of the front was closed by four press snaps. Three upper parts of press snaps were positioned at 1.5cm distance from the left front edge and 2, 13 and 22cm respectively below the collar seam, and a fourth upper part was positioned at a horizontal distance of 6cm from the uppermost snap. The four lower parts of the press snaps were accordingly positioned at the right front.

The lay-down collar was made of double-laid fabric with a stiffening inlay. Its stand-up portion was 1cm high at the front and 4cm high at the back, and the width of the lay-down collar was 6cm at the front and 5cm at the back. When the collar was worn open, both upper front edges were turned outwards in the length to the center press snap, and thus formed short lapels. When worn in this manner the collar of the flyer's blouse was frequently turned outside the collar of the smock.

Frhr. v.d. Heydte wears the 2nd model jump smock.

Below: The 2nd model jump smock in wear with rank insignia.

The slight curved sleeves narrowed from the elbows down. By an order (BLB 38, No.550) dated 11 August 1938 the front panel was prolongated by a 6cm long wedge-shaped attachment to the panel to allow better movement of the arm. The rear seam was slashed at the end for a length of approximately 11cm. The slash was closed by a press snap. The sleeves ended in a blouse fashion with a 5cm wide band with two upper parts of press snaps and one lower part to fasten or narrow the sleeve ends. A 17cm long inner sleeve was sewn to the sleeve 20cm from its end, to serve as protection against the wind. Its rear seam had an 8cm long slash, which was buttoned by a press snap, and the seamed end had an inside rubber band.

The seam of the armpit was covered on the inside by a twill tape. For ventilation, the connecting seam between body portion and sleeves was open at the bottom for a length of 10cm. Below the slash six eyelets of 5mm in diameter each were positioned on the side of the body to allow for additional ventilation.

The lateral seams of the body were reinforced on the side by a tape of basic fabric, which was approximately 13cm wide a the armpit and tapered downwards to a width of 4cm, and ended 15cm above the end of the legs. A 20cm long opening, closed with a zipper, was positioned at either lateral seam and from the waistline down to reach into the trouser pockets. Three eyelets were positioned in either lateral seam at the waistline and spaced 1.5cm apart, to put through the belt hooks of the flyer's blouse to facilitate carrying the leather belt with full field equipment. At the ends of the legs and immediately forwards of the lateral seam one upper part of a press snap was affixed from the inside, with the lower part about 10cm towards the rear. The purpose of the snap was to narrow the legs when the parachute harness was worn.

Gibbons

Guards, dressed in the 2nd model jump smock with horizontal thigh pockets, secure a field headquarters after the fall of Crete.

There were several variants of the smock, which were probably produced in early 1940. The pockets were of the inserted variety, and were closed with metal zippers without a covering tape. Smocks with pockets may be regarded as transitional models to the third model smock. The variants were as follows:

- pattern as above, but buttoned at the front and with a concealed buttonhole tape at the left front.
- with breast pockets at either breast, which were positioned slightly lower and slightly more slanted as with the third model smock.
- with one breast pocket only at the left breast, and with or without thigh pockets.
- with pockets at the upper thighs with a horizontal zipper.
- with breast and thigh pockets; this variant also came as a camouflage smock.

Unidentified Oberst, wearing the 2nd model green or grey smock, confirms his units' location with another officer of his command.

A camouflage version of the 2nd Model smock in wear.

Flock

Bernhard Ludwig/Jim Haley

- Third Model Jump Smock: Since about mid-1940 a third model smock was introduced. The basic pattern of the second model smock as retained, but it now took the more practical form of a front buttoned coat. Its inserted pockets were with zippers and covering flaps. Except for early manufactured smocks made of the same green mottled fabric as the second model, they now came in three distinct camouflage patterns, which were those used by the army. The use of the various patterns was based on availability of fabrics. The patterns of camouflage were as follows:
  - "Splinter" equipment as used on the groundsheet: It depicted the colors in an irregular geometrical "splinter" pattern, with the colors clearly divided from one another, and with short, narrow green or dark stripes all in the same direction across any color. The emphasis seemed to be on the green colors.

Standard 3rd pattern "splinter" smock with horizontal thigh pockets with tape cover. Note the "holster" at the right rear of the smock.

Feltrin

399

Charita

General Student decorates paratroops who are wearing the 3rd pattern "splinter" smock. Note the horizontal thigh pockets and the wear of the web tropical belt.

Klaus Peters

The 2nd and 3rd pattern smocks in wear.

Note the array of smocks, in particular the one third from the right, and their camouflage patterns.

- "Water" pattern as used for the winter suits: Soft, dissolving, "watering" various color transitions, with emphasis on the brown colors. Used since 1942.

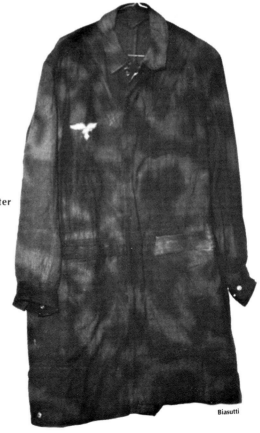

3rd pattern smock with "water pattern" camouflage.

Biasutti

- Italian pattern: A sand-brown pattern with large color splotches of different colors. Smocks of Italian pattern fabrics were manufactured in limited number after the surrender of Italy in fall of 1943 when Italian army stocks were captured.
- Tan tropical pattern: Designed to be used for the planned invasion of Malta. Few were actually produced.

This painting of a German paratrooper in Italy during the 1943/44 time period clearly shows the tropical jump smock in wear. It was painted by Olaf Jordan.

Cut and make of the smock was with the front buttoned by four of five 2.3cm diameter buttons from the collar to below the waistline, with a concealed buttonhole tape along the left front edge. The length reached to nearly the knees. The skirts could be fastened around the leg in a trouser-like fashion, and secured by press snaps on the inside of the thighs. The press snap at the end of the lateral seems was retained.

The inserted pockets were closed by metal zippers, which were covered by narrow rectangular tapes of basic fabric. The tapes were sewn on with the edges of their narrow sides and one broad side, with open edge outwards with the breast pockets and downwards with the thigh pockets. The breast pockets were positioned very high and slanted inwards, and the thigh pockets were positioned horizontally and with the flaps above the height of the crotch.

The opening at the lateral seams was omitted. At the waistline a short flap with a press button was sewn into the lateral seams, to allow for the narrowing of the waist by two lower parts of press buttons positioned forwards. At the right back was a holster for a flare pistol, which later was omitted. The holster consisted of a small pocket for the end of the barrel, and a larger pocket with a flap (with press snap) for the grip of the pistol. Some smocks had sewn on fabric loops and/or D-rings for attaching articles of equipment.

    b. Dragging Smock: A special dragging smock (Schleifanzug für Fallschirmschützen) was stocked at the parachute school only, and issued to trainees for basic training to preserve the jump smocks. The term was derived from one of the first steps in training when the trainee was dragged over the ground by his parachute, which was driven by the air stream caused by the propeller of a wind-machine, with the purpose to learn to free himself from the parachute harness. As the smocks obviously were exposed to heavy wear and tear a 2m long bale of basic fabric was provided for each dragging smock.

The smock was of the step-in pattern, and made of olive-green strong fabric. The weight was approximately 2.2kg. The front consisted of one panel, and the back was cut of two panels with a horizontal seam at the waistline. The short legs reached to about mid-calf length. The front slash opened in full length to 6cm above the crotch seams, with the edges prolongated to reach over the center breast line for 2.5cm at the left side and 6cm at the right. The opening was buttoned by a concealed buttonhole tape with eight buttonholes on the left edge and eight 2.2cm diameter buttons at the right edge. Four tucks each about 20cm long were distributed on the left and right front and back. A

The troopers are positioned on the ground behind the wind machine.

20cm long opening of the lateral seams at either hip was closed by zipper, which was covered by a flap sewn on at three sides.

The lay-down collar was made of two layers of basic fabric. It was closed by two leather straps of 1.6cm in width and 23cm and 25cm in length, which were sewn to the left stand-up part of the collar and the underside of the lay-down part. For fastening they were pulled through a pair of 2.5cm diameter rings which were correspondingly sewn on by short leather tabs at the right side of the collar.

The sleeves were made of two panels, and lined with olive-green lining fabric. The rear seam ended in a slash, which was fastened towards the rear by two buttons at the center and the end and two buttonholes. A second button was placed rearwards of the lower button to narrow the sleeves. The legs had a slash at the outward lateral seam, which was narrowed by leather straps with a buckle.

> c. Trousers: The trousers were officially termed "Fallschirm-schützen-Hose" (paratroop trousers). They were made of green mottled cloth of the color of the field blouse of the army. The lining was fieldgrey twill fabric. The cut was in two front and two rear panels. The weight was approximately 1kg.

The waist edge was horizontal and had two tucks at the back distanced each 15cm apart from the lateral seams. The lining of the waist measured 6cm wide around the front between the tucks and 10cm wide at the back. It was connected with the panels by a horizontal seam running at the front between the lateral seams at a distance of 5cm below the waist rim and at the rear 3cm below the rim. The fly was buttoned by a concealed buttonhole tape with four buttonholes at the left edge of the front slash and a fifth button (right) and buttonhole (left) below the rim. The seams of the crotch were covered on the inside by a rounded patch of lining of about 17cm in length and 20cm in width.

To adjust the width of the waist, there were two narrow straps of basic cloth on the left and right hip, and 7cm below the waist rim. Each rearward section of the straps measured 13cm long and 3cm wide at the rear and where it was sewn into the seam of the tuck, and tapered to 2cm at the pointed forward end. The friction buckle was held by a loop of double-laid twill, which was sewn into the lateral seam.

Cloth loops below the waist rim allowed to hold the leather belt when the trousers were worn without a suspender. The loops had a vertical inner width of 6cm. Three cloth 1.5cm wide loops were positioned at either front. They were made of double-laid basic cloth, and sewn into the seam at the rim and sewn on below. Two buttons for the suspender were sewn on one beneath the other at the upper end. If not needed the ends were tucked inside the trousers, and secured in place by a narrow horizontal tape with a center seam. Two pairs of suspender buttons were positioned 2cm below the rim on the left and right front inside.

Two side pockets were with a slanted 18cm long opening beginning 7cm below the waist rim and 9cm forward of the lateral seam, and ending 2cm from the lateral seam. The bag of the pocket was made of twill, and mea-

Note the waist adjusting belts and slanted side pockets.

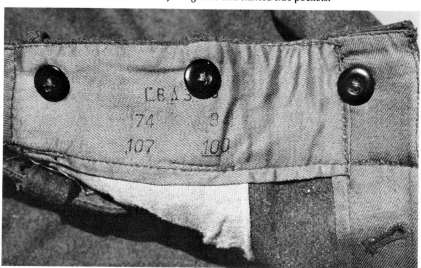

Internal markings on the waist rim.

sured 17cm wide and 27cm high. The scalloped flaps were lined with twill, and were closed by a press snap. The width of their ends was 4.5cm.

At the right rear was a rear pocket with a horizontal 18cm long opening and 4cm rearwards of the lateral seam. The bag was made of nettle, and measured 20cm wide and 18cm high. The scalloped flap was 4cm wide at the ends. A pocket for two first aid packets was positioned at the left rear with a

405

Right leg opening with snap flap.

Ed Anderson.

Left leg opening with button.

13cm wide opening 5cm from the lateral seam. The bag was made of twill, and was about 18cm wide and 10cm high. the flaps of both pockets were lined with twill and were buttoned.

An 8cm wide and 10cm high watch pocket was positioned at the rear front, and was with a 7cm wide opening 13cm below the waist rim. The flap was lined with twill, and was with an end width of 2cm and a center width of 4cm. It was fastened by a press snap. Centered above the pocket was a sewn-on metal ring of 1.5cm diameter for hooking the watch chain.

There was a 20cm high opening in either outward lateral seam at the height of the knees. The purpose of the opening was to permit the internal knee protectors to be removed following the jump. Both openings were closed by three (later two) press snaps, and had a 24cm high and 5cm wide basic cloth underlay. The shape of the pocket flap varied. To the rear of the right opening was a narrow lateral pocket to hold the utility knife. Late pattern pants were produced without the side openings.

The ends of the legs were tapered from a width of approximately 28cm to and end width of 18cm by four tucks (each 10cm long), and were positioned at the front and rear center. At the outer lateral seam was a 15cm long slash. The edges of the slash and the end of the legs were lined by a 4.5cm wide twill tape. A 1.5cm wide and 30cm long grey ribbon was sewn to the bottom corner of the slash. To fasten the leg ends the ribbon was put through a 1.5cm wide opening of the front tuck and tied. Some personnel, as a personal preference, removed the ankle ties, and installed elastic stirrups to prevent the pants from riding up out of the boots.

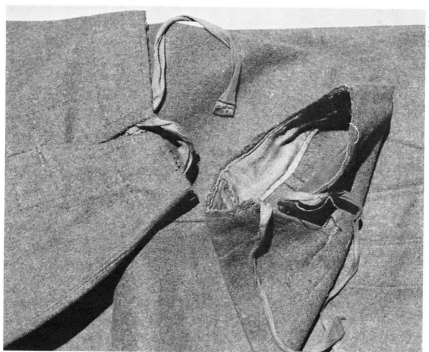

Ed Anderson

Ends of tapered legs with ankle ties.

When worn, the ends of the trouser legs were bound above the ankles by means of the ribbons, tucked into the jump boots and bloused at the tops.

A slightly different trouser was made of blue-grey cloth, possibly a wartime production. It was without the lateral opening to take out the knee protectors after a jump. The outside seam of the right thigh had an opening with an inside pocket and was secured by a flap which was secured towards the rear by two press-buttons. the seam of the left thigh was open in a length of 12cm and held together by three short horizontal seams. The purpose of this slit is not known. Anyway, it was not possible to take out the knee protector pads.

The utility knife was fitted to the inside rear of the right leg opening (in this case a two-snap flap closure).

The earlier pattern jump trousers tended to have a three-snap closure on the right leg opening. Note both men are army paratroopers.

d. Jump Boots: The boots were officially termed "paratroop boots" (Fallschirmschützen-Stiefel). They were of black (sometimes brown, but rarely) leather with tops reaching nearly mid-calf. The weight was approximately 1,850 grams. The vertical rear height as measured from the upper edge of the heel was 25cm. The circumferences of the leg were 27cm at the ankles and 32cm at the rim. The toe end was reinforced by an internal cap made of celluloid. the panels were sewn together at the rear and along the very front, with the seams covered by outside leather tapes. The slightly curved edges of the lateral lace-up slash (referred to as "side-lace") were reinforced by a leather tape, and were with 12 pairs of metal eyelets. The soft leather tongue was 22cm wide at the end and was sewn on its entire length. Since about early 1940 the boots were manufactured with a front lace-up slash.

Charita

1st pattern leather "side-lace" boots in wear. At right is Max Schmeling. Note also wear of the double decal helmets.

The construction of the sole was with two leather soles—a 5mm thick soft rubber sole, a 4mm thick rubber sole and the rubber heel—all made of artificial rubber ("Buna"). Soles and heels were molded with large chevron-pattern ridges to prevent slipping.

A fabric patch was sewn onto the inside of the tongue to indicate the size, model number, manufacturer and year of production.

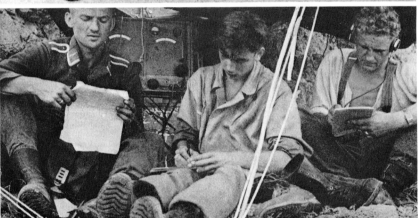

Paratroopers at Crete wear the side-lace boot with chevron-pattern heels and soles.

A new model jump boot was introduced by an order (BLB 41, No.243) dated 25 February 1941 together with a "appertaining rubber cover for half-soles" (with no further description). The boots were slightly lower, and laced in the front. Soles and heel were made of leather, and were studded at the edges with nails. The heels were grooved to accommodate ski bindings. These boots were also provided for use as mountain shoes.

The manual L.Dv.300 "Regulations for the Economy of Clothing of the Luftwaffe during the War" of 25 September 1943 listed "Fallschirmjäger-Galoschen" (paratroop galoshes). Introduction orders and details have not been found, however. There is a possibility that these were identical to the rubber cover mentioned in the above order of 25 February 1941.

2nd pattern leather front-lace paratroop boots being worn during ground training.

2nd pattern paratroop boots. Note grooved heel for ski bindings.

e. Gloves: The paratroop gloves ("Fallschirmschützen-Handschuhe") were of the gauntlet type, and made of black (pre-war), dark brown or grey leather. The hand portion was 24cm long, and the sewn-on cuff portion measured 12cm long. The width was 27cm long at the wrist and 44cm at the end of the cuffs. Two elastic bands were positioned at the end of the cuffs and at the wrist. On the outer side of the cuff were three inside 2mm diameter elastic bands and equidistanced from each other. They served the purpose of narrowing the cuffs.

The gloves were unlined for summer wear, and fur-lined for winter wear. A variant version had approximately 15cm long cuffs without the inside elastics.

Short version.

Personnel retrieve equipment from the drop container. Note the short paratroop gloves on the container lid, as well as the knee pads stuck in the belt. Of further interest is the smock at the left is the camouflage pattern, while the one at the right is not.

This paratrooper climbs on board a Ju 52 for a training jump. Note he wears the long version gauntlets.

    f. Knee Protectors: The first internal model of paratroop knee pads (or protectors—"Fallschirmschützen-Knieschützer") was worn underneath the trousers. Since 1940 a second external model was introduced, which was more practical as it was worn over the trousers. Following the jump, the knee protectors were removed to allow for better mobility.

    • Internal Knee Protectors: As the protectors were fastened at the outer side of the knees they were made in pairs as a mirror image. They consisted of patches of rubberized cotton tricot which were sewn together, and were with a 5cm wide border of sewing-silk along the upper rim. The trapezoid patches were 22cm high, and with a 30cm width above and 27cm below. The padding was sewn onto the patches near their outer edge. It consisted of a rectangular patch of nettle fabric measuring 15 x 18cm with a filling of kapok in four vertical tubular ribs. A horizontal 8cm long narrow leather loop was sewn on above the padding and near the upper rim, the purpose of which was to facilitate removing the pads through the slash of the trousers. It appears that some pre-war protectors were made of leather.

Both outer edges of the pads were trimmed by a double-laid 3.5 - 4cm wide stripe of blue-grey trousers cloth which was prolongated downwards for 3.5cm. The edge nearest to the padding was with 13 cut-out loops, each 8mm wide and distanced 12mm from each other. The cloth stripe of the outer edge had 13 corresponding metal oval eyelets. For the rather complicated fastening, the loops were put through the eyelets and secured by a leather lace running through the loops from above. To facilitate the passing of the lace through the loops, a steel needle was first passed through the loops from below, then the lace was secured to the eye at the end of the needle, and finally the needle with the lace was drawn downwards. The upper end of the lace was bound to a metal ring. The needle was 25cm long and 3mm thick, and was with a short wooden handle at the end opposite to the eye.

Teilbarer Knieſchützer für Fallſchirmſchützen
Maße für Größe 8

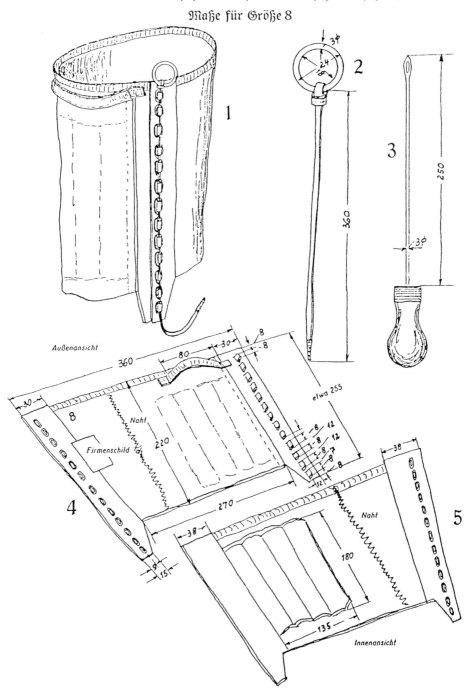

Außenansicht

Naht

Firmenschild

Innenansicht

Order dated 15 March 1938 (BLB 38, No. 140).

The knee protectors were removed through the lateral slash of the trousers in a way that first the lace came out of the loops by pulling its ring, and then the pads were removed by the leather loops.

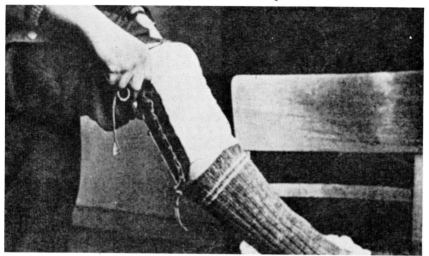

The internal knee protectors are shown being put on.

- External Knee Protectors: The pads were made of dark brown leather (later blue-grey fabric), and consisted of five or six tubular ribs with an inside filling of foam rubber which came in horizontal or vertical variants. The pads covered the knee from side to side. Two strong elastic straps, which were adjustable by slides, were sewn at one side of the pads. When worn, they were crossed behind the wearer's knee and clipped to a pair of button-hooks at the opposite side of the pad.

Reverse view.

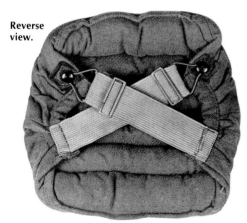

Charita

External knee pads being worn just prior to exiting aircraft. These authors have never seen a photo of the elbow pads being worn.

2nd pattern smock with two horizontal opening thigh pockets with tape cover. Note the knee protectors and boots without lacing.

Splinter-pattern knee protectors which are extremely uncommon.

g. Elastic Ankle Bandages: Additional support of the ankles during a jump was provided by the elastic ankle bandages (elastische Binden), which were wound around the ankles under the socks. They were made of 8cm wide linen in an elasticized weave. When stretched out the full length they were approximately 8m.

h. Other Protective Articles: The above mentioned L.Dv.300 dated 15 September 1943 additionally listed a face mask ("Fallschirmjäger-Gesichtsmaske"), elbow protectors ("Fallschirmjäger-Ellbogenschützer"), and shoulder protectors ("Fallschirmjäger-Schulterschützer"). Neither introduction orders nor descriptions of the articles have been found.

Elbow Protective Pads (Fallschirmjäger-Ellbogenschützer): These were used only during the very early days of the paratroops. The basic construction was similar to the knee protectors, but somewhat longer and a bit narrower.

> i. Steel Helmet: Two models of the "paratroop steel helmet" (Fallschirmschützen-Stahlhelm) were produced—the first model being a test and evaluation model, and the second the standard production pattern for distribution. The second varied considerably from the first, lacking the lateral slits, and with an entirely new improved liner and strap system.

The double pattern decals of both models were those as used on the M1935 helmet—the national tri-color shield on the right side, and the national emblem on the left—Luftwaffe pattern worn by Luftwaffe units, and army or Luftwaffe pattern for those army units. The army pattern shield was worn until mid-1940. Order (BLB 40, No.726), dated 12 June 1940 specified that the tri-colored shield was to be omitted, and the national emblem was ordered in a "color adapted to the camouflage" of the blue-green shade. In 1943 it was eventually omitted as well. It should be noted that the emblems were omitted only with newly produced helmets or overpainted whenever a new paint was necessary. This resulted in helmets with one or two decals occasionally being worn until the end of the war.

> • First Model Steel Helmet: The helmet was based on the M1935 helmet. Its bottom rim was considerably shortened by cutting off the eye visor rim almost completely, and by reducing the side and neck rim to a length of about 2cm.

Stacey

1st pattern double decal paratroop helmet as indicated by the slot in the rim at each side. This was nothing more than a modified M35 helmet with shortened rim.

Skötte

1st pattern, army double decal paratroop helmet with modified M1931 liner and strap system.

418

Skötte

1st pattern, Luftwaffe paratroop helmet with later
liner system. Note that
spanner bolts have been
used and the holes which
were utilized with the old
liner are evident.

The M1931 liner (Innenausstattung 31) was retained, but modified by adding a rubber padding and a new Y-pattern chin harness. The rear strap of the chin harness was sewn onto the front strap below the chin. Rear and front straps were adjusted by slide buckles at either side near the carbine spring hook by means of which the straps were hooked to rectangular metal eyes hanging down from the metal ring of the liner at the sides and at the back of the neck. A 2cm long narrow slit was placed at either side, which was possibly intended originally for the attachment of the chinstrap. Apparently the chin harness proved unsatisfactory. Therefore, a limited number of helmets was modified by exchanging the M1931 liner and strap system with the liner and straps of the final design steel helmet, which was affixed in the same way.

Army paratrooper wears the 1st pattern helmet with Luftwaffe insignia.

- Final Model Steel Helmet: The final design was introduced by an order (BLB 38, No.239) dated 16 June 1938. A description contained in the above-mentioned order of 15 March 1938 apparently was wrong in some minor details, and was revoked and replaced by the 16 June 1938 order.

The steel helmet was pressed from sheet steel of 1.15mm thickness, and came in one piece and three sizes of 66, 68 and 71 inner width. The sizes of the head width number 53, 54, 55/56, 57, 58/59, 60 and 61, and were gained by the liner sizes. The weight was approximately 1,000 grams.

The field-grey color of the steel helmet was altered to matte blue-grey with a roughened finish by an order (BLB 40, No.726) dated 12 June 1940, with the proviso that units which were "not employed," i.e., training or home garrison units, were permitted the continued wear of helmets with the field grey paint. Camouflage paints of any colors, to include white-washing, were expedients by individuals or units. Paratroop units fighting in North Africa had their helmets painted olive drab. A wide range of camouflage paint pat-

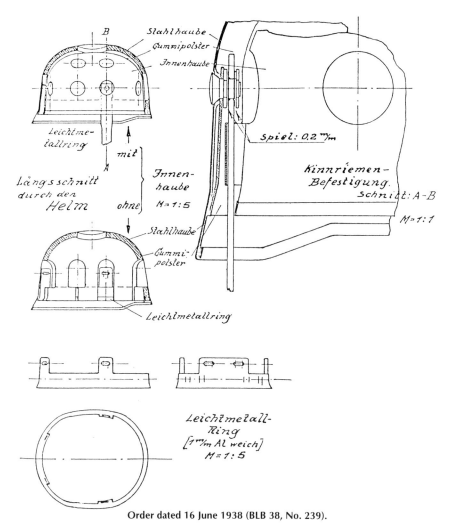

Stahlhelm für Fallschirmschützen
Baumuster: 142–7 A

B

Stahlhaube

Gummipolster

Innenhaube

*Leichtme-
tallring*

mit

*Längsschnitt
durch den
Helm*

ohne

*Innen-
haube
M = 1 : 5*

Spiel: 0,2 ᵐ/ₘ

*Kinnriemen-
Befestigung.*

Schnitt: A–B

M = 1 : 1

Stahlhaube

*Gummi-
polster*

Leichtmetallring

*Leichtmetall-
Ring
[1 ᵐ/ₘ Al weich]
M = 1 : 5*

Order dated 16 June 1938 (BLB 38, No. 239).

terns are encountered, and can be largely associated with tactical area of operations.

The basic form of the first model helmet was retained. The slightly slanted side and neck rim was about 1.8cm wide, and the bottom rim was turned inwards for 4mm all around. The liner was affixed by special screws in four holes, which were positioned on at either side and two at the rear. The centers of the holes were set at a distance of 7cm above the bottom rim of the helmet, and the centers of the rear holes were spaced 6cm apart. The screws were 6mm in diameter, and came in three types.

- Type 1: The first pattern had a 34mm wide center bore in its length for ventilation and a small hole at either side of

Stahlhelm für Fallschirmschützen
Baumuster: 142—7 A

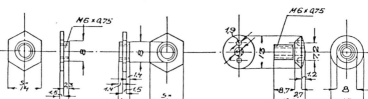

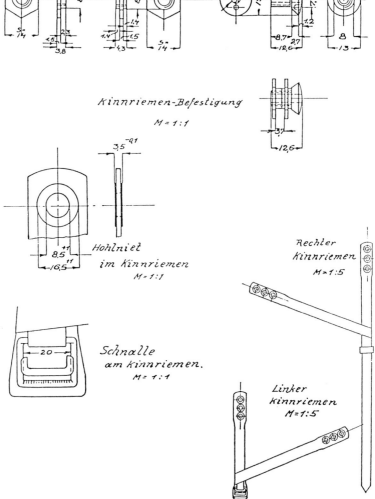

Kinnriemen-Befestigung

M = 1:1

Hohlniet
im Kinnriemen
M = 1:1

Schnalle
am Kinnriemen.
M = 1:1

Rechter
Kinnriemen
M = 1:5

Linker
Kinnriemen
M = 1:5

Order dated 16 June 1938 (BLB 38, No. 239).

it, which served for the two-prong spanner wrench. As this special tool was not always available, this pattern gave way to the second pattern.

- Type 2: The second pattern screw was adopted from the vent bore and a slot so that a standard screw-driver could be used.

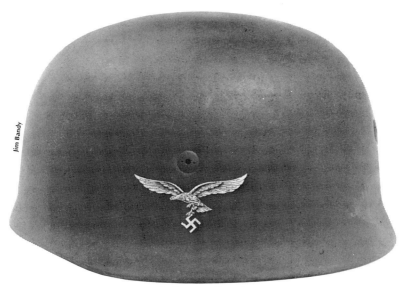

2nd pattern, Type 1.

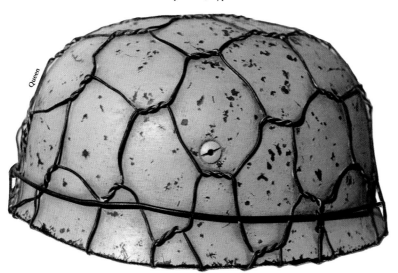

2nd pattern, Type 2, with vent hole and slot in each screw. Specimen is with a tan paint and chicken-wire to affix camouflage.

- Type 3: The final pattern was used in helmets of later war production and as replacement on earlier helmets. The screw had a slot, but with the vent bore omitted.

Steel screws were later replaced by light-metal (aluminum) screws. The screws were held in place on the inside by a lock washer, and one or two nuts. The screws also held the chin harness in place.

2nd pattern, Type 1, with stenciled Luftwaffe national emblem.

Hatton

2nd pattern, Type 3, with screw-driver slot screw. The purpose of the stripes at left and right rear is not known, but probably a tactical control sign.

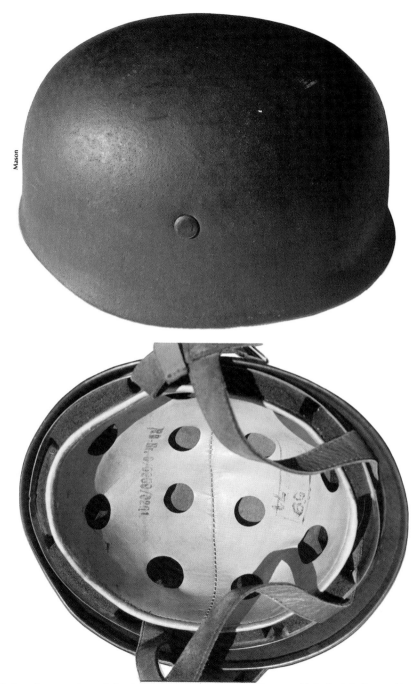

Late pattern paratroop helmet with split-pin brads in lieu of screws. Note the interior markings.

Variant pattern "screws"—probably more like a spread brad rather than a screw.

The liner system consisted of a cap-shaped sweat lining and a shock-absorbing foam rubber cap. The lining was made of natural-colored soft leather, and had several ventilation holes. Four holes of 2.5cm in diameter were at the top, and seven holes of 3cm diameter each were distributed above the bottom. Since 1940, it was permitted to glue together the cap of several pieces of leather. A flexible light-metal alloy aluminum ring was attached at its outward bottom. At its upper edge, the ring had three riveted or welded metal patches of 1cm in height for attachment to the steel shell by means of the screws. The lateral patches were 3mm wide with one hole each, and the rear patch was 8.5mm with two holes. Seven shock-absorbing pads of foam rubber were inserted between the leather and the ring, measuring 3.5cm high and 13mm thick with sixes 56, 59, 61, and 10mm thick for all other sizes. The pad colors varied as follows: M1937 (Prototype) orange; M1938 creme;

M1940 black. Between the leather and the rubber pads was an additional leather band of 3.5cm in width and 2mm thick. Metal ring, pads and leather ring were sewn together. The inner top portion of the shell was cushioned by 10mm thick foam rubber cap, which could be glued together from several pieces. The top of the rubber cap had a hole of 7cm in diameter, and the bottom rim was with several cut-outs which were 6cm high. The ends between the cut-outs were glued to the shock-absorbing pads at the bottom edge of the liner system.

The top of the liner cap was stamped with the usual markings—manufacturing firm or, later, the RB-number, year of manufacture, control stamp and size. War production helmets did not have all these markings, however.

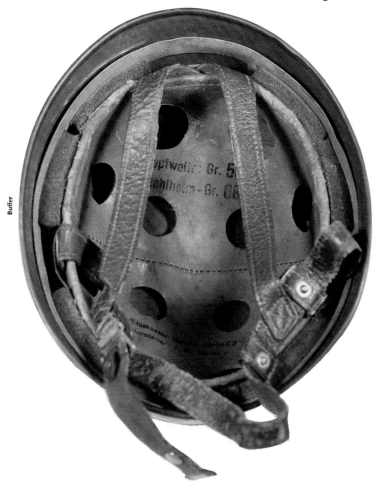

Standard pattern liner for the paratroop helmet showing the rubber crown padding, the leather cap with vent holes.

The chin harness consisted of the 1.6cm wide chin and rear straps, which were made of grey leather with leather lining. The rear strap was sewn to the chin strap in an acute angle. The upper ends of the straps widened to **427**

2cm for a better hold of three metal grommets each, which served to affix the chin harness to the steel shell by the screws of the liner. The holes allowed to adjust the harness to the wearer's head form. The rear straps were crossed in height of the rim of the helmet. To hold the straps in place they were pulled through leather loops at the bottom of the liner. The right chin strap was longer and was put through a friction buckle, which was sewn to the left chin strap immediately below the junction with the rear strap. It was then pulled back and held in place by a leather loop at the right side of the chin strap.

Alexander

Camouflaged double decal helmet with the 1st pattern chin harness featuring the friction buckle and plain running-end strap.

Apparently, the buckled chin strap did not prove satisfactory for jumps. Therefore it was replaced by an improved harness system at a later date. All straps were 2cm wide. The left chin strap was prolongated, and was with three press snaps at the end, with the lower parts of the snaps at the right end. For additional security, a 1.6cm wide leather strap was strapped over the press snap straps, and buckled at the left side. A variant system, which may be regarded as a test harness, was identical, but with a sewn-on triangular leather patch covering the angle between the chin and rear straps. At the ears a vertical slash opened rearwards.

Since 1944 the liner system was modified and somewhat simplified. The chin harness eventually was similar to the harness of the first test model.

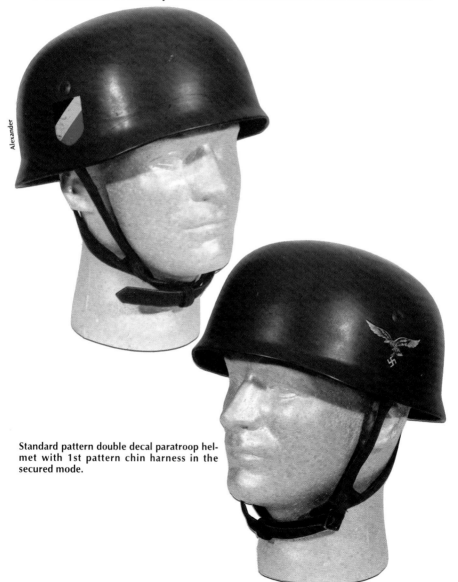

Alexander

Standard pattern double decal paratroop helmet with 1st pattern chin harness in the secured mode.

429

Make-shift leather chin harness affixed to a standard pattern double decal paratroop helmet.

- Helmet Band and Camouflage Net: These were introduced for the paratroop helmet by order (BLB 38, No.140) dated 15 March 1938 for the helmet band, and by order (LV 42, No.2326) dated 3 September 1942 for the camouflage net. Both articles were identical with those of the M1935 helmet, and will be described with the M1935 helmet in the chapter dealing with equipment.

Corpsman wears a tight-knit helmet cover and same material as a face net. This netting is typical of the British style.

This Oberjäger wears a maneuver band directly over his helmet cover.

431

Various forms of netting in wear.

Paratroop military policeman with rope netting on his helmet.

Rope net cover at left, while at the right is a discarded helmet clearly showing the interior markings.

Camouflage painted paratroop helmet with rope netting cover to affix foliage for additional camouflage.

General Meindl, at Normandy in 1944, wears the Meindl badge on the left side of his cap.

von Hungen

Meindl badge.

k. Camouflage Cloth Cover: Since late 1940, a cloth cover was frequently worn with the steel helmet. The cover was introduced in the fall of 1939, and was originally made of green mottled or, less frequently, of grey fabrics as used with the smocks. Since the spring of 1941 the covers were made of camouflage cloth of the same patterns as used for the smocks. The basic construction of all issue covers was identical, but with minor variations existing, however. The cover was sewn together of four to six panels with the addition of an oval piece of cloth forming the top. It fitted tightly over the helmet, and was secured to it by four or six wire hooks, which were equidistantly sewn to the bottom edge. As the hooks tended to break, they were replaced on covers of later production by a drawstring construction with the string running in the bottom seam and fastened tightly under the rear rim of the helmet. A band of greenish or grey fabric was sewn around the body of the cover by several vertical seams spaced 5 to 7cm apart thus forming a series of loops. The width of the tape varied between approximately 1.5 to 3cm. Two narrow ribbons of the same material and color were sewn to the oval top cross-wise, and in the same way. The loops were intended to hold camouflage material such as twigs or grass, etc.

Klaus Peters

The helmet cover with wire hooks in wear.

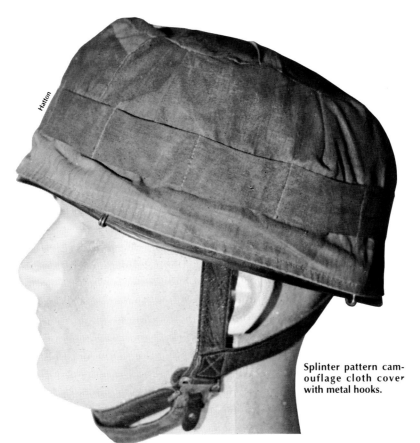

Splinter pattern cam-
ouflage cloth cover
with metal hooks.

Major Walter Gericke wears the cloth cover with metal affixing hooks. 435

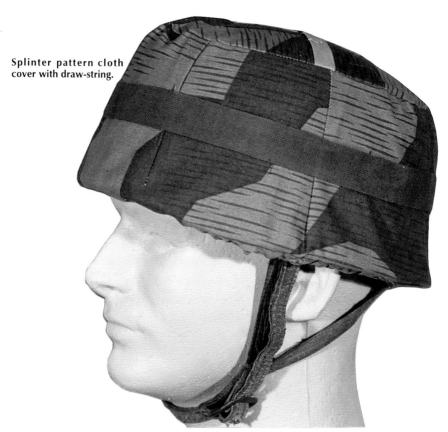

Splinter pattern cloth cover with draw-string.

Wear of the cloth cover as above.

Camouflaged cloth cover affixed to paratroop helmet.

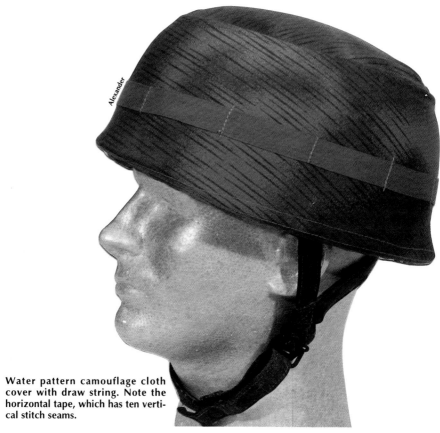

Water pattern camouflage cloth cover with draw string. Note the horizontal tape, which has ten vertical stitch seams.

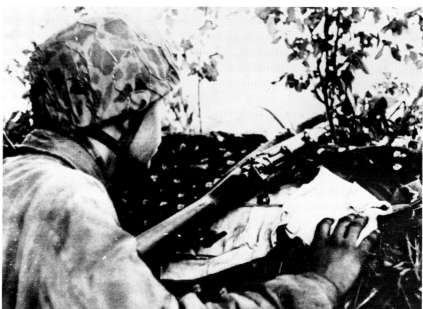

Chicken wire is worn over a camouflage material, probably from a parachute.

The above helmet covers are fabricated of Italian camouflage material.

Note the white helmet cover.

There were white covers for winter camouflage and tan covers for use with the tropical uniform and smock and of the same basic construction, but lacking the looped bands. Besides the standard issue helmet covers numerous other methods of camouflage were employed by individuals or ordered by units. Cloth covers were of a makeshift construction, commonly of two panels rather than the more complicated construction. Frequently the helmets were covered by wire nets, which allowed to hold camouflage material. Wire nets were occasionally also worn over the issue covers for additional means of holding camouflage material.

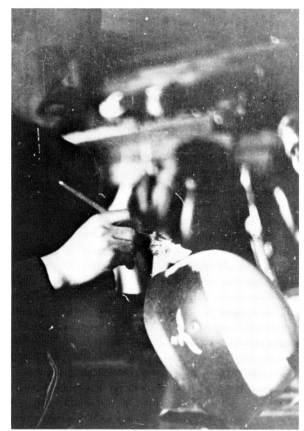

This helmet is being painted white for use in winter warfare.

Paratroopers in winter dress wearing the helmet with white (snow) finish. Note the 1st Sgt. position rings about the greatcoat sleeve.

Paratroop helmet with winter finish.

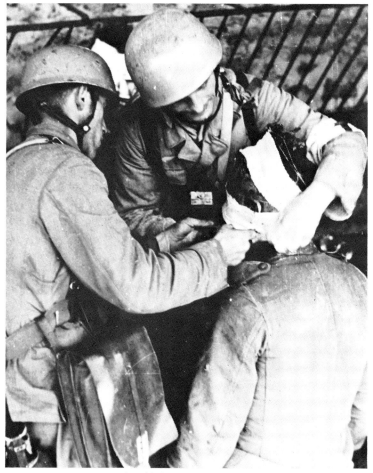

Tan painted helmets worn in Italy, 1944.

One of Ramcke's paratroops in North Africa (1943) wears the 2nd pattern chin harness with securing snaps. The helmet has a camouflage pattern.

This tan finished paratroop helmet was taken off a member of the Ramcke Brigade by an Australian veteran.

The above tan, turtle shell pattern was used extensively in Italy.

R.L. Lyons

This brown and green painted helmet was captured at Normandy.

443

Tan and green airbrushed camouflage finish.

Reddish-brown and green camouflage paint.

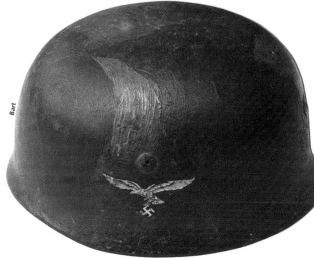

Camouflage paratroop helmet in brown, tan, and green.

444

A medical corpsman paratroop helmet (single decal) with red cross insignia painted on the front and back.

Al Barrows

Lautenschläger

Chicken wire over the paratroop helmet for the purpose of adding camouflage.

445

446   Chicken-wire net affixed to a standard pattern paratroop helmet.

Another version of chicken wire
attached to a paratroop helmet.

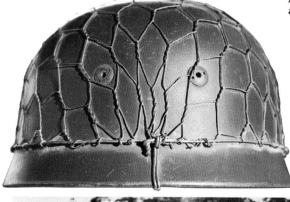

American soldiers gathering up paratroop helmets after a Normandy battle.

447

A beautifully painted souvenir of the Normandy battles.

Front

Rear

top

1. Utility Knife: The utility knife (Flieger-Kappmesser) was introduced by an order (LV 37, No.666) dated 24 May 1937 for parachutists and members of aircraft crews. It served the purpose to enable paratroopers after the jump or crew members after bailing out to cut off the lines of the parachute or the harness after a bad landing. By its special design as a gravity blade knife it could be opened with one hand. The blade was housed in a metal housing with wood handle covers. If the knife was pointed downward, and the lateral spring-tension bar lever pressed, the blade was freed, and could slide from the handle. Releasing the lever locked the blade. For housing the blade, the process was reverse.

Order dated 24 May 1937 (LV37, No. 666).

1. Blade
2. Covering plates
3. Metal case
4. Wooden plates
5. Metal head
6. Peg
7. Slit
8. Flat spring
9. Cam
10. Press lever
11. Pricker
12. Hinge of the pricker
13. Spring of the pricker
14. Rivet
15. Wire ring

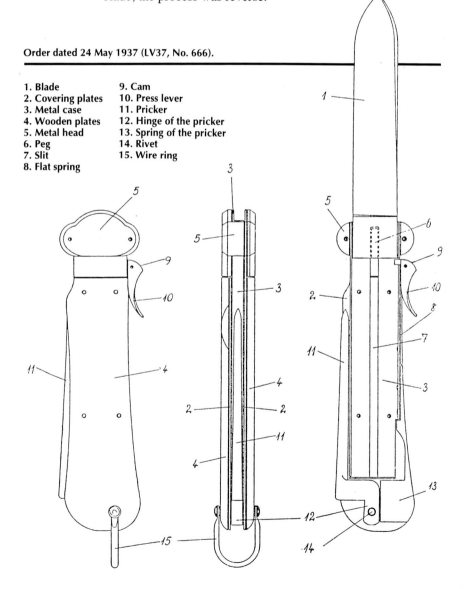

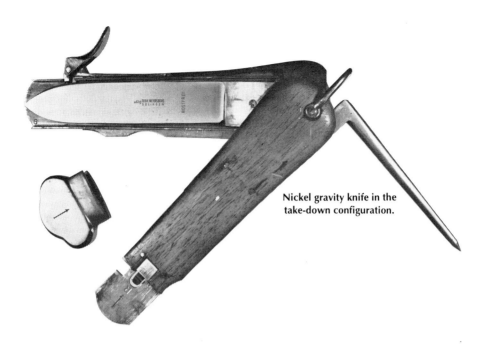

Nickel gravity knife in the take-down configuration.

The broad side of the handle were covered by riveted brown (of varied colors) wood plates. One end of the handle had a metal head with a slit to allow the blade to slide out or in. This cap was either fixed by rivets, or of the type that could be removed by pressing a square tension button. At the other end was a wire loop to secure it by a chain or cord. A fold-out splicing pick was affixed at the narrow side of the handle opposite the lever. Its angled rear end was covered by the wooden plate, and was affixed by the rivet of the wire loop. NOTE: The example shown in the schematic is the type with the fixed (1st pattern) metal head. Examples with the removable (2nd pattern) metal cap could the opened, thus allowing full access to the blade. The metal handle parts could be blued or nickle-plate. The blade of the 2nd pattern, when without the manufacturer's logo, was often stamped with the RB Nr.

A generic utility cord, approximately 2' long, and with a metal clip at both ends, were sometimes attached to the wire loop, with the other end attached normally to the belt.

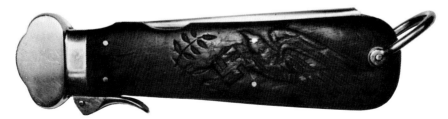

Non-take-down nickel version, but with paratroop emblem (diving eagle with swastika) carved into the wood grip-plate.

Blued (top) and nickel (bottom) take-down versions of the utility knife. Twisted about the blued version is the standard pattern securing utility cord with fastening hooks at both ends.

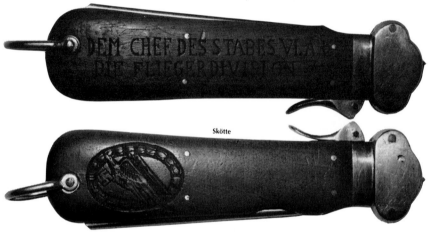

Skötte

Handle of a gravity knife carved with the designation indicating it belonged to the Chief of Staff of the VIth Artillery Corps, Fliegerdivision 7.

m. Gas Mask Canvas Container: As the standard metal cylindrical canister of the gas mask was not very practical while jumping, a special canvas container was issued. It was a short tubular bag of greenish or blue-grey canvas with a zipper along its length covered by a flap secured by two press snaps. The adjustable carrying strap was identical to those of the metal canister. The earlier pattern was worn suspended from the neck, and laying on the chest. Inside was a pocket with press-snap button to hold replacement lenses, and a brown leather reinforcement pad at the position of the filter (at the chest side). An introduction order has not been found.

Gibbons

1940 pattern gasmask
with press snap flap
closure worn at the
chest.

Gibbons

453

A simplified bag was probably introduced in late 1940. The bag was made of dark green or blue-grey fabric as used for breadbags, was open at one end and closed by a flap with a press snap. A pocket for the reserve anti-fogging lenses was sewn to the inner side of the flap.

Paratroop units employed in the role of ground combat troops since 1942 were normally issued with the standard metal canisters.

Normally, the gas mask and container were worn inside the jump smock.

    n. Ammunition Bandoleer: Because the standard issue leather ammunition pouches were too bulky for jumps, an ammunition bandoleer (Fallschirmjäger-Patronengurt) was introduced mid 1938. Introduction order and official descriptions have not been found. The basic model underwent several improvements. The bandoleers were made of strong canvas fabric of various colors—usually early patterns were green mottled (1938) or blue-grey (1940), while later patterns (since 1941) were made of tan or splinter camouflage.

Bandoleers were hung around the neck by a slightly curved band of double-laid fabric, which was approximately 45cm long and 6cm wide. By an order (LV 44, No.1188) dated 21 August 1944 an improvement was ordered by sewing on a 2.5cm wide tab of fabric at the right angle and at the center of the band. By two buttonholes and one button a loop was formed to connect the bandoleer with the rear ring of the Y-straps holding the leather belt, thus preventing sliding off. Bandoleers in wear were to be altered by the units.

An array of camouflaged, tan and blue bandoliers. Note the variations in flap closures.

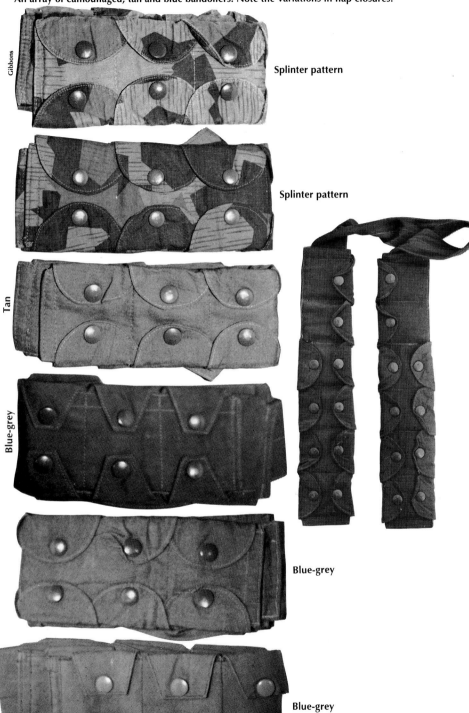

Gibbons

Splinter pattern

Splinter pattern

Tan

Blue-grey

Blue-grey

Blue-grey

455

A wider band with the ammunition pockets was sewn to either end of the neck band. Each of the separately sewn-on pockets held one or two clips of five each, which were put in from the outward sides. Apparently, the pockets of the first model bandoleer were without flaps as an order (BLB 41, No.362) dated 24 March 1941 required sewn-on flaps closed by a press snap. Bandoleers in wear were to be altered by the units by sewn on flaps. The flaps were triangular with a snap positioned near the cut-off point, but there exist some patterns with a squared flap.

The pockets were sewn to the band in the following order: top two pockets for one clip each with opening and flaps at the outward side, and below these four pockets with opening at either side. With these pockets a clip was inserted from either side, and a patch of the same size as the pockets was sewn in to separate the clips. To hold the bandoleer in position in connection with the leather belt, there was a strap of double-laid fabric sewn to the reverse side. The strap was approximately 25cm long and 3cm wide, and was sewn to the band at the seam between the second and third pocket. For wear it was put behind the belt, and then through a horizontal loop of about 5cm in length and 2cm in width, which was sewn on at the reverse center of the second pocket from below, and then the strap was reversed upwards and secured by a press snap at its end. Bandoleers of early production were without this attachment, and were held in place by wearing the leather belt over the ends of the bandoleer. The reverse of later specimens was usually stamped with the control markings.

Klaus Peters

Paratroop at right wears the bandolier with the angular flap closure.

An ammunition bandoleer for the M1942 paratroop rifle (Fallschirm-jägergewehr 42—FG42) was of a similar construction, and with four pockets at either band each holding one ammunition magazine. These were commonly made of splinter, water or blue-grey colored fabric.

Ammunition bandoleer in the splinter camouflage pattern and the standard rounded flaps. The bandoleers also came in tan and blue-grey, and with squared flaps.

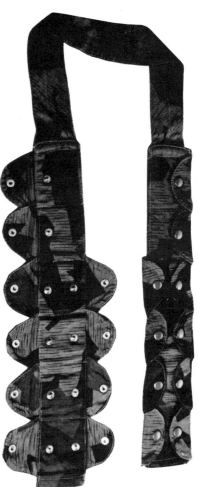

The blue-grey bandoleer is worn with the tropical uniform.

A splinter pattern of the FG42 ammunition bandoleer in wear.

The paratrooper in the center wears the FG42 ammunition bandoleer.

o. Carrying Straps for Ammunitions Cans: By order (LV 41, No.962) dated 5 August 1941 carrying straps were introduced to carry two metal ammunition cans each containing 300 belted rounds of 7.92 standard cartridges for machine guns. The order stated the straps were worn "as the back pack," and that the back strap was hooked to the leather belt and with the two cans attached by web straps. This would lead to the conclusion that the straps took the form of Y-straps made of leather or webbing during the final months of the war.

Ammunition cans being carried over the shoulders and as a back pack.

459

p. Hand Grenade Bags: The above mentioned L.Dv.300 of 25 September 1939 lists "paratroop hand grenade bags" (Fallschirmjäger-Handgranatenbeutel). Details have not been found, however. Providing they conformed to the standard pattern, they were a pair of fabric bags with zipper closures at the top of each bag, and connected by two heavy web straps, and slug around the neck. Each bag held about five M1924, M1939 or M1943 stick grenades. Bag fabric varied from splinter or dark green fabric.

Army paratroops on maneuver. The one at left wears the grenade bags (and the ammo bandoleer) about his neck. Note the wear of the army and Luftwaffe helmets.

Other grenade bags also existed, to include a single bag with shoulder strap. Zippers were either metal or white plastic.

q. Parachute (Fallschirm): The parachute was not an item of individual issue, but rather a unit item. It is mentioned here as it was distinctive to the paratroops. The parachute consisted of the semi-circular canopy (Kappe) with 20-28 panels and open apex, suspension lines (also termed shroud lines—Fangleinen), short double riser joined at a single point (Tragetauc), backpack in the form of two brownish-olive reinforced canvas bags

(Packhüllen) and harness—and no reserve parachute! Sewing was with white silk or grey silk-like synthetic fabric since 1940. The folded canopy was packed into the inner bag, which was packed into the outer bag along with the bundled suspension lines, and connected with two D-rings at the shoulder straps of the harness.

Each parachutist was required to pack his own chute, thus gaining a confidence in the equipment he would jump. Additionally, there were unit riggers charged with packing additional chutes. The rigger log was filled out as to date of packing and the individual doing the packing. Issued with the parachute for the purpose of storage was a burlap kit bag with a cover flap with snap closures, and with two fabric reinforced carrying straps. The parachute and a small bag with tools were packed into the kit bag.

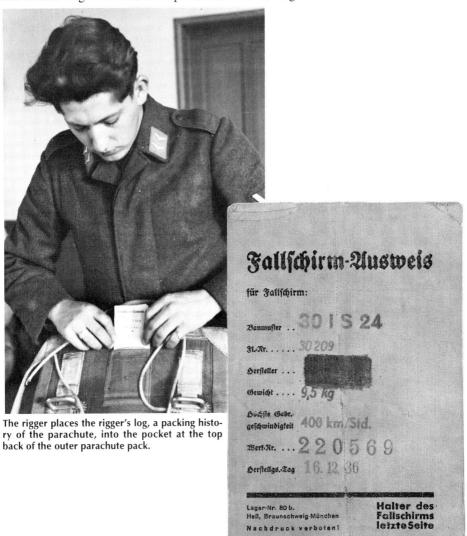

The rigger places the rigger's log, a packing history of the parachute, into the pocket at the top back of the outer parachute pack.

Fallschirm-Ausweis

für Fallschirm:

Baumuster .. 30 I S 24

Fl.-Nr. 30 209

Hersteller ...

Gewicht .... 9,5 kg

Höchste Gebr.
geschwindigkeit 400 km/Std.

Werk-Nr. ... 2 2 0 5 6 9

Herstellgs.-Tag 16. 12. 36

Lager-Nr. 80 b.
Heß, Braunschweig-München
Nachdruck verboten!

Halter des Fallschirms letzte Seite

Riggers check out their tools before beginning their task.

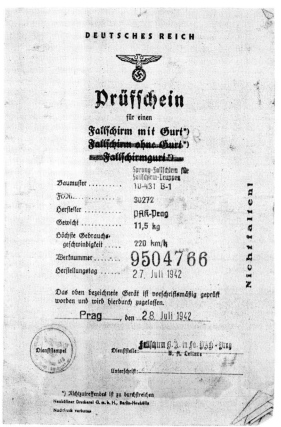

DEUTSCHES REICH

Prüfschein

für einen

Fallschirm mit Gurt*)

~~Fallschirm ohne Gurt*)~~

~~Fallschirmgurt*)~~

	Sprung-Fallschirm für Fallschirm-Truppen
Baumuster	10-431 B-1
Fabr.	30272
Hersteller	PAR-Prag
Gewicht	11,5 kg
Höchste Gebrauchs-geschwindigkeit	220 km/h
Wertnummer	**9504766**
Herstellungstag	27. Juli 1942

Das oben bezeichnete Gerät ist vorschriftsmäßig geprüft worden und wird hierdurch zugelassen.

Prag, den 28. Juli 1942

Dienststempel

Dienststelle: Fallschirm-P.-A. in Fa.-PAR-Prag
P. R. Leitner

Unterschrift: _____

*) Nichtzutreffendes ist zu durchstreichen

Neuköllner Druckerei G. m. b. H., Berlin-Neukölln

Nachdruck verboten

Nicht falten!

Blue-grey, fabric control log of the manufacturer, accompanying the parachute from the factory to depots, and then to respective units.

When jumping, the static line (Aufziehleine) was hooked to the frame of the aircraft door and connected with the inner bag. When the parachutist jumped the static line would pull the parachute from its bag (with the outer bag remaining connected to the harness), deploying the canopy. The static line and the inner bag remained connected with the aircraft, and had to be pulled back in. It was necessary to have a special permit for free-falls requiring manual activation of the parachute.

Photographic depiction of the parachute sequence:

Paratrooper boards the Ju52, holding the static line in his teeth in accordance to procedure. The hook at the end of the static line was snapped to the anchor line cable just prior to exit.

The "spread eagle" exit. Note the static line attached to the anchor line cable (inside aircraft).

463

The moment just prior to the start of parachute deployment.

Deployment sequence from moment of exit to the full deployment of the parachute.

The long ride down with no control.

464

The nature of the suspension usually caused the parachutist to land "spread-eagle" even though they were instructed to do the shoulder roll during parachute swing-landing training.

For reasons of safety, the normal jump altitude during training and field exercises was between 200 and 600 meters, and 100 meters during combat, with the parachutist falling to 40 - 60 meters before the parachute activated.

Because the parachute effectively had only a single riser, the jumper was unable to control his descent, and his aircraft exit was dictated to be a forward "swan dive" with arms and legs outstretched. It was not unusual that the jumper was spun around by the prop blast, thus twisting his suspension line. If all went well, the jumper was still subjected to the oscillation, and the impact of a hands and knees landing.

The 1st model parachute (RZ1) is put on by army paratroopers.

465

- Parachute Model 1 (Rückenfallschirm mit Zwangauslösung 1—RZ1): The first of a series of paratroop parachutes, it was developed by the Luftwaffe experimental station at Rechlin, and remained in service until early 1940. The harness (Gurtzeug) made of strong web consisted of two shoulder straps, a chest band, a wide belly band (Gürtelgurt), and two crotch straps—all connected by rectangular and diagonal seams at the connecting points. Fitting was such that straps were passed through heavy metal buckles, and the running end secured under the main strap or in the case of the leg straps, with two large carbine hooks snapped to a large "D" ring at each hip. This was the principle parachute used during operations at Narvik (Norway—9 April 1940), Aalborg (Denmark—9 April 1940), Eben Emael (Belgium—10 May 1940), and Amsterdam/Rotterdam (Holland—10 May 1940).

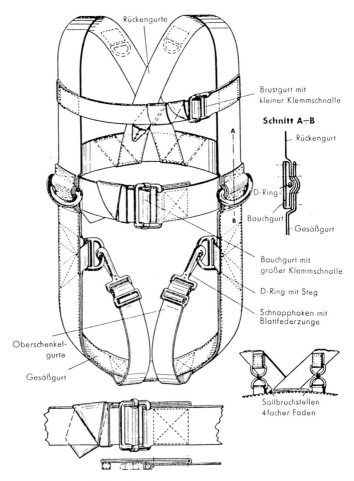

The jump harness.

Parachute Model 1. Note the crotch straps secured to the harness "D" ring by means of a carbine hook. The paratrooper wears the 1st model helmet as denoted by the slit at the rim.

The RZ1 harness in wear by army parachutists.

467

Harness as found on the Model 1 parachute. Harness is as worn for parades and special ceremonies.

Parachute Model 16 in wear. Note the addition of the upper back cloth.

- Parachute Model 16—RZ16: This reflected a minor modification of the static line stowing, resulting in improved safety. Additionally, a wide pack cloth was added, which covered the upper back, and passed over each shoulder. The harness was otherwise the same as Model 1.

- Parachute Model 20—RZ20: The major modification was in a quick- release system thus allowing the parachute and harness to be quickly jettisoned for immediate entry into combat. Additionally, the white canopy gave way to a green/brown camouflage pattern. This parachute was first placed into operational use during the assault on Crete (20 May 1940), and was retained until mid-1943.

B. Burk

Parachute Model 20 as denoted by the quick-release buckles on the harness.

Klaus Peters

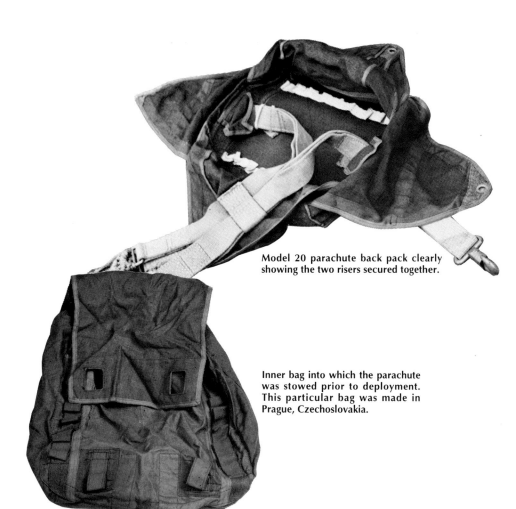

Model 20 parachute back pack clearly showing the two risers secured together.

Inner bag into which the parachute was stowed prior to deployment. This particular bag was made in Prague, Czechoslovakia.

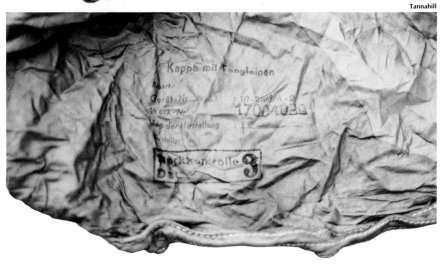

Marking on the skirt of a camouflaged parachute, Model 20.

Tannahill

Burlap kit bag for stowing the parachute.

- Parachute Model 36—RZ36: Introduced in October 1943, the canopy was initially modified to square, but this was soon changed to triangular in shape. This model never saw operational service.
- Cargo Parachutes (Lastenfallschirme) were the same as those used by personnel. They were made of grey silk or artificial silk. These were attached to drop-containers (wooden rectangular cases or metal bomb-like cases) containing rifles, ammunition, small equipment, etc. Large equipment, such as light-weight guns, were dropped using bundles (Traube) of up to five parachutes.

Note drop-containers being dropped from this Ju-52.

A drop-container being packed with equipment.

Two patterns of the cargo parachutes.

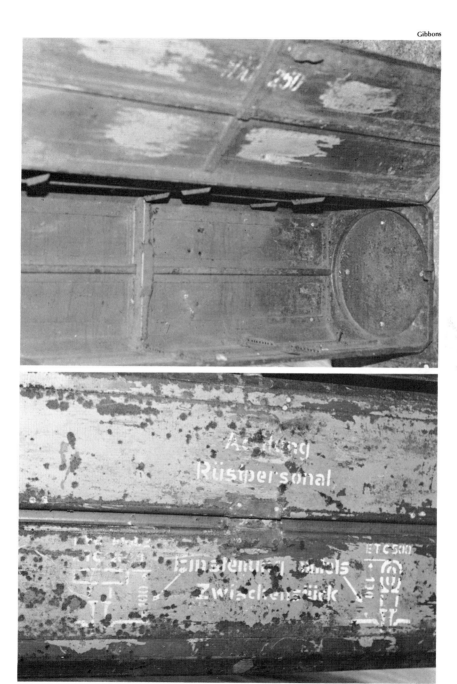

Interior view (top) and exterior loading markings (bottom) of the Model 10-4505 A-1 "crate-form" container.

Above: Paratroop medical personnel unload a crate-form drop container of its medical supplies.

Right: Crate-form weapons container with boggie wheels for better mobility being towed during action on the Isle of Crete.

Below: The more common bomb-like container being unloaded.

Tail section of the bomb-like container.

Luftwaffe MP40 accessories—center left is the rarely encountered "6-pack" magazine pouch (as compared to the standard pattern three pouch at center right); bottom is the dust cover; bottom right is the web tropical sling.

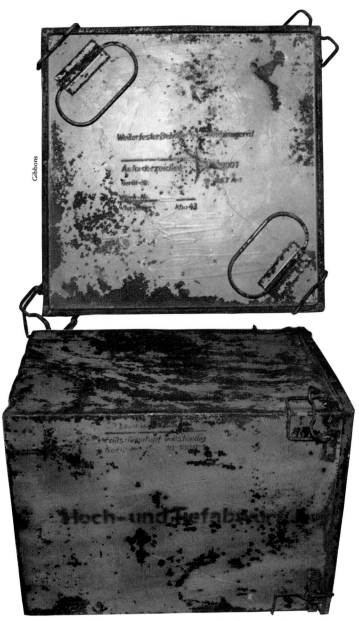

Storage container, Model 10-167-A1, for the cargo chute.

r. Paratroop Tropical Uniform: For details, see the chapter dealing with the tropical uniform.

s. Dust Covers: A protective blue-grey fabric dust cover reinforced by brown or black leather trim as affixed to the bolt
assembly of the K-98 and MP38/40 during the jump or to keep
the weapon clean in the field.

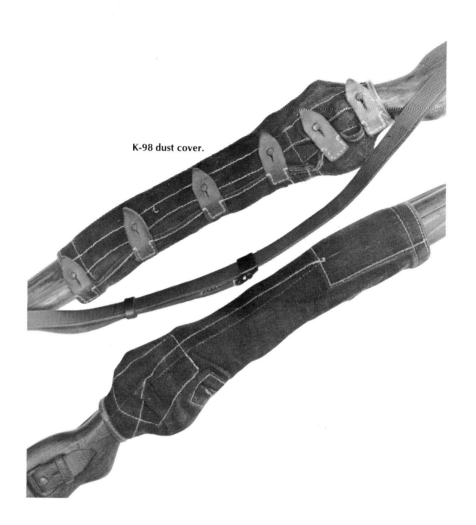

K-98 dust cover.

The following topics will be covered in Volume 3 of "Uniforms and Traditions of the Luftwaffe":

Luftwaffe Field Divisions
Male Luftwaffe Auxiliaries
Female Luftwaffe Auxiliaries
Miscellaneous Equipment
Individual Equipment
Special Garments of Flying Personnel
Special Equipment of Flying Personnel
Other Special Garments
Chemical Warfare Equipment
Small Unit Weapons
Colors of the Luftwaffe
Reich War Flag, Personal and Command Flags
Music Bands, and Fife and Drum Corps
License Plates and Paint of Motor Vehicles
Aircraft Types, Markings and Paint